SUFFOLK IN THE MIDDLE AGES

To A. L.

in admiration, gratitude, and the spirit of the Bacons:
MEDIOCRIA FIRMA

SUFFOLK IN THE MIDDLE AGES

Studies in Places and Place-names, the Sutton Hoo Ship-burial,
Saints, Mummies and Crosses, Domesday Book, and
Chronicles of Bury Abbey

NORMAN SCARFE

THE BOYDELL PRESS

First published 1986
The Boydell Press, Woodbridge
Reprinted in paperback 2004, 2007

Transferred to digital printing

ISBN 978-1-84383-068-9

The Boydell Press is an imprint of Boydell & Brewer Ltd
PO Box 9, Woodbridge, Suffolk IP12 3DF, UK
and of Boydell & Brewer Inc.
668 Mt Hope Avenue, Rochester, NY 14620, USA
website: www.boydellandbrewer.com

A CiP catalogue record for this book is available
from the British Library

Library of Congress Catalog Card Number: 85-28005

This publication is printed on acid-free paper

Contents

List of Plates

List of Maps and Plans

ACKNOWLEDGEMENTS

We are grateful to the following for their kind assistance in providing illustrations:

Michael Nicholson for end-papers
Trustees of the British Museum for Plates 1, 2, 3, 4, 5, 6, 7, 9, 10, 11
Trustees of the Dunwich Museum for Plate 7
Photo Rex (B. Saltel), 6 rue des Chalets, Toulouse, for Plate 8
Mrs Edwin Smith for Plate 12
The Suffolk County Council for Plates 13, 25
The Master and Fellows of Corpus Christi College, Cambridge for Plates 14, 16
The Metropolitan Museum of Art, New York, The Cloisters Collection, (Inventory 63.12) for Plates 15, 17, 18, 19, 20, 21, 22. We are especially grateful to Dr Charles T. Little, of the Metropolitan Museum of Art, for obtaining for us the use of their latest (1985) photographs for Plates 15, 17, 18, 20, 21 and 22
Mr Bob Carr, Mrs Valerie Fenwick and Mr Paul Fincham for Plate 23
Cambridge Committee for Aerial Photography for Plate 24
Hilary Evans for drawing the maps

Preface

History writers have two main options. They can train their wide-angle lenses on some broad, disparate subject, like the United Kingdom, the United States, the U.S.S.R., and shorten the range of time (Hugh Brogan's recent *History of the U.S.A.* stays brilliantly in focus over 700 pages); or they can explore a smaller patch over a correspondingly longer period. My own instinct is always to focus on a relatively small landscape, or on a community, one that I think I know; and then examine its development, if possible from its origins. In this book we get glimpses, sometimes sharp, more often fleeting, of Suffolk, the southern half of the ancient kingdom of East Anglia, over about 1,500 years. We start with the naming of the places by Romans and British and — mainly — English (Angles) after they began to settle alongside the descendants of Boudicca's Iceni at *Camborito* (halfway between Bury St Edmunds and Mildenhall). We end with one of the *Hundred Mery Talys* of 1526, the year after the scaffolding came down to reveal the great bell-tower of Lavenham. In accents uncannily familiar, the tale shows people who are still rather easily alarmed and superstitious, yet being prepared for the Reformation.

I have to acknowledge too many debts. It was my friend W. G. Arnott whose book *The Place-names of the Deben Valley Parishes* first showed me how much these names can tell us about landscape and people in aboriginal and later circumstances. Professors Kenneth Cameron and Kenneth Jackson have patiently encouraged me, and I have greatly profited from Margaret Gelling's books on the subject. I am equally greatly indebted to Oliver Rackham, the remarkable botanist-historian, whose book *Trees and Woodland in the British Landscape* is a seminal work comparable with W. G. Hoskins' *The Making of the English Landscape*.

The Suffolk of a few surviving Celtic place-names is the one we try to glimpse through finds in the Sutton Hoo ship-burial. The coins in that glittering purse start a train of thought leading to Brian Hope-Taylor's Bernicia and back. His book on *Yeavering*, Rupert Bruce-Mitford's great official *Sutton Hoo* tomes, and Martin Carver's vigorous and imaginative direction of current research on that site (which I can see across the river from my home) can hardly fail to provoke constant questioning and speculation. The possible relevance of Bawdsey's place-name, or Shottisham's, occurred to me only as I began to write this book.

The stimulus to write about Iken came from Stanley West's marvellous discovery of that fragment of a cross in January 1977, and he has kindly supplied the drawings that accompany chapter 3. The work of the County Archaeological Unit he directs is inestimably valuable. His work at West Stow and Keith Wade's at Ipswich hold the attention and admiration of archaeologists across Europe: so will Bob Carr's extraordinary revelations at Brandon when he concludes and publishes. Incidentally, it is through research for the Unit that Mavis Baker came upon the clue that leads us to think that at last we know the whereabouts of *Haegelisdun*, where St Edmund was slain.

My examination of the strange fate of Edmund's embalmed corpse began in time for the celebrations in 1969 of his death eleven hundred years earlier. The current research includes not only the location of *Haegelisdun* but also the chance that may soon be presented for Edmund's supposed relics from St Sernin's in Toulouse to be tested by carbon-dating.

It is appropriate that chapters 1, 5, 6 and 11 should make their appearance in 1986, the ninth centenary of Domesday Book. Those four chapters owe most to the Domesday commissioners and scribes, as parentheses and foot-notes abundantly acknowledge. This book could never have been contemplated without that magnificent record. Like some other reference books, notably the great Oxford English Dictionary, Domesday Book rewards consecutive reading: my copy of the *facsimile* for Suffolk, published with rubrics properly in red, by Colonel Henry James of the Royal Engineers in 1863, is one of my best 'worn' books.

We come to Bury abbey. It is the very good fortune of Suffolk that two of the most lively chronicles of contemporary life ever written in medieval England were written in Bury, in circumstances I explore again in the wake of Professor Ralph Davis's brilliant edition of *Abbot Samson's Kalendar* in which he showed that the chronicler Jocelin of Brakelond was one of the leading monastic administrators, the cellarer, very much in the heat of the action he described. That discovery alone made H. E. Butler's edition of Jocelin's *Chronicle* seriously out-of-date, but it has never been re-edited. I stress that Jocelin's was a *Cronica*, and not a *Vita*, since it is regularly described as 'a biography' and that is to mistake its author's intention. Rodney Thomson, in his valuable edition of the *Chronicle of the Election of Hugh* described Jocelin's chronicle as biography, though he recognises its true purpose. My own purpose in paraphrasing here so fully the narratives of these two chronicles is, apart from their incomparably vivid picture of life in the cloister and chapter-house at Bury, to compare them in the light, or shade, of their political messages: the main concern of them both is to record rights — in Jocelin's case the rights of the cellarer against the abbot, in the *Electio* (its author on less clear ground) the rights of the Church against the King. The resolution of the wrangle over Hugh's election came at Runnymede a day or two before the celebrated 'concord' between John and the barons. It could hardly be a more spectacular or theatrical end to a sordid squabble, of the kind familiar to politicians the world over, and not least in the olive grove of Academe.

Some of the greatest pleasures of my life in Suffolk since World War II have sprung from my connection with two very different bodies, the Suffolk Institute of Archaeology (founded in 1848) and the Aldeburgh Festival (founded in 1948). Four of the last five chapters in this book are rebuilt around pieces I produced for various Aldeburgh Festivals. Re-shaped, they shift the story back from Bury to the Aldeburgh hinterland: not wholly, though, and it is pleasant, for instance, and for the first time, to have located the house of Richard de Calne to which the 'green children of Woolpit' were taken.

I must thank my colleagues on the Council of the Suffolk Institute of Archaeology and History — which, after nearly 150 years of scholarly activity, is in better shape than ever under Dr John Blatchly's Presidency — for so willingly allowing the re-use of material I first published in our *Proceedings*. I am grateful to the staff of our very hard-pressed Suffolk Record Offices — with the most used, but by no means the most funded, Search Rooms in the country; and to its photographic section under Trevor James. My friends Geoffrey Cordy of Felixstowe and Nigel Luckhurst of Cambridge have also been swift to help over photography. Paul Fincham's constant help I cannot adequately acknowledge. Richard Barber and his colleagues at the Boydell Press have my hearty thanks for suggesting the book on Medieval Suffolk I had been working towards for the love of it for many years. Frank Collieson has again run his kind and expert eye over my page-proofs. Mrs Christopher Hibbert has produced an exemplary index. Finally, it is a pleasure to express thanks to St Edmundsbury Press for their distinguished printing of a book so often pivoted on the story of Bury.

N.S.

Woodbridge
1 July 1985.

SETTLERS AND MISSIONARIES

1

Place-names and Settlements in the Landscape: an Introduction, and some Themes

The earliest verbal records of Suffolk are its place-names. They face us on sign-boards every two or three miles; more frequently in Suffolk than elsewhere. We are apt to look rather blankly at them, for we need a dictionary — E. Ekwall's *Concise Oxford Dictionary of English Place-names*[1] — to get the hang of most of them. Ekwall consulted their earliest forms of spelling, and from those resolved their meaning with much assurance. In Suffolk, most of them go back at least to Domesday Book, so one depends on his expertise in Old English, Old Scandinavian, etc. The surprising thing, though, is how little they have changed over all these centuries. Despite amusing variations in the spellings of the same name by the Domesday scribes,[2] the place-names we use today are easily identifiable in the great record of 1086.

The meaning of many of them is obvious enough; for instance where they describe the vegetation that seemed to the namers, the early English settlers, to characterise their land: alders at Alderton, ash at Ashbocking, Campsey Ash and the Ashfields, broom at Brome, elms at Elmham, Elmswell, and so on. Nothing very sensational about this, though it is moderately moving to find ash-trees still thriving in 'their' places, and melancholy to contemplate the sudden modern absence of the noble elm. In the most illuminating book on the British landscape since W. G. Hoskins' classic *Making of the English Landscape* (1955) Oliver Rackham warned of the mantraps here: at Alderton there might have been just one conspicuous alder, at Elmham one elm! I have tried to choose examples where this seemed at least improbable.[3] Some familiarity with these names, and with the tests of interpretation, sharpens our appreciation and our pleasure in travelling. It also provides valuable clues for our detection of the past, as Margaret Gelling demonstrated so expertly in her recent book on this theme: *Signposts to the Past*.[4] Hers is the main theme I want to develop here, in relation to this county.

1 4th edn., 1960. Its 1st edn. appeared fifty years ago in 1936. An up-to-date revision is needed: Ekwall was not in a position to assess the reliability of Old English charters as they are now understood, nor was he strong on Celtic roots. Serious students need to resort to the recent publications of The English Place-name Society. For quick reference by interested laymen, Ekwall's *Dictionary* remains indispensable and this chapter is offered as one student's celebration of a notable jubilee, 1936 – 1986.

2 Kelsale, for instance, was spelt in five very different ways in Domesday Book: Norman Scarfe, *The Suffolk Landscape*, London 1972, 151.

3 Oliver Rackham, *Trees and Woodland in the British Landscape*, 1976, pp. 55 – 56.

4 London, 1978.

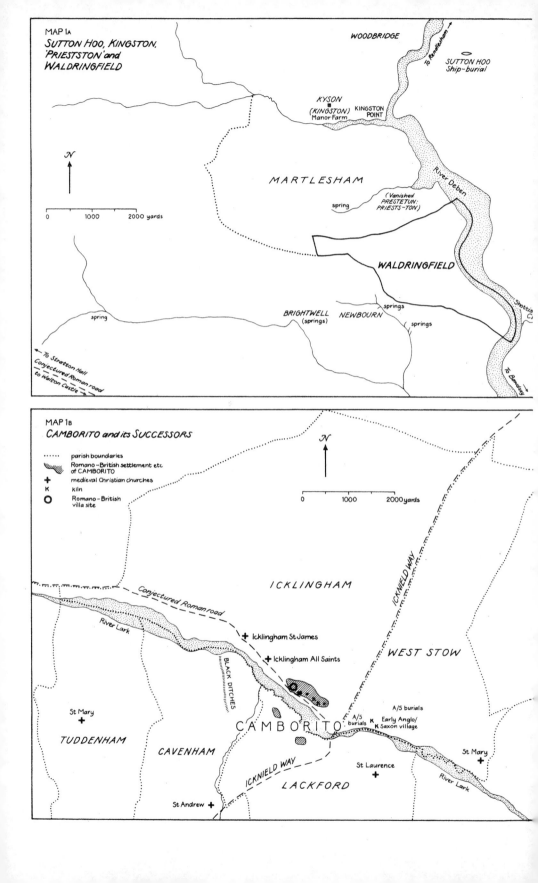

MAP 1A
SUTTON HOO, KINGSTON,
'PRIESTSTON' and
WALDRINGFIELD

WOODBRIDGE

To Kesgrave

SUTTON HOO
Ship-burial

KYSON
(KINGSTON)
Manor Farm

KINGSTON
POINT

River Deben

N

0   1000   2000 yards

MARTLESHAM

(Vanished
PRESTETUN:
PRIESTS—TON)

spring

WALDRINGFIELD

Shottisham C.

spring

BRIGHTWELL
(springs)

NEWBOURN

springs

springs

To Stratton Hall
Conjectured Roman road
to Walton Castle

To Bawdsey

MAP 1B
CAMBORITO and its SUCCESSORS

.... parish boundaries
▨▨▨ Romano–British settlement etc.
       of CAMBORITO
✝ medieval Christian churches
K kiln
⊙ Romano–British
   villa site

N

0   1000   2000 yards

ICKLINGHAM

Conjectured Roman road

ICKNIELD WAY

River Lark

✝ Icklingham St James

✝ Icklingham All Saints

WEST STOW

BLACK DITCHES

CAMBORITO

K
DKN

A/S burials

A/S burials

K
K

Early Anglo/
Saxon village

St Mary
✝
TUDDENHAM

CAVENHAM

St Mary
✝

ICKNIELD WAY

St Laurence
✝

River Lark

LACKFORD

St Andrew ✝

Eyes

Do you think of islands when you think of Suffolk? I, for one, did not. Yet eight fairly well-known Suffolk places have names embodying the Old English word for an island (*eg*, which has become *-ey*, and Eye itself). Centuries of draining marshes and improving water-courses have lowered the river-levels and removed or reduced the original watery surroundings that distinguished these places. But once you are alerted, you will have no difficulty in seeing that the market-town of Eye, in the middle of Suffolk, is built on a small island, surrounded by low-lying, willow-growing, sedgy land. (Much of it is the 'Town Moor', which in Suffolk means Town Fen, or Marsh: A. H. Smith shows how in the eastern fens 'moor' came to mean 'marsh'.) In the years 1066 — 1071, when the Conqueror's magnate, William Malet, built his castle here and laid out the market-place, he chose the place for its defensible 'island' qualities — those of a moat.[5]

Kersey is no longer easy to think of as a 'cress-island', though visitors always remember the water-splash a little higher up-stream, where it crosses the village street below that steep church-path. The cress-island was eclipsed during the Middle Ages by the fulling-mill beside that stream, so that 'kerseys', popular textiles, entered early into the imagination of Shakespeare: 'Russet yeas and honest kersey noes' (*Loves Labours Lost*). So did next-door Lindsey, in the same way as 'linsie wolsy' in *All's Well*; for at least one of Lindsey's three running brooks must have turned a fulling-mill: in the 12th century one of them was used to fill the moat of Adam of Cockfield's 'adulterine' castle — which was built, perhaps, on the original 'island'.[6]

The most startling of Suffolk's *-eys* is Bawdsey, at the northern lip of the Deben estuary. As you descend and rise from Stangrove Hall and the Alderton 'mainland', on the one road leading into Bawdsey, you easily perceive how it stood islanded by the river and the sea. But a most tantalising enigma lies hidden in the first part of the name, which Ekwall reveals as 'Baldhere's island'. Whoever this particular Baldhere may have been, we can hardly ignore his namesake Balder, Odin's son, in Scandinavian mythology, slain by the inevitable mistletoe spear and sent blazing out to sea on his funeral ship as in Matthew Arnold's 'Balder Dead' — not an inspired poem, but an endlessly evocative title. Bawdsey's name by itself might have prepared us, years earlier, for the uncovering of the great burial-ship seven miles up river at Sutton Hoo. (*Hoo* is a hill-spur, and Sutton, south-*tun*, southern estate.) Perhaps this explains why it has proved so hard to find a body in the ship-burial at Sutton Hoo.

---

5 A. H. Smith, *English Place-name Elements*, II., 1970, p. 42; Scarfe *op. cit.*, 152 and Pl. 25.
6 *Victoria County History: Suffolk*, I, 1911, 601 — 2, with plan. Visited by Suffolk Institute of Archaeology in 1976. This link between places and cloths needs more research.

Sutton Hoo

Here, very dramatically, are 'sign-posts to the past'. Across the river from Sutton is a part of Woodbridge called, usually, Kyson, a corruption of the Kingston (*Cyngestune*) that was given to Ely soon after 1002. Kingston means, quite simply, King's estate, or King's manor, and its significance, across the river a mile downstream from the ship-burial is one of those elements in the problem that might have been considered by those medievalists who declined to believe that the finds were magnificent enough to be 'the regalia of a king'. In his revised note on 'The Graves of Kings', J. M. Wallace-Hadrill, with reluctance, finally allowed that the Sutton Hoo treasure is important enough to be royal.[7] He continues to 'keep an open mind about the identity of the body', but so does everyone concerned, while allowing that the likeliest candidate, after decades of research, is Raedwald. Meanwhile there is Rendlesham, three and a half miles upstream on the same bank, which Bede specifically called a *vicus regius*, a royal place, or estate.[8]

What Rendlesham means is disputed by the experts, despite Bede's early interpretation, '*ham* of Rendil', the otherwise forgotten pioneer settler. Dr Gelling thinks it may mean 'little shore', a diminutive of *rand*.[9] Professor Cameron is content to follow Bede. This kind of difference is hard to resolve. Here I wanted to show how two inconspicuous names, Bawdsey and Kingston, relate interestingly, perhaps productively, with the archaeology of Sutton Hoo, one of the most absorbing problems of its kind in our own Age. A third such name is Shottisham, between Sutton Hoo and Bawdsey, where aerial photography has revealed one of the most interesting groups of circular crop-marks, like poached eggs, or shooting-targets:[10] perhaps Bronze Age barrows, but linear-marks also suggest ritual. Our business is with the place-name: *ham* of the Scots, which is the Old English word for the people from Ireland. Was there a Celtic community settled near Sutton Hoo? If so, could they be responsible for the workshop-collaboration referred to in the following chapter, at p. 37 below?

---

7   In his *Early Medieval History*, Oxford, 1975, pp. 39—59. In the same Hundred as Kingston, a curious carucate of 'wasteland' in Domesday Book (fol. 425) was called *Kingesland*. In N.W. Suffolk, Coney Weston's early spellings, *Cunegestun*, etc., show that it was another Kingston, and deserves archaeological attention. Kenton, too, may mean royal manor. Bury (*Betrichesworde* in his day) is another of Bede's royal *vici*. There must have been some royal estates in Suffolk attested by neither Bede nor place-names: Blythburgh was undoubtedly one. Then Athelington means *tun* of the young princes; and the Chiltons, beside Sudbury and Stowmarket, may mean *tun* of the young nobles. Both Sudbury and Stowmarket (which was originally called *Thorney*) are likely to have been royal manors. Two of them, Rendlesham and Kingston, are significantly close to Sutton Hoo: this is the point.

8   Colgrave and Mynors, *Bede's Ecclesiastical History*, 1969, p. 284.

9   Gelling, *Signposts to the Past*, p. 189.

10   Scarfe, *op. cit.*, Pl. 9.

The British Predecessors: A First Fifteen

In his masterly survey, *The Anglo-Saxons*,[11] James Campbell declared roundly: 'It is inconceivable that the few score pre-450 A.D. burials from East Anglia can indicate that all the British inhabitants had been driven out. Indeed, for all we know, all or part of the area may have been ruled by Britons till the 6th century.' If we adopt this start-line, the way is clear for some constructive deduction in both archaeology and toponymy. We shall notice later that the place-names of the Lothingland district, immediately north of Lowestoft, are largely Danish or Scandinavian, and indicate a clear predominance of such settlers. Enough of an Anglo-Saxon element in the names enables us to feel certain that, in the absence of very strong archaeological counter-evidence, there was no draconian, genocidal clear-out by the Northerners of the earlier inhabitants.

Somerleyton is a re-assuring example: Somerlidi's *tun*. Somerlidi is the Old Norse word for 'summer-warrior', a clear enough description, for the Danes and Vikings were warlike 'summer-visitors' from across the North Sea: the re-assurance comes in the word *tun*, Anglo-Saxon for farm or estate. The name is a hybrid and illustrates an amalgamation — of language, and presumably of people. If James Campbell and others are right, and the earliest English were settling in the same way alongside their Celtic precursors here, are there place-names to indicate a similar amalgam? Dr Brian Hope-Taylor, in his magnificent excavation and report on Yeavering (Northumberland), has shown King Edwin (and by inference his English predecessors) ruling Bernicia according to the very forms and even structures of the Romanised native British of previous centuries. By Edwin's day, the natives had again accepted tributary status, as they had in the Roman hey-day.[12] Is there evidence of tributary Britons in Suffolk place-names? Edwin was Raedwald's protégé. Is there evidence that native institutions were as hardy in East Anglia as they were in Bernicia? It seems highly unlikely, but we must look.

Margaret Gelling has shown that Wickham contained the Old English word *wīc*, borrowed from the Latin *vicus*, and so became 'a term used for a Romano-British habitation site',[13] with *ham*, a common Old English word for farm-settlement or village. She is content to show that the examples she lists coincide with, or are not more than a mile from, Romano-British habitation sites. She was on stronger ground than she knew with her Suffolk examples: Wickham Skeith, beside the Colchester-Caistor-by-Norwich Roman road; Wickham Market, where the making of a recent by-pass revealed, just north of the present little market-town, a large, sprawling,

11   Oxford, 1982, p. 29.
12   B. Hope-Taylor, *Yeavering: An Anglo-British centre of early Northumbria*, 1977, p. 281.
13   Gelling, Margaret, *Medieval Archaeology*, XI, 1967, 'Place-names derived from the compound WĪCHĀM', p. 93.

prosperous settlement, comparable with a medieval market-town;[14] Wickhambrook, near a large Roman corridor-villa revealed in 1971 by aerial photography at adjacent Lidgate.[15] Margaret Gelling omitted the Wicken, or Wyken, Hall in Bardwell, which Domesday Book revealed as one of her *Wichams* (at folios 421 and 439b); that *Wicam* is made up of four estates, each of one 'carucate'; it is an outlier of Bardwell parish and adjoins Ixworth, one of the largest of Suffolk's Romano-British settlements (excavations continuing in 1985), which lies on Peddars Way (Chelmsford-Ixworth, etc: Map 2a).

Here, one must deviate for a moment to introduce Grim, 'the masked one', the Devil, a nickname for Woden, who — like Zeus — was always going around in disguise. A part of Pakenham running towards Ixworth, between Mickle Mere and Pakenham Fen, is called Grimstone End. It was *Grimstuna* c. 1200,[16] and stood among a series of ancient earthworks including a triple-ditched rectangular Roman fort, below ground now, but once mysterious and awe-inspiring, like Grim's Ditch, the Devil's Dyke, etc. In the 13th century there was a Grim's Ditch in Thornham Parva:[17] it remains as a sunken lane along the south side of the churchyard, and originally ran east across the Colchester-Caister-by-Norwich Roman road, obviously a defence-work against attackers from the south (Maps 2a and 2b). The Suffolk Domesday *Grimestuna* (fols. 292 and 341b) is now Grimston Hall in Trimley St Martin, and was the boyhood home of the Elizabethan circumnavigator, Thomas Cavendish. Whether it owes its name to fears of Woden and the Devil is less obvious: no sign remains of formidable earthworks close by, and Ekwall errs when he says (*sub* Grimsbury) that Grim was not a man's name: indeed, a Grim was one of six freemen living in *Guthestuna* in 1086 (it is in Kirton, which adjoins Trimley St Martin; fol. 340b). On the other hand, this Grimston Hall lies alongside Stratton Hall (*Strattuna* in D.B.: fols. 342b–343); and *Straet-tun* usually means estate on, or near, a Roman road. This *straet* must have been an important one, linking Colchester with Walton Castle, the (now submerged) Roman fort guarding the mouths of the Deben and Orwell estuaries. This line of road has not been determined by precise archaeology, only by approximate toponymy. It may have run on an embankment-causeway at the edges of this peninsula: it may have seemed to a newcomer as alarmingly impressive as almost any piece of Roman engineering.

14   In her book, *Signposts*, p. 35, Margaret Gelling puts Stoke Ash into Norfolk. Its Romano-British settlement site adjoins Wickham Skeith. (Skeith is the Old Norse word for a racecourse.) In 1985 the Wickham Market by-pass archaeological 'rescue-dig' remains unpublished.

15   Scarfe, *op. cit.*, Pl. 12.

16   R. H. C. Davis, *Kalendar of Abbot Samson*, 1954, p. 105. In 1985, Judith Plouviez and the County Archaeological Unit have been excavating the fort, apparently immediately post-Boudiccan, and surrounding successive periods of civilian settlement.

17   B.L. Harl. 52 A. 49.

If four Suffolk Wickhams refer to places the Romano-British were living in, what other Latin and Celtic words, compounded perhaps with English ones, like *ham*, suggest the presence of Britons in the landscape the English occupied in gradually overwhelming numbers? In the 'British Names' map included with A. H. Smith's *The Place-name Elements*,[18] only three British place-names and one river-name appear on the Suffolk section of the map: Dunwich, derived from Celtic *dubno*, 'deep'; Walton, *tun* of the Welshman or the British (not itself a Celtic word, but English, implying they had Celts alongside); and Clare, perhaps Celtic for 'bright', a reference to the river, the Stour, Suffolk's one Celtic river-name, probably meaning 'powerful'. Four names, then, may be added to the four Wickhams: so far eight names to signal the British presence. Notice that the three new place-names are closely associated, like the Wickhams, with Romano-British archaeology: at least one Roman road heads directly for Dunwich (itself mostly submerged): Walton lies alongside the (submerged) Roman fort at Felix-stowe;[19] and Clare is the little town lying beside the British fort the early English called 'Erbury'.

In his text (II, 244), though not on his map, A. H. Smith allows that Walpole means 'pool of the British'. This, too, is highly probable, for the pool lay in a confluence of the Blyth river, less than two miles south of the Roman villa at Chediston, and perhaps directly on the route between two major Roman roads at Halesworth and Peasenhall. What about Walsham-le-Willows? Here the experts, A. H. Smith and Ekwall, seem reluctant to accept '*ham* of the Welshman or Celt', now sanctioned by Professor Cameron. Walsham adjoins not only Wyken Hall, Bardwell (one of the four Wickhams) but also Stanton, with its Roman villa-site at 'Stanton Chare'. In my book, Walpole and Walsham take the tally to ten: see p. 17−18, further on, for confirmation.

Brettenham seems to be a key English word to denote *ham* of Bretta, 'the Briton'. Suffolk's Brettenham lies in remote, brook-watered farmlands between Lavenham and Stowmarket: its eastern parish-boundary follows a straight strip of Roman road,[20] the road that once joined the Peddars Way at Stanton Chare, from Bildeston and perhaps Colchester (Map 3). Across Brettenham's eastern parish boundary lies Hitcham, with remains of a Romano-British building. In 1902, a new library at Brettenham Park was built 'on the side of an old burial ground, probably Roman'.[21]

Tuddenham's name, the *ham* of Tuda, adds two, brings the total to

---

18   In *Part One*, 1956, reprinted 1970.

19   Gelling, *Signposts*, p. 93, discussed the 'division of opinion concerning *walh*'. The most recent, very comprehensive, analysis is by Kenneth Cameron: 'The Meaning and Significance of Old English *walh* in English Place-names', *Journal 12*, English Place-name Society, 1980, pp. 1−53: see p. 27 for his acceptance of Walsham-le-Willows.

20   I. D. Margary, *Roman Roads in Britain, South*, 1955, p. 226, Roman Road no. 330.

21   *Proceedings Suffolk Institute of Archaeology and History*, XVIII, 1924, pp. 219−221 and XXIV, 1949, p. 167.

thirteen: it is agreed by the leading Celtic place-name authority, Professor K. Jackson, that Tuda derives from the British *Toto*.[22] An Angle *could* have a personal name borrowed from Celtic, without being a Celt, but it seems unlikely. Tuddenham St Martin, on steep slopes above a tributary of the Deben just north of Ipswich, lies a little over two miles east of the Castle Hill Roman villa within the Ipswich Borough boundary. We come to the other Tuddenham in a moment. Meanwhile a third Toto-name to consider is Dodnash, spelt *Todenes* in Domesday Book (fol. 295b), and now within Bentley parish: Bentley's boundary with Capel St Mary is a Roman stretch of the A12, Margary's 'Pye Road'.[23] A Romano-British house-site is recorded in Capel St Mary. I think Dodnash may be reckoned a fourteenth reference to the British in Suffolk's names, but Professor Cameron thinks that that is 'scraping the bottom of the barrel', so we reject it. Nor can the manor of Kentwell in Long Melford safely make a fourteenth: its Domesday spelling is *Kanewell* (fol. 355): but, further west, the Kennet may be counted a Suffolk river as well as a Cambridgeshire one, for it is crossed in Suffolk at Kentford. Here, at *Ceneteford*, famous enquiries were held, c. 1071–1087, into the lands of Ely.[24] And Kennet is a British river-name. For a fifteenth name we go to Bulcamp (D.B. fols. 333 and 356: *Bulecampe*), on the north bank of the Blyth river opposite Wenhaston, with its scattered remains of Romano-British farms. That they should have extended to these low, south-facing fields across the river would not be surprising; but that English settlers, with their own words for fields, should have adopted the Latin word for a field, *campus*, seems to argue some peculiar circumstance. Most likely, they adopted the name with no knowledge of the original meaning of *campus*, but such an adoption implies a period of hand-over or transition. At all events, Dr Gelling includes Bulcamp among her examples of this kind of name-survival through from the Latin.[25] (See Map 7.)

So far, fifteen names have been found that reasonable people would regard as very probable indicators of the survival in Suffolk of Celtic or British names in the English vocabulary. It is not a large number, but already it looks less flimsy than the four that are marked on the map in A. H. Smith's *Place-name Elements*, which it may soon be time to re-draw. The possibilities are by no means exhausted, but before we look any further it would be good to have these fifteen names agreed. Some of what follows is more speculative: rejection of the speculation should not involve the dismissal of the cases for the first fifteen. In view of the extremely high density of the English settlement in Suffolk, the survival of fifteen names is an impressive hint of British survival and British-English overlap.

22 *Language and History in Early Britain*, 1953, pp. 554–555.
23 Margary, *op. cit.*, p. 233: road 3C.
24 *Liber Eliensis*, p. 29, *passim*.
25 Gelling, *Signposts*, p. 77.

Camborico/Camborito, Icknield Way, Ickworth, etc.

Round the Roman place-names that may survive in Suffolk we must walk warily. It is amazing enough that hundreds of names recorded in 1086 remain in an identifiable form in 1986. For place-names to have survived, recognisably, six additional centuries, from late Roman times, seems against all probability. The language of Romans and Britons differed much more radically than ours does from that of the English in 1086.

In Suffolk, two place-names in the Antonine Itinerary can be fairly closely located: *Ad Ansam* in Stratford St Mary below the sharp bend in Dedham Gun Hill, where the river makes a similar bend, aptly enough described by *Ad Ansam*, 'at the handle'. *Sitomagus*, from the road-measurements in the Itinerary, must lie in the coastal strip east of the A12, perhaps in the hinterland of Aldeburgh. But nothing of these two names remains in a modern place-name. In Bernicia, the British name *Ad Gefrin* ('at the hill of the goats') survives almost intact as Yeavering. But *Ad Gefrin* was a local British capital, and the word *was* British. *Ad Ansam*, 'at the handle, or loop', is a Latin word, and marked a mere main river-crossing. The death of that name, and of *Sitomagus*, by no means implies the extinction of the British in East Suffolk.

What seems (to the inexpert linguist) to survive from Roman place-names into our own is, often, the first syllable, as we saw (however 'borrowed' and at one remove) in the Wickhams. Other obvious examples are *Glevo* (Roman) — *Cleawanceeaster* (Anglo-Saxon) — Gloucester: *Corstopitum* — Corbridge: *Letoceto* — *Liccidfeld* — Lichfield. And what this suggests is that the successive generations of post-Celtic English have not understood the meaning of the original Latin or Celtic word accurately, and have 'rationalised', over several centuries, substituting -bridge or -feld or -ham for the original ending, and sometimes substituting an imaginary English personal name for a word they did not understand. This seems to me the only possible explanation of those three examples. It seems to me a possible and *permissible* explanation of a few very important Suffolk place-names that can only otherwise be explained by an *unacceptable* degree of coincidence. I write this defence of the next page or two, remembering Margaret Gelling's warning, on the first page of *Signposts*: 'Philologists, for their part, are acutely aware that historians and archaeologists are embarrassingly disaster-prone when discussing place-names.' A mere historian, one can only try to understand and follow their precepts. It may be that any philologist should skip the next page or two, but I very much hope not. I will make them as brief and explicit as possible.

One of the three or four most remarkable archaeological sites in Suffolk lies where the Icknield Way crosses the river Lark and where four medieval parishes made common boundaries: Cavenham with Icklingham, Lackford and West Stow; see Map 1b. Local archaeologists and historians agree with

Margary:[26] this place was the *Camborico* of the Antonine Itinerary, Iter V. I imagine we would all accept Professor Jackson's 'suggested emendation' and think of it as *Camborito*,[27] which means 'crooked ford'. The Lark certainly bends here and the Icknield Way changes direction and crosses it at an oblique angle: See Map 1b. (One notices with pleasure that philologists allow themselves to amend the recorded version of a word if it makes more sense, and where the letters are confusingly similar in shape.)

Camborito, this open area around the crooked ford, including adjacent parts of the later Cavenham, Icklingham and Lackford parishes, had a villa excavated in the 19th century. It has also yielded some of the most spectacular Romano-British finds uncovered anywhere in East Anglia — more British, perhaps, than Roman. An Eygptian bronze statuette, Isis nursing the infant Horus, represents a phase in Celtic religion before Christianity substituted the Virgin and Child; so does the small bronze figure riding a prodigious phallus; and the bronze wheel of the Celtic god Teranus.[28] Then there are bronze crowns, thought to have been worn here by Celtic priests; there is also a bronze plume, almost certainly an attachment of one of the crowns. This is the point at which pagan Celtic ritual at *Camborito* may have moved to Celtic Christian ritual: for at Water Newton, in Huntingdonshire, other plumes have been found, identical in shape but made of silver and bearing the Chi-Rho monogram, the first two letters of Christ. This Christian monogram occurs at *Camborito*, on the Icklingham side of the Lark, inscribed on no fewer than three, and conceivably four, lead tanks. What they were used for we can only conjecture: some kind of holy-water stoup? Some kind of vessel for ablution: one of them seemed to be connected with the little apsed building that is thought to have been a baptistry? This stands in prolongation of other, unexplored buildings, so that we are almost reminded of 7th-century Yeavering, and even Canterbury. But in Christian *Camborito* we are back in the 4th century, 'the best days of Roman Britain', its population perhaps as high as in 1348, or in 1500, 'a Britain more like its medieval than its Anglo-Saxon self'.[29]

The advent of Celtic Christianity in the middle of the 4th century may have involved the destruction of *Camborito*'s pagan temple; for a small Barnack pillar, once perched perhaps on the wall of a portico, was found in a pit under a general sealing layer of chalk, which may represent a general purging of the pagan ground. Cisterns and 'baptistry' imply congregations. Congregational churches were usually separate from churches with cemeteries. *Camborito* had become, by the 4th century, altogether more than just a place by a crooked ford. Strong linear earthworks, 'the Black

26   Margary, *op. cit.*, p. 245.
27   Gelling, *Signposts, op. cit.*, p. 39.
28   These objects from local museums were brought together in an Exhibition of Religious Art in Suffolk in 1984 at Christchurch Mansion, Ipswich. The catalogue contains an excellent review, by Mrs Hilary Feldman, of the Celtic material: pp. 1—4.
29   J. Campbell, *The Anglo-Saxons*, p. 9.

Ditches', in Cavenham seem designed to protect more than just a river-crossing against attack from the south-west, at a later, uncertain date. Was there an attack? Door-hinges and nails, found in one of the Christian tanks, suggest the dismantling of a building in the face of danger, rather than a massacre.[30] At West Stow, the fourth of the parishes that meet at *Camborito*'s crooked ford, Dr S. E. West showed conclusively that an Anglo-Saxon community was established alongside the British of *Camborito*, probably from c. 380 onwards.

The fact that *Camborito*'s name, the crooked ford, was replaced by Lackford, means no more than that the English no longer understood *Camborito*'s precise Celtic meaning. Its use in the Itinerary of Antoninus showed that it was a place of some note when the itinerary was made, in the late 2nd or early 3rd century. We have glimpsed its importance in the 4th century, when the English first settled at West Stow, alongside. It seems likely that the memory of such a place, and so of its name, would have survived. It may be only a concidence that one of the succeeding English names was Cavenham, but we saw *ham* being added to *wīc*, derived from *vicus* to become Wickham. It seems just possible — one claims no more — that *Camborito* became jumbled and perhaps 'rationalised' in the first part of the name which had in Domesday Book (fols. 391b, 403) become *Canavatham* and *Kanavaham*. Since we may presume to start here with *Camborito*, we can see how *Cambor* might, to a superior Anglo-Saxon, sound like *Canava*, v and b being so easily switched. Ekwall suggests a personal name, Cafna, or Cafnoth. But neither Ekwall nor, we suppose, the locals in 1086, knew about *Camborito*. We noticed that, of Roman names, only the first syllable survived as a rule: here, slightly more may have come through.

The British who lived in the villa and the sprawling settlement at *Camborito*, and worshipped in pagan temple and Christian church, were members of Boudicca's old tribe, the Iceni. Their rebellion brought severe reprisals, but not extermination. Theirs was a name to remember. Professor Jackson has explained[31] that they would have pronounced it Ickénni, with the stress on the short e. An individual would have been called an Icenos. (The Roman alphabet used only c to express k.) Archaeology has shown clearly that, from the first, their areas of settlement were most concentrated in the Breckland, spreading into the Fens in the west and to the coast in the east, but centred on the light lands of what became N.W. Suffolk and S.W. Norfolk.

The Icknield Way runs through the heart of their homelands, crosses the Lark at *Camborito*, the Little Ouse at Thetford, and on past Ickburgh in Norfolk. It seems natural that East Anglian archaeologists should continue

---

30 S. E. West and J. Plouviez, 'The Romano-British Site at Icklingham': *East Anglian Archaeology*, Report No. 3. Suffolk County Planning Department, Ipswich, 1976, p. 122. And cf. S. E. West, 'The Anglo-Saxon Village of West Stow', *Medieval Archaeology*, XIII, 1969, 1−20.

31 In a letter to the author.

to suppose that the Icknield Way carries the name of the Iceni[32] (even though as a track it was here earlier than they were) so long as the philologists echo Ekwall: 'the etymology of the name has not been found.' The early spellings are *Icenhylte weg*, 903, *Icenhilde weg*, 1043, etc. Nor are philologists very convincing when they translate Ickburgh (Norfolk) as Ica's *burgh*. One understands their inclination to give personal names to small estates whose forms are mostly no earlier than Domesday Book. I personally feel that the *burg* of an Icenos *might*, after six centuries of Anglo-Saxon language, have become Ica's *burg*. In the same way, I believe Iken — beside Ica's stream, according to Ekwall — not only might have been, but is more likely, in the light of its choice by Botolph for his monastery[33] some centuries earlier, to have been a place still related to or frequented by one or more Iceni. In short, I believe that, however indirectly, individual or plural Iceni may have been involved in at least some place-names beginning with Ick- when they lie within the territory of that British tribe. The proposition seems no more outrageous than the survival of the Latin word *vicus*, however indirectly, in Wickham. Finally, if it is argued that tribal, as distinct from personal, names are unlikely to have been commemorated in what were, presumably, personal estates, how do we square this with, for instance, Freston, *tun* of the Frisian, or Saxham, the *ham* of the Saxons (a clear indication that settlers at Saxham could think of themselves as distinctively Saxon among the predominant Angles, or English, of East Anglia),[34] or Swaffham and Swavesey in neighbouring counties — the *ham* and landing-place (*hythe*) of the Swabians? We have already noticed Shottisham, the *ham* of the Irish; to which Shotley may be added. Professor Cameron objects that Saxons 'were odd men out in the area', whereas the Iceni were not. I fear they may, brusquely, have become so. The settlements echoing their name are few.

Three places take their names from (now vanished) *tumuli*: the clue is *hlaw*, 'an artificial mound, a mound with buried treasure.' Bux*low*, by Knodishall, is in the coastal heath, a major area of vanished mounds: it is roughly where *Sitomagus* seems to have been. Thur*low*, in the south-west corner of Suffolk, was early spelt *Tritlaw*, which means either 'assembly hill' or 'famous tumulus': wherever in Thurlow was it? Thurlow's elongated shape makes one wonder if there was a cursus: see Map 5a. Lawshall means 'mound-shelter': perhaps the linear earthworks known as 'the Warbanks'

32   N. Scarfe, 'The Place-name Icklingham: A preliminary re-examination', in *East Anglian Archaeology: Report No. 3*, Suffolk County Planning Department, Ipswich, 1976, pp. 127–132. A generous and comprehensive discussion of that article by Mr R. W. I. McConchie, of Wollongong University, New South Wales, is soon to be published. He concludes, from the available linguistic evidence, as I see he must, that the Old English name *Ycel* is 'the most probable' source of the place-name Icklingham. He understands with admirable clarity the gap between archaeological probability and the limit beyond which linguistic scholars may not tread. If it could ever be bridged, he has, I think, the patience, the will, and the ingenuity, to do it.

33   See p. 46, fn. 29, below.

34   Scarfe, *op. cit.*, p. 85.

once associated with a mound. The one *hlaw* that survives is Eastlow Hill in Rougham, described in the piece on the three Bradfields, on p. 76. Which brings us to the

Place-names ending in -feld (later -field)

These form perhaps the most significant group of all Suffolk's place-names from the point of view of using them to read the early settlement of the landscape. Here we consider only the major settlement-names.

There are approximately 500 'places' in Suffolk. One hesitates to call them 'villages' since so many of them lack the 'Midland' kind of nucleus, a village-street, or even a village-green in the normal sense of the phrase. They were called 'vills' in the Middle Ages. Usually their boundaries are those of the medieval parish. This is one reason why the medieval church remains such a symbol of identity for Suffolk country-people. It is also why it seems to us characteristic of the ignorance and dim secularity of the officials who make decisions increasingly from remote corridors that the boundaries of these ancient places are no longer shown on the Ordnance Survey's 1:50,000 sheets — themselves a pale form of the one-inch-to-the-mile sheets that were the pride of all who could read them and liked to know where they were. In Suffolk we are literally dislocated without maps to show where we cross from one vill, or civil-parish, to the next. Without them, the study of the main English place-names is doubly difficult and the point of them is lost.

For these 500 'places' in Suffolk there are only about 400 different names. There are eight Elmhams (ten if you include Homersfield and Flixton, of which more later); there are four Ilketshalls, four Creetings, and a great many examples of two or three parishes with one name between them.

A useful way to begin grouping and classifying these 400 is by looking at the suffixes, the name-endings. We find that 97, about one in four, end in -ton, originally *-tun*, one of the commonest of suffixes and much analysed. If applied early to a settlement, it was a farmstead: applied later, it was an estate, a village, or early *town* (same word). Next we find 81 Suffolk suffixes are *-hams* (including *-inghams*): again nothing remarkable, for it seems to cover everything from farmstead to *hamlet* to village. So 178 Suffolk names, almost half of the total, were either *tuns* or *hams*, and referred to farm-settlements. Conceivably these were early settlements, and *ham* seems to indicate, as a broad and general rule, an earlier naming than *tun*. Many desperate articles have been written on the theme of -ingham as an indicator of earliness (as in Framlingham, which Ekwall translated as 'the ham of the people, -ing, of Framela'). It used to be thought that the direct reference to 'a people' in this way, as to a tribe, suggested a pristine, aboriginal settlement, early in the settlement period. But all these main place-names suggest a 'first' settlement by the namers. Only archaeology can help to show 'how early', or whether the English namers were moving into settlements of earlier farmers. Unfortunately, field archaeology in the later 20th century, is still a long way from being able to give clear signals for many of these 400 names.

However, in Suffolk, after -ton and -ham, the third commonest suffix is -field, originally -feld. This is well worth exploring. There are 31 of them, which is some way behind the 81 hams, but still a sturdy family of Suffolk names: of the total 400 it represents one in every thirteen. It compares with only eight -felds in Norfolk and fifteen in Essex. In Britain, Margaret Gelling has counted 'about 250 major settlement-names containing feld'.[35] Suffolk has one for every eight of that total, and here, at least, they represent places with very interesting features in common.

What does the name itself suggest? The linguists, Ekwall and Gelling, start off in unison: it means 'open country: land free from wood: a plain' (Ekwall). Gelling begins, briskly: 'open country'.[36] She goes on to explain that in Anglo-Saxon literature the meaning of the word seems to change, implying 'grazing-land, common pasture' to begin with, but by the later 10th century moving to what it tends to mean today — plough-land, arable.[37] These literary references are not numerous, but are worth noting. Gelling then remarks[38] that among English place-names already recorded in writing by AD 730, ten had the suffix -feld, which 'indicates that it was a prolific name-forming term in the early Anglo-Saxon period'. As we shall see, one Suffolk instance (Homersfield) seems to be as late as the 9th century, and another, Metfield, might be, but probably isn't, later still. Yet there is every reason to suppose that the remaining twenty-nine survive from the early Anglo-Saxon period — indeed, from the main period of English settlement in the Suffolk of the Romano-British, the Iceni.

I was coming to this conclusion when I published my book on The Suffolk Landscape in 1972.[39] I was encouraged in correspondence with Professor Kenneth Cameron, the Hon. Director of the English Place-name Survey, and my views were confirmed by reading Oliver Rackham's brilliantly illuminating book, Trees and Woodland in the British Landscape, 1976, and by correspondence with him in 1979. In his book, the key passage was:[40]

'In Roman Britain . . . it is plausible that . . . areas of woodland were managed for the purpose of growing small and medium-sized trees . . . Some kind of permanent coppice must have stood behind the ironworks of the Weald . . . the potteries of Wattisfield (Suffolk) . . . and the wattle-and-daub of rural buildings and (on a smaller scale) behind most bath-houses and hypocausts in forts and villas and behind every grain-drier on a farm.'

35 Place-names in the Landscape, 1984, p. 239. Minor feld-names abound, e.g., in Essex.
36 op. cit., p. 235.
37 op. cit., p. 236.
38 op. cit., p. 237.
39 op. cit., pp. 87, 183—187.
40 op. cit., p. 51.

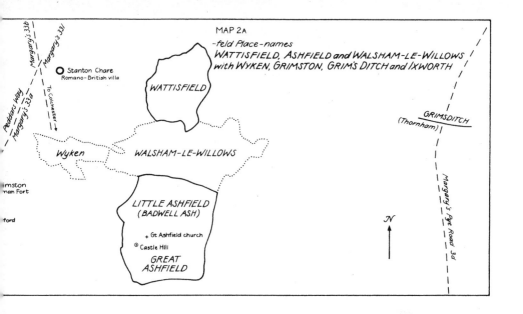

MAP 2A
-feld Place-names
WATTISFIELD, ASHFIELD and WALSHAM-LE-WILLOWS
with WYKEN, GRIMSTON, GRIM'S DITCH and IXWORTH

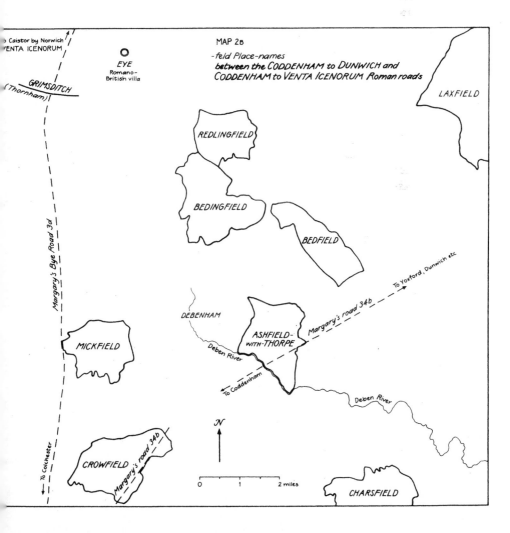

MAP 2B
-feld Place-names
**between the CODDENHAM to DUNWICH and
CODDENHAM to VENTA ICENORUM Roman roads**

On the following page, Oliver Rackham added:

> 'It is just possible that some of the oldest coppices in counties with strong Roman connexions, such as Suffolk and Essex, might go back as managed woodland to the Romans.'

It has long been known that the potteries of Wattisfield go back, with presumable interludes, to Roman times. It had never occurred to me to link the supply of firing-material to the place-name, which certainly means an open space (in contrast to woodland), and possibly means 'open space for wattle-growing' — i.e. for supplying the main primitive and medieval wall-filling in these parts. It is seventy years since Basil Oliver[41] and C. F. Innocent[42] showed how, from Roman times, twigs or wattles had been interwoven with stakes and, in stouter buildings, posts, to create walls which were then sealed with daub — clay, mixed with short straw and chalk and worked into the wattle. The rain was kept off the daub by widely overhanging thatch and by fine plaster keyed into the daub panels. In this way, wattle-and-daub survived for centuries. The wattle was usually long split saplings of hazel and ash. The provision of housing involved the production of coppices of both hazel and ash, and my first thought on reading that paragraph by Oliver Rackham was that Wattisfield might well have been concentrating on the production of building materials (much as nearby Sapiston perhaps specialised in the production of soap, according to Ekwall). But at Wattisfield the main need was obviously for fuel for the potteries. (Incidentally, yet another Roman kiln in very good order has emerged seven miles down the road at Grimston End, near Ixworth, in the 1985 excavation: there must have been very great demand for fuel as well as for wall-building.)

Now the main needs for kiln fuel have lately been reviewed by Vivien Swann in her survey, *The Pottery Kilns of Roman Britain*.[43] As I suppose everyone who has ever made a fire knows, you need a ready supply of quickly combustible material to get the kiln really hot, and then a slower, steady burner, like ash. It so happens that a mile or two south of Wattisfield you come to Great and Little Ashfield (see Map 2a). These two Ashfields together cover a rough square of about three miles. The boundaries are very unusual: they are curiously straight, and two, if not three, of the four corners are noticeably rounded: the fourth's sharp angle is formed by a stream. These rounded corners are features of a medieval (and presumably earlier) park: they simplify the erection of park-pales. The purpose of ordinary park-paling is to keep the deer enclosed. If my guess is right, that Ashfield lay within a big Ash-coppice wood to help fuel the industrial pottery at Wattisfield, then here the object would have been to keep such creatures

41 *Old Houses and Village Buildings in East Anglia*, 1912, pp. 10 and 37.
42 *The Development of English Building Construction*, 1916, pp. 126—133.
43 Vivien G. Swann, *The Pottery Kilns of Roman Britain*, R.C.H.M., 1984.

out. Again the hint came from Oliver Rackham, who pointed out that ash, like hazel, as saplings and coppice shoots are the favourite food of cattle and deer.

There is still an abundance of ashtrees in Great Ashfield. By the time of Domesday Book, Robert Blund had succeeded Achi, a landowner with an East Scandinavian name, in several estates around Ashfield (fols. 438b – 440). They included the main part of Ixworth, with a park and a vineyard; in Ashfield itself, woods of various sizes survived as pannage for feeding pigs, and there were ten hives of bees and a church. The Blunds (or was it the Achi's?) seem to have found it necessary (it can hardly have been erected for convenience of living, or for fashion) to build themselves a round motte, 24 ft high, to reside on. From about the time of the Northman Achi, a tall (10 ft 6 in) carved stone cross survives, bearing up its side a baffling inscription. Whether it related to a boundary, or to Christian preaching, is not clear. A Christian use may be inferrable from the fact that it was serving as footbridge across the churchyard ditch when Lord Chancellor Thurlow had it removed to his garden in Ashfield. (Pl. 23)

But my conviction is that Ashfield and Wattisfield were given their pure English names long before this Anglo-Danish period. Achi's Ashfield entry in Domesday Book reads: 'In *Easce*feldam tenuit *Achi* . . .' Those are the usual spellings in the Suffolk Domesday of both Ashfield and Achi. However, on the following folio (439b), the scribe spelt his name Aki. This implies that Achi was pronounced with a hard ch. We need not for a moment wonder whether perhaps Ashfield, like Ilketshall (see p. 28) and Alpheton (Ch. 5), happened to take its name from an 11th-century landowner. *Easce* really does mean ash. And *feld* implies open spaces in the woodland. This supposes that the woods were being regularly cleared, or coppiced, when the English named these places. From what we know of the industrial scale of the Romano-British potteries of Wattisfield and elsewhere round here, these processes of coppicing and clearing were taken over by the English from the British. We know from Dr Stanley West's discoveries at West Stow that at *Camborito*, the primitive English and less-primitive British over-lapped. The evidence of these -*feld* names suggests to me that such overlapping was widespread in Suffolk. This would bear out, on a large scale, what Oliver Rackham suggested about the possibility that some of the oldest coppices go back as managed woodland to the Romans. In the case of the Bradfields (see Map 3) there is still coppicing to show. Here, at Ashfield and Wattisfield, there is one more powerful support from the place-names.

If the ashwood at Ashfield was wanted to fire potteries at Wattisfield, why were they not adjacent? The answer lies in the name of the place that divides them (Map 2a): Walsham-le-Willows,[44] which means village of the

44 Walsham's charming affix is a comparatively recent development: in John Kirby's *Suffolk Traveller*, 1735, it is 'Walsham in the Willows'; Willows, like hazel and ash, had a function as building material. Thatchers, with perhaps the key role in the whole process of local building, liked to use split willow for the stakes or broaches, hairpin-shaped, with

Welshman, or *walh*, or the Romano-British (presumably Iceni, but their name is already used, as I believe, at Ixworth and elsewhere in the neighbourhood). The fact that the English named this place '*ham* of the Welshman' is for me conclusive argument that Oliver Rackham was right to suggest a date as early as the Romano-British for the kind of woodmanship we have been considering. At Walsham, the English settled alongside that 'Welsh' farmer whose men — family or subordinates — were, as I think creating open spaces, *felds*, in Wattisfield and Ashfield, to north and south of their village.

These arguments are strengthened by Oliver Rackham in patient replies to my letters.

'A coppice panel,' he says, 'normally ceases to be "open space" within a year or two; abandoned wood-pasture commons revert to woodland within about 20 years; and abandoned arable usually becomes more impenetrable than an ancient wood within 30 years. Open spaces survive as such *only if they are used*, and it takes a lot of grazing to prevent them from being bushed over.'

Elsewhere he affirms:

'The survival of so many Roman roads implies that there has continuously been a population to use them and to keep them open. If not used, a road becomes overgrown within a few years; in 15 years at most it becomes more impenetrable than the surrounding country. (Disused roads have a particular attraction for blackthorn.)'

Historians or archaeologists still feeling that the *adventus Saxonum* occasioned wholesale slaughter of the British and the flight of the survivors to Wales and Cornwall will be hard-pressed if they are to make their theories fit the evidence of the place-names we are considering, these -*feld* names of Suffolk.

As well as the Bradfields in their group with Stanningfield and Cockfield, Map 3 shows Waldingfield and Whatfield, linked closely not only to Roman villas, and roads, but also to the neighbourhood where Oliver Rackham has shown the small-leaved lime to be growing in the ancient woods.[45] These woods, he says, 'are almost certainly the fragmented remains of parts of the Wildwood that were particularly rich in *Tilia* (limes).' They are represented by Assington Thicks and Groton Wood (and a scatter of nearby smaller woods). Margaret Gelling translates Waldingfield as 'open land of the dwellers in the wold'.[46] If she means 'dwellers in the Wildwood', that might

which they fixed the thatch in place — indeed, like a hairpin. Harrison, the Elizabethan Alec Clifton-Taylor, wrote that 'in former times', willow, sallow (goat willow), plum, hard-beam (hornbeam) and elm were used before the insistence, in his day, on oak for ordinary buildings.

45   Oliver Rackham, *op. cit.*, p. 43 and fig. 8.
46   *Place-names in the Landscape*, p. 242.

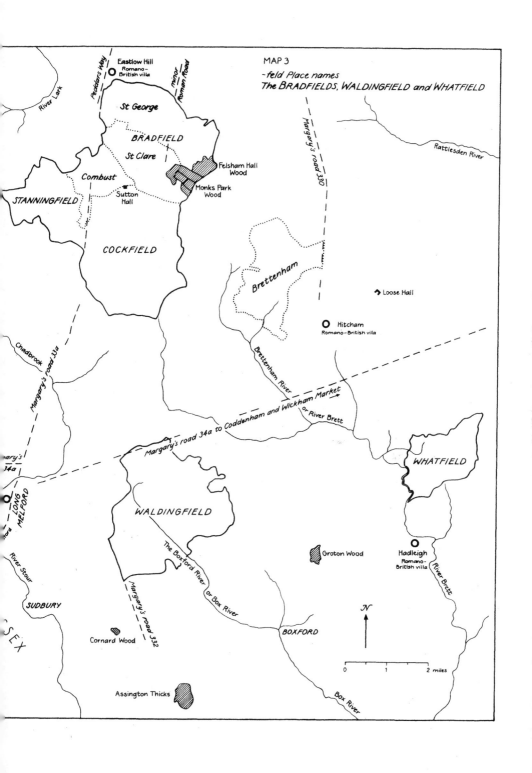

MAP 3
-feld Place names
The BRADFIELDS, WALDINGFIELD and WHATFIELD

Eastlow Hill
Romano-British villa

Peddars Way

minor Roman Road

River Lark

St George

BRADFIELD

St Clare

Felsham Hall Wood

Combust

Monks Park Wood

STANNINGFIELD

Sutton Hall

COCKFIELD

Margary's road 33a

Chadbrook

Margary's road 33a

Brettenham

Rattlesden River

Loose Hall

Hitcham
Romano-British villa

Brettenham River

Margary's 34a

LONG MELFORD

Margary's road 34a to Coddenham and Wickham Market
or River Brett

WHATFIELD

WALDINGFIELD

The Boxford River or Box River

Groton Wood

Hadleigh
Romano-British villa

River Brett

River Stour

SUDBURY

SSEX

Margary's road 332

Cornard Wood

BOXFORD

N

Assington Thicks

Box River

0   1   2 miles

be right. But the close proximity of the Romano-British villa and settlement at Melford, and the conjunction of major Roman roads, must be related to the meaning of those open lands at Waldingfield. If they were really wide open, like Bradfield, when the English arrived, then they were probably being grazed. Whatfield, itself near the villas at Hadleigh and Hitcham, means 'open space where wheat was grown', and so that was already an arable open space.

The position of Whatfield in the valley of 'the Briton' at Brettenham, and that of Waldingfield, watered by the stream of 'the Box' demonstrates that Margaret Gelling is mistaken when she suggests that 'the main characteristic of the area of Suffolk where *feld* names predominate may be comparative dryness'.[47] The main characteristic of the area of Suffolk where *feld* names predominate is rich, heavy boulder-clay. It is famous for its wheat-growing qualities, as it probably was when Whatfield was named. In the 16th century it was equally famous for its dairies, for the pastures were not confined to the valley-meadows. The kind of clay that will grow good wheat will grow good grass. It is *moisture-holding*. The first job any boulder-clay farmer tackles is draining the water from the fields, in pipes and ditches that run into the streams forming the east-flowing rivers. There is only one of Suffolk's thirty-one *feld* names that might be thought 'comparatively dry'. It is Waldringfield, flanking the heathland of Martlesham, and echoing the impressive curve of Martlesham's southern boundary: Martlesham's landscape suggests prehistoric settlement (see Map 1b, p. 2). It faces Kingston, the *tun* of those Sutton Hoo kings, across Martlesham Creek. And it contains a vanished Priests-*tun*, *Prestetun* in Domesday Book, a 'carucate', and an 'acre' of meadow, approximately located by W. G. Arnott.[48] Waldringfield itself, with at least one early Anglo-Saxon cremated on the site of the graveyard of All Saints' church, was an 'open space' belonging to 'Waldhere's people', upstream from 'Baldhere's island', and presumably pasture or ploughland for its own benefit and that of its neighbours: its newly arrived or imminent neighbours to the north were probably Swedish 'royals', and to the south were at least well-watered by the springs still welling up at Brightwell and Newbourn. In the early days there were the British of Walton, serving the Saxon Short fort there of the Romans. Their landscape was already supplied with roads like that running to the fort from Stratton and presumably Colchester. Patient field-walking in Waldringfield may one day establish whether that open space was devoted to coppicing, grazing, corn-growing, or all three. (Sutton Hoo's own site is pre-historic.)

The maps of these Suffolk -*feld* place-names need little comment. These ancient 'open spaces' are shown to be, with the exception of Waldringfield, in the heavy boulder-clays that stretch across Suffolk from north-east to

47   *Loc. cit.*
48   Domesday Book, fol. 424b. *Place-names of the Deben Valley Parishes*, Ipswich, 1946,   p. 12.

south-west, and their proximity to, and sometimes coincidence with, Romano-British positions. Two of them it seemed unnecessarily extravagant to map: Bredfield, which lies just across the Coddenham-Wickham Market Roman road from Charsfield — which has its own Roman vestiges and appears on the southern edge of Map 2b — and Sternfield, which does just appear at the south-east corner of Map 4: it is very close to Knodishall (possibly *Sitomagus*) and Aldeburgh (with its Roman remains, like Dunwich's, under the sea), and is a mile and a half from the villa-site at Langham Bridge, Farnham (OS 372583).

Map 5a is mostly self-explanatory. Aerial photography in 1971 revealed the Lidgate villa in amazing detail — like one of the greater Elizabethan or Jacobean houses in plan.[49] Wickhambrook's name we noted as an example of a word borrowed from Latin and transmitted to the English namers here. We can hardly doubt that the 'open space' at Withersfield, Badmondisfield and Stansfield were created, by Romano-British woodmen or farmers, for coppice, pasture or arable. Stradishall's name sends us looking for a *strade*, or Roman road; Chedburgh's, as at Chediston which we are coming to, makes us wonder whether the *beria*, or *beorg*, was a mound in some way associated with the great founder of Christianity in Essex, Cedd: Chedburgh's little valley enfolds a tributary of the river Linnet, and the only episcopal monument in sight is the obelisk commemorating the earl of Bristol who made such an impression as bishop of Derry. Similarly Thurlow (*thryth-hlaw*, a famous tumulus) has nothing to vindicate its striking name save the straightness of its boundaries, which suggest a line of Roman road or possibly a ritual *cursus*.

On Map 5b, the likelihood of Ringsfield and Shadingfield being made 'open' by Roman-British farmers is clear. Two points to note are the first element in Ringsfield, which could refer to a circular wood-henge monument, of which no other sign has emerged; and Stoven is the Old English (or Old Norse) word *stofn*, a stump. Oliver Rackham, describing the first clearing of the Wildwood, observed that 'the stumps and bigger logs would have to be ploughed around, as in 19th-century North America, for many years.'[50] Stoven could be a reference to an exceptionally big ash-stool, such as he illustrates in Plates VII (Felsham Hall Wood, Bradfield) and IX (near Saffron Walden). This might suggest an extension of coppicing from adjoining Shadingfield. At present we do not know what either clearance was made for, only that it seemed worthy of a name that has not changed since the days of the early Anglo-Saxon settlers. Pakefield is now almost swallowed, by the sea in the east and by Lowestoft in the north.

The -*feld* implications shown in Map 4 were what first caught my curiosity. As with the Bradfields, which we look at separately in Chapter 6, it is hard to get a picture of so many separate adjacent 'open spaces'. Sitting in

49   Scarfe, *op cit.*, Pl. 12.
50   Oliver Rackham, *op cit.*, p. 47.

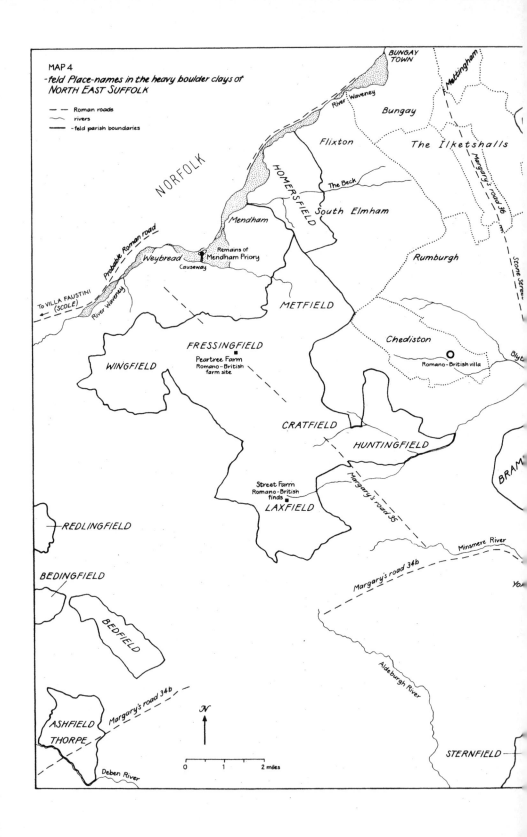

MAP 4

-feld Place-names in the heavy boulder clays of
NORTH EAST SUFFOLK

— — Roman roads
〰 rivers
━━ -feld parish boundaries

NORFOLK

BUNGAY TOWN

River Waveney

Bungay

Mettingham

Flixton

The Ilketshalls

HOMERSFIELD

The Beck

South Elmham

Rumburgh

Mendham

Remains of
Mendham Priory

Weybread

Causeway

Probable Roman road

To VILLA FAUSTINI
(SCOLE)

River Waveney

METFIELD

Chediston

Romano-British villa

Blyth

Margary's road 36

Stone Street

FRESSINGFIELD

Peartree Farm
Romano-British
farm site

WINGFIELD

CRATFIELD

HUNTINGFIELD

BRAM

Street Farm
Romano-British
finds

LAXFIELD

Margary's road 35

REDLINGFIELD

Minsmere River

BEDINGFIELD

Margary's road 34b

Yo

BEDFIELD

Aldeburgh River

Margary's road 34b

N

ASHFIELD
THORPE

Deben River

0   1   2 miles

STERNFIELD

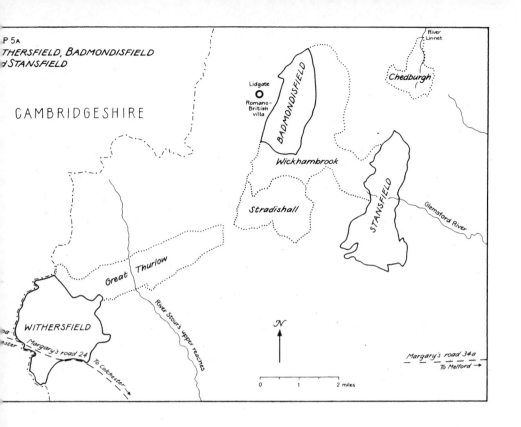

MAP 5A
WITHERSFIELD, BADMONDISFIELD
and STANSFIELD

CAMBRIDGESHIRE

River
Linnet

Chedburgh

BADMONDISFIELD

Lidgate
O
Romano-
British
villa

STANSFIELD

Wickhambrook

Glemsford River

Stradishall

Great Thurlow

WITHERSFIELD

River Stour's upper reaches

Margary's road 24

To Colchester

N

Margary's road 34a
To Melford →

0   1   2 miles

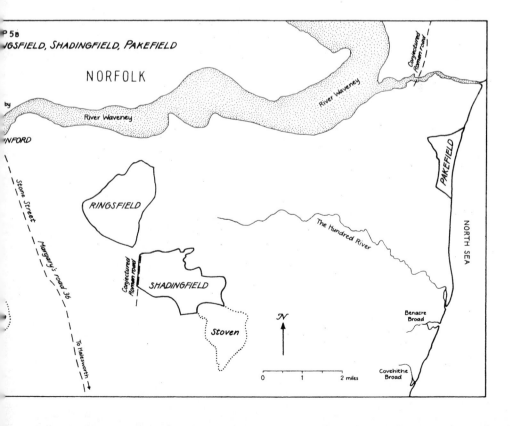

MAP 5B
RINGSFIELD, SHADINGFIELD, PAKEFIELD

NORFOLK

Conjectured Roman road

River Waveney

River Waveney

by

NFORD

PAKEFIELD

Stone Street

Margary's road 36

RINGSFIELD

The Hundred River

NORTH SEA

Conjectured Roman road

SHADINGFIELD

Stoven

Benacre
Broad

To Halesworth

N

Covehithe
Broad

0   1   2 miles

this rich boulder-clay, they must have been spaces in woodland. Again, the framework of Roman roads and the proximity of the villa at Chediston make it fairly obvious who organised and maintained these great clearings until the early English took over. It is possible that a better toponymist than I am may be able to make more appropriate sense of the first elements of all these names — as at Ashfield. I feel faintly discontented with 'open land of Wiga's people' for Wingfield, 'open land of Craeta' for Cratfield, 'open land of Leaxa' for Laxfield, and so on, but presumably Wiga, Craeta and Leaxa were not at all discontented with their farmland and woodland on this fertile clay. They would certainly have to work hard to keep their clearings grazed or ploughed or coppiced. Already, families and friends are involved at Huntingfield, 'the open land of Hunta's -ing, his people'. Fressingfield supplies momentary relief: it *may* mean 'open land of the Frisians' — the rest being presumably Angles, by contrast, of racial origin. (In West Suffolk, we find Flemings at Flempton and Saxons at Saxham: at least in the settling, or naming, period, East Angles *were* distinguished from each other racially, however muddled they soon became. The pagan Essex men, indeed, practised a religion unlike that of all other Saxon and English invaders.)[51] For Fressingfield's woods, see chapter 11, p. 146.

The implication of this welter of new personal, and occasionally family, tribal or racial names, may be that they were carving into individual farms what had been managed by their British predecessors from large estate-centres, villas like Lidgate and Chediston, and from working villages like Walsham-le-Willows (Map 2a), Brettenham (Map 3) and Walpole (Map 7). In his study of the development of settlement in Blything Hundred,[52] Peter Warner detected a scatter of main Romano-British 'settlement complexes' — at, notably, Wenhaston (Map 4), Reydon (near Southwold), Darsham (Map 7) and Knodishall, near Aldeburgh. In the main -feld cluster on Map 4, an early Romano-British farm was detected at Peartree Farm, Fressingfield, very near the line of Roman road running to Weybread, the *way* referred to in the name. The finds at Street Farm, Laxfield, could indicate remains of another disused (north-east to south-west) Roman road if Street Farm proves to be an old name.

The name of Metfield looks at home among this great cluster of -felds on Map 4, but it is different. First, its meaning is 'open land with meadow'. That is lovely: for once, we have a picture, a named use of one, or part of one, of these -felds. But have we? The only place in Metfield that could possibly be thought of as meadow is the very small green just east of the church: it has a forded stream running round two sides of it, and a large pond. But then there is another difference to take into account. All the remaining thirty -feld names we are examining appear in Domesday Book.

---

51   Scarfe, *op cit.*, pp. 84—85; and *Essex: A Shell Guide*, pp. 9—10.
52   Leicester University Ph.D. thesis: microfilm copy in Suffolk Record Office, Ipswich, J.440/1.

Metfield's name does not. However, at adjacent Mendham, a minster, a church with a monastic community, featured in a will in c. 942−951:[53] it was clearly the mother-church of Metfield. Sure enough, Mendham in Domesday Book is assessed on two separate churches and three-eighths of another. Since Metfield was later regarded as a hamlet and chapelry of Mendham, we may assume that Metfield's was one of these Domesday churches assessed as Mendham's. It lies concealed and anonymous in the long descriptions of that place. We may therefore be justified in thinking more easily of Metfield as 'open land, in woods, with meadow'. For this meadow can now be imagined as lying among those delectable water-meadows of Mendham, down in the wide Waveney valley.

We come to the last of the -feld names to be considered, a key example in the elucidation of Suffolk place-names: Homersfield (Map 4). Homersfield adjoins Mendham, with its old minster, and is itself a part of South Elmham, also with an old minster. The facts are succinctly set out in Domesday Book,[54] which lists first the lands of the East Anglian bishop and, next, the 'fee', the feudal possessions of the bishop.

In Suffolk, the two great estates of the bishop, virtually his only lands in Suffolk, were Hoxne, with a church (a former cathedral of the diocese), and the greater part of Homersfield, with another church. His feudal possessions were substantially concentrated in this same small neighbourhood: two small-holdings and a second church in Homersfield, various other smallish estates in 'Halmeham' (South Elmham) with 5 churches; then two small estates in Flixton with half a holding of a church. The only other considerable feudal possession of the bishop was in Lothingland Half-Hundred, at least sixteen miles away down the Waveney valley. By a most extraordinary coincidence, it, too, was called Flixton, and it has a church dedicated to St Michael and so well endowed that it, too, must have been a minster. Those are the bare facts. Now, in Domesday Book, Homersfield was spelt Humbresfeld, and toponymists agree that it means Hunberht's feld. It is embedded in this tight-knit bundle of estates and churches of the bishop's fee — the historic endowment of the East Anglian bishop — known as South Elmham. It so happens that Hunberht was the name of the last bishop of Elmham before the Danes put an end to the sequence of bishops, and to King Edmund. The late Professor Dorothy Whitelock recorded: he is 'said to have anointed Edmund king of East Anglia in 856; post-conquest writers identify him with the bishop present with king Edmund in 869, and Symeon of Durham makes him share his martyrdom.'[55] She does not say these things are impossible, only that such things were suggested because his was the last name on the surviving list of the bishops. She did, in correspondence, dismiss outright the idea that Hunberht's -feld might have

53   D. Whitelock, (ed.), Anglo-Saxon Wills, 1930, I. Michael Hardy has found Romano-British sites in Metfield.
54   Domesday Book, fols. 379−381.
55   'The pre-Viking age church in East Anglia', Anglo-Saxon England, I, 1972, p. 22.

been named after a bishop who was last on the list of pre-Danish bishops and might have died with Edmund: 'such places had been named very much earlier'.

But, similarly, the coincidence of having two places called Flixton in two widely separated estates of the East Anglian bishops, made no impression. They, too, could not be named after the first of those bishops, Felix, whose endowment they all inherited. Such names were thought to belong to much earlier stages of the English settlement than the first half of the 7th century, so that was that. Happily, we all try to keep open minds about open land. In chapter 5 I have demonstrated, I hope conclusively, that for whatever reason, Alpheton took its name from a lady living as late as the 11th century. I am not suggesting that Hunberht's -*feld* was the first name of this place. It had, of course, been part of South Elmham and may have had a Celtic name before that. One of the Flixtons, too, was part of South Elmham. (The other, in the 12th century, lost a lot of its territory to Oulton.)[56] It is my considered judgement that Homersfield took its name from the last bishop of Elmham before that first Danish visitation, whether or not he died with Edmund: my guess is that he did. In those days there were two bishops at work in East Anglia, one at Elmham, the other at Dunwich. Hunberht's colleague, over at Dunwich, was Aethelwald — the last pre-Danish bishop there. By an extraordinary chance his seal, with wolf's heads glittering with garnet eyes, was found early in the 19th century at Eye (Pl. 7). Hunberht was commemorated more securely at Elmham. And so, I suppose, was their 7th-century forerunner of Felix: both at Elmham and at Oulton, which was so probably named Flixton on being given to him. His palpable success as the apostle of East Anglia we celebrate in chapter 3. I know that 'this is the sort of speculation no place-name student would indulge in'. In circumstances like these, of inescapable and extraordinary coincidences, it may be that they should.

-tun *and* -stan, *a caution*

Words ending now in -ton usually started as *tun* and, as we saw, there are 97 of them in Suffolk. They are seldom prefixed by personal names, but when we see Chediston's name, we might suppose we had found an example. We have not. The Domesday spellings are *Cidestan* and *Cedestan*, which means 'Cedd's stone'. No one is surprised that -*stone* (which is how Chediston's name *should* end) is a very rare suffix in this county: there are so few stones lying about to be worth naming a place after. Chediston is unique in Suffolk, which is enough to arouse curiosity. Its prefix, too, is something to conjure with.

The Romano-British villa-site at Chediston, immediately east of the church, has not been excavated. A little further to the east, behind

56   Scarfe, *The Suffolk Landscape, op. cit.*, pp. 125 – 127 and fig. 9.

Chediston Hall, and again just beyond the Chediston boundary at Rockstone Manor, the name is immediately explained by the presence of enormous erratic stones deposited here by a glacier along with the surrounding boulder-clay. The Chediston Hall specimen has long been concealed in woodland, but the Rockstone from which the manor (in Cookley: 'woodcock-glade'; confound Ekwall with his 'Cuca's leah'!) took its name is to this day said to have been used by druids as a sacrificial stone! This seems to the rash romantic in me to be the moment to remember bishop Cedd, the apostle of Essex, who had been consecrated by the Scots (Irish), who served so well as mediator between Roman and Irish traditions at the Synod of Whitby, and who ended his long life by founding and ruling the monastery at Lastingham. In Essex he founded Christianity in the ruins of Othona, the Roman fort at Bradwell-juxta-Mare. Bede says 'he established churches in various places and ordained priests and deacons to assist him in preaching and baptism, especially in the city of *Ythancaestir* (Othona).' It was this Cedd who baptised an Essex prince 'in vico regio qui dicitur Rendlaesham'. King Aethelwald of East Anglia, brother and successor of king Anna, supported the prince as he ascended from the holy font.[57] The formidable Cedd was not a stranger, then, in Suffolk. Divining the magic that must have surrounded these gigantic, unaccountable stones, I see very well how Cedd might have come here to preach and to try to dispel pagan fear of them. That the place bears his name may be a coincidence, but it could mean that he succeeded as he generally did.

The remaining place-name suffixes, including -halh

After *-feld*, the next commonest name-ending is *-ley*. This is not surprising in a county so largely covered by boulder-clay in which woodland flourishes, so long as it is not cut down or intensively browsed; for *-ley* implies 'a glade', different in degree, in the minds of the namers, from the more open *-feld*. They occur side-by-side at Charsfield and Otley, Stanningfield and Brockley. The remaining suffixes are worth enumerating, for their mere number has significance in terms of the landscape: -ley 26; -ford 20; -ing (place of the people or family of) 17; -halh 15 (I will return briefly to these); -stead (place or site) 12; -burh (a fortified place) 12; -worth (a homestead or enclosure) 10; -den (a valley) 10; -ey (an island, as we saw) 9; -don (a hill, a very relative concept in Suffolk and most obvious south-west of Bury) 7; -well 7, a disappointing total, for few walks are more enjoyable than those taken in search of an eponymous water-source; -brook 5; -grave (grave or ditch) 4; -bourn 4. There are still 43 unclassifiables, such as Hengrave, where -grave = grēd, a meadow; or Groton, which is *groten-ea*, a sandy stream.

As things stand, *-halh* has a slightly pejorative modern equivalent, 'a nook'. Margaret Gelling discusses it at length in her section on 'Valleys and

---

57   Colgrave and Mynors, (see p. 30 below), *Bede's Ecclesiastical History*, pp. 282–4, 298.

Remote Places' in her latest book.[58] In her 'glossarial index' she gives Ilketshall as 'Ulfketill's nook'. Now, a glance at the four parishes that make up Ilketshall (Map 4) will show that it is no kind of a nook, nor was it when it was named at the start of the 11th century. In her discussion, however, Margaret Gelling says: '*halh* sometimes means "piece of land projecting from, or detached from, the main area of its administrative unit" '.[59] This does seem to describe Ilketshall's case. The unit in question was a quarter, a 'farthing' or 'ferthing', of the Hundred of Wangford, administered from Wainford, Bungay, where the Roman road plunged through the Waveney. South Elmham (including Homersfield and Flixton) made one 'farthing', while 'the Seven Parishes', as they are still sometimes called — of Bungay (2), Mettingham and Ilketshall (4) — made a second farthing.

As with Hunberhtsfeld, one risks an assertion of the identity of the Ulfketel whose name is preserved here. His valour got East Anglia known as Ulfkill's Land all over the Norse world, and his great benefactions to St Edmund's abbey we come to on pp. 77–78. The Bigot earls of East Anglia had based themselves on Bungay by the time of Domesday Book, and soon erected a castle from which to defy Henry II. Whether their famous predecessor Ulfketel was based at Bungay is not yet clear, though I have no doubt that his name is remembered in Ilketshall. Professor Cameron reminds me that we have no irrefutable proof, and thinks such statements of belief are rash. I naturally base my belief on reasons, and await the possible emergence of proof, either documentary or archaeological. Absence of proof should not signal the termination of all thinking.

Because Ilketshall's name dates in this way from the beginning of the 11th century, we may not imagine for a moment that it was not actively settled under an earlier name, or names, during the preceding centuries. It was at this time that Bedericsworth became St Edmundsbury. Valiant preliminary excursions into the subject of this earlier settlement have been made by Peter Warner and P. G. Bigmore.[60] Bigmore suggested the survival in Ilketshall of an area of Romano-British centuriation, based on 20-actus units. It seems that Bigmore's theories have been dismissed because Ilketshall's name indicates relatively late colonisation! The Ilketshalls need much more patient research, in those heavy clays and among the documents. I think, as Peter Warner clearly does, that Bigmore is on the right lines.

Margaret Gelling has suggested this rather curious and useful alternative meaning for *halh*. I wonder whether we may not be too firmly dismissing the possibility, when we come to these late 10th/early 11th-century Anglo-Danish names, that the word may occasionally mean hall as well as nook? Domesday Book makes twenty-six references to halls in Suffolk, using the

---

58   *Place-names in the Landscape*, pp. 100–111.
59   *Loc. cit.*, p. 100.
60   'Blything Hundred: A study in settlement, 400–1400', and 'Suffolk Settlement: A study in continuity.' Ph.D. theses, Leicester University.

word *halle*. In Sudbury, for instance, sixty-three burgesses attached to the hall are described as *'halle manentes'*, with two horses on the demesne of the hall, again *halle*. Most of these *halle* references are to numbers of horses kept there. Unluckily, the forms of the various references to *Ilcheteleshala* and *Ilcheteshala* among the possessions of earl Hugh in *Wenefort* Hundred rule out verbal evidences of his hall there. The name must be explained by some kind of 'detachment from an administrative unit'. There is an excellent candidate for the site of whatever it is, in Ilketshall St John, at the great mound, 23 ft high, with its horse-shoe shaped bailey and fosse.[61]

The place-names of the Danes and Norsemen

Compared with Norfolk, the place-name evidence for Danish/Norse settlement in Suffolk is significantly sparse. It is largely confined to the coastline, and particularly to the Lothingland strip north of Lowestoft — itself an old Norse name. But the message of these names is largely one of co-existence, and probably collaboration and inter-marriage, with the English — as we hinted in the section on 'The British Predecessors' early in this chapter. These are almost all 'hybrid' names — Scandinavian prefixes to the English -ton: Gunton, Corton, Belton and Somerleyton — the *tun* of the 'summer-warriors'. Ashby's name did not appear till late in the 12th century, along with its church and round bell-tower. Lound is the delightful Scandinavian word *lundr*, a grove.

Moving south along the coast, there is Westleton, *Weslidi-tun*, farm of a Norseman who had travelled west! Minsmere, nearby, is the mere at *Mynni*, Old Scandinavian for 'mouth of a river' — the one that flows down through Yoxford. Another hybrid in that neighbourhood is Ubbeston. Still further to the south, Eyke is simple Scandinavian for oak: near Staverton Thicks it must be highly plural, not one of those conspicuous solitary oaks Oliver Rackham warned of. A final trio of Domesday Book hybrids remains in the Felixstowe peninsula — Morston (Hall, Trimley), Grimston (Hall, Trimley) and Nacton, *Hnakki's tun*.

Inland, Wilby is a pleasant trip-wire: what looks like the Danish *byr* is really English *beag* — ring of willows that still thrive in hedgerows near the church. Risby really is Danish. Wickham *Skeith* must have had a Danish racecourse, perhaps on the green: skeith = racecourse. Finally there is Thwaite, a late Danish clearing at the heart of the woods beside the Roman 'Pye' road from Colchester to Norwich. Eight Thorps are scattered from Aldringham (near Aldeburgh) and Hasketon (Thorpe Hall), across through Hoxne and Westhorpe, Stanton, Ashfield and Ixworth, to Thorpe Morieux. According to the place-names, the Danish conquest of Suffolk was hardly colonisation. It was political, a foretaste of the Normans of 1066.

61 *Victoria County History: Suffolk*, I, 1911, p. 600, with plan.

2

Raedwald's Queen and the Sutton Hoo Coins: Dishonour, Diplomacy, and the Battle at the Idle River

In his *Ecclesiastical History of the English People*,[1] Bede did not give the name of the wife of Raedwald, ruler of East Anglia from 599 to, perhaps, 624; he was writing a century later in far Northumbria, but he did provide two vivid illustrations of the influence she exercised over her powerful husband. Bede's great saga of the coming of Christianity to the early English celebrates, almost with approval, her devotion to the pagan priority of loyalty to one's best friend and her dread of the dishonour that would lie in betraying him for gold. In this essay, I hope to establish the possibility that the gold in question was the collection of gold coins buried in the Sutton Hoo ship, in one of the most richly bejewelled purses ever made. The argument leads, via Northumbria, to the whetstone-sceptre and the large hanging-bowl in that ship.

Bede, a monk of Wearmouth-Jarrow, naturally deplored the East Anglian queen's faith in the old northern gods. He was recalling how King Edwin of Northumbria (a significantly tardy convert to Christianity) was responsible for persuading Eorpwald, Raedwald's son and successor, to leave idolatry and embrace the faith of Christ. The story reminded Bede that Raedwald himself had once, long before, in Kent, been initiated into the mysteries of Christianity, but with scandalous results. 'On his return home, he was led astray by his wife and wrong-headed teachers who undermined his faith, so that his last state was worse than his first': he combined both forms of worship in one temple. It is usually supposed to have stood in what Bede called a *'vicus regius*, a royal estate, at Rendlesham'. But this sole reference by Bede to Rendlesham was to a royal baptism that took place there at least thirty years after Raedwald's death. Martin Carver, on being appointed Research Director for Sutton Hoo, quickly observed that Raedwald's temple and hall, going back to the 6th century, might quite possibly have been at Kingston, just across the river about a mile below Sutton Hoo: Kingston simply means 'royal manor'. Here is a familiar archaeological uncertainty, until the two places can be fully explored. Raedwald's great-nephew Aldwulf, who ruled East Anglia from c. 663 to 713, well into Bede's day, testified that that dual temple lasted possibly as late as c. 650, for he saw it 'when he was a boy'. Unless Aldwulf was an extremely old man in 713, that blatantly Laodicean temple-church would have been a source of

1   Bertram Colgrave and R. A. B. Mynors (eds.), *Bede's Ecclesiastical History of the English People*, 1969, 188–191 (hereafter, C. and M.).

vexation throughout the highly effective ministry of St Felix (c. 630—648), but all the more remarkable a physical memorial to the strength and personality of Raedwald's queen.

Bede continued with the note that, soon after his conversion by King Edwin, Eorpwald, Raedwald's son, was killed: 'and after that, the kingdom lapsed into error for three years until Eorpwald's brother Sigeberht came to the throne, a very Christian and learned man'. Bede's earlier description[2] of the circumstances of Edwin's acceptance of Christianity in the year 627, in council with his chief friends and advisers and the chief priest, underlined the essentially political nature of that king's 'conversion'. It was eleven years since Raedwald had taken up his cause, defeated his enemies and set him on his throne. The delay in his conversion is fairly obviously connected with his allegiance to Raedwald, who had made himself paramount king south of the Humber by 616, and in Northumbria in the course of 616, when he set Edwin up as his client king there. But Raedwald died in about 624 and Edwin waited till 627 before adopting Christianity. If Raedwald's widow was still a dominant figure in her kingdom in those two or three years, that might partly explain Edwin's political reluctance to abandon the old gods in whom she believed. He owed her, and them, his life;[3] and loyalty to friends was a fundamental of their belief. The fact that he quickly converted Eorpwald, probably in that same year, 627, suggests that the old dowager may by then have died. Eorpwald's speedy death, and East Anglia's 'lapse' for three more years till Sigeberht's accession, attest that her influence and example survived during those final years of formal, Established paganism in the pre-Danish kingdom.

The nature, survival and strength of the queen's influence are highly relevant to anyone considering the circumstances of Raedwald's burial. If she herself outlived him, she would probably have had a major part in the ordering of his funeral, as H. M. Chadwick recognised and largely believed, in the earliest speculation on this subject.[4] It has long been understood that the silver spoons with *Saulos-Paulos* inscriptions most probably refer to the conversion of the buried person.[5] Now that the dating-evidence of the coins makes it likeliest that Raedwald was that person,[6] we must suppose that the spoons, and possibly the nine silver bowls with cruciform decoration, were presented to him in Kent at that early, ineffectual initiation into the Christian mysteries; and that, at his death, his pagan widow would be anxious to bury with him these symbols of his half-hearted and unresolved lapse from

2 C. and M., 182—187.
3 C. and M., 180—181.
4 H. M. Chadwick: 'The Sutton Hoo ship-burial: who was he?', *Antiquity*, XIV, no. 53, 1940, 76—87.
5 R. L. S. Bruce-Mitford, *The Sutton Hoo ship-burial: a provisional guide*, British Museum, London, 1947, 49.
6 Bruce-Mitford, *The Sutton Hoo ship-burial*, British Museum, London, Vol. 1, 1975, ch. IX, 578—682, and X, 683—717.

the truth as she saw it. All this is fairly familiar thinking. It seems worth rehearsing because what has not been suggested hitherto is that the presence of coins in that fabulously adorned purse[7] may be explained in a rather similar way. (Plates 4 and 5.)

Bede heard, and wrote down, a circumstantial, credible account of Edwin's exile at Raedwald's court. The date was about 615−616 — immediately before Raedwald, supremely powerful south of the Humber, went into battle on Edwin's behalf and defeated Aethelfrith of Northumbria 'at the borders of Mercia and on the east bank of the Idle'. This decisive battle is likely to have been fought just south of Bawtry in north Nottinghamshire; after Bawtry, the river idles due east towards the Trent. Here is Bede's account:[8]

> Aethelfrith sent messengers who brought (*offerent*) Raedwald much money (*pecuniam multam*) as inducement to kill Edwin. That did not work. He went a second and third time, with more lavish (*copiosora*) gifts of silver, and threats of war if the gifts were turned down. Raedwald, whether swayed by the threats (*minis fractus*) or seduced by the bribes (*corruptus muneribus*) yielded to the entreaties (*cessit deprecanti*) and promised to slay Edwin or to hand him over to the messengers.

This passage certainly suggests that the money-inducement was sent and accepted. Then came a strange interview outside Raedwald's hall at dead of night between Edwin and a shadowy stranger, presumably Paulinus.[9] Professor Whitelock[10] noticed Bede's omission of the stranger's name. Bede may have thought that to name him destroyed the mysterious, indeed, miraculous, effect of his story. The Roman mission seems already to have marked Edwin down as a key figure for conversion. They were evidently waiting only for Raedwald's rule to end before bringing Edwin to declare himself. The formidable Paulinus was quietly at work on this, preparing for the conversion of Northumbria and the creation of the archiepiscopal province of York, as early as 601.[11] But now, to encompass Edwin's survival, the mission was in the embarrassing predicament of having to invoke, and to trade on, the East Anglian queen's high standards of pagan honour.

Bede described the dramatic outcome. When Raedwald told the queen of his intention to kill Edwin,

> she talked him round with the warning that it ill became so great a king to exploit the misfortune of his best friend and sell him for gold; still less to lose his own honour, more precious than all adornments, for the love of money

---

7 The gold-inlaid jewellery decorating and framing the purse-lid alone contained no fewer than 1,526 individually shaped garnets and 33 millefiori insets.

8 C. and M., 176−177, 180−181.

9 C. and M., 178−179.

10 Dorothy Whitelock, 'The pre-Viking age church in East Anglia', *Anglo-Saxon England*, Vol. 1, 1972, 1−22.

11 C. and M., 104−105, and 192−193.

(*amore pecuniae*). What more (Bede continued rhetorically) is there to say? Not only did Raedwald not hand Edwin over, he even helped him to gain his kingdom. As soon as the messengers had gone home, he assembled a large force and attacked and slew Aethelfrith at the edge of Mercia on the east bank of the Idle before he had time to get his whole army together.

Naturally, Bede knew nothing of the strategy behind Raedwald's march to the Idle. Though Raedwald caught and killed his Pompey with one clean lightning strike, there is a touch of Caesar in the action. Not for nothing was his terrible headgear fashioned with models from Constantine's workshops somehow still in mind.[12] Not entirely for nothing did Raedwald's family, the Wuffingas, put Caesar with Woden and Frealaf at the top of their family-tree.[13] One thing more we would like Bede to have said is whether Raedwald returned Aethelfrith's money with the messengers. On this he is silent, leaving us to decide for ourselves whether it seems more in Raedwald's character to have packed them off empty-handed. To me it does.

What Bede seems to have said is that Aethelfrith sent money, and that money changed hands. Where would Aethelfrith have acquired any money? In Northumbria in the second decade of the 7th century, a very strong likelihood — perhaps the only real possibility — is by way of a diplomatic gift.

Reviewing *The Sutton Hoo Ship-Burial, Vol. I,* in *The Antiquaries Journal,*[14] Professor Rosemary Cramp wrote: 'To my mind the coin group makes most sense as a diplomatic gift put together in an area where such coinage was common so that selection could have been easily effected.' (A salient fact about the thirty-seven coins is that all are different, none duplicate.) Hitherto, the possibility has been considered that some such gift as this had been made direct to Raedwald.[15] No-one has considered Aethelfrith, yet he is not an unlikely recipient for such a gift. By the time of his attempt to bribe Raedwald, c. 615–616, he had ruled Northumbria twenty-three or twenty-four years: he and Raedwald were the two most powerful men in Britain. Bede described Aethelfrith in Book I, chapter 34[16] as

a very brave king and most eager for glory, who might indeed be compared with Saul except that he was ignorant of the Christian religion; for no ruler or king carved out more land for the English people to settle after either exterminating or subjugating the natives.

Irish and British slaves may have been Aethelfrith's main export-commodity to Europe. Just before his time, some angelic-looking boy-

12   Bruce-Mitford, *The Sutton Hoo ship-burial,* Vol. 2, 1978, 220.
13   *op. cit.,* Vol. 1, 693–695.
14   Rosemary Cramp, *Antiquaries Journal,* XVIII, part II, 1978, 220.
15   Bruce-Mitford, *op. cit.,* Vol. 1, 1975, 585.
16   C. and M., 116, 117.

slaves had caught Pope Gregory's eye, in one of Bede's most often-quoted stories:[17] that they were from Northumbria is less well remembered. Later,[18] Bede described Aethelfrith's resounding victory over the British at Chester, sometime between 613 and 616. The most celebrated episode in the battle was Aethelfrith's slaughter of about 1,200 monks from Bangor who had misguidedly taken up a praying position in full view of both armies. After such a victory, a diplomatic gift from the Merovingian king Chlothar II (613 – 629) could well have been a response to a present of slaves, or conceivably to a manumission of a number of Christian slaves, possibly some survivors from Bangor. J. P. C. Kent's brilliant dating of the Sutton Hoo coins seems to fit into this kind of programme perfectly.[19] In a much later passage,[20] Bede described how St Aidan in Northumbria made a point of 'distributing gifts of money (donaria pecuniarum) either for the use of the poor or for the redemption of those who had been unjustly sold into slavery'.[21]

If Aethelfrith received such a diplomatic gift, he was the kind of king who would not scruple to make practical use of it. Nor would he have been much surprised that it did not bring immediate results. The resort to the 'more lavish gifts of silver' may also, as Rupert Bruce-Mitford thought on reading the first draft of this piece, relate to part of the Sutton Hoo treasure — the Anastasius dish, the fluted bowl and, conceivably, the nine silver bowls. But equally, as he pointed out, the phrase might be taken, strictly, to imply that the first gift was also 'of silver', and thus could not be the gold coins. The text, on which we depend, remains ambiguous and inscrutable on this point. The contents of the purse contrast relatively meanly with the surrounding splendours aboard the burial-ship. Birgit Arrhenius has equated them with a mere two ounces Roman weight.[22] Even so, there is one person who might have wanted these gold pieces buried with, or in tribute to, Raedwald. If they were part of a bribe, and if his queen felt so strongly that acceptance of such a bribe tarnished her husband's character intolerably, she would on that score alone have wanted to bury the thirty-seven coins, three blanks and two small ingots intact, as evidence to her gods that it had

17   C. and M., 132 – 135.
18   C. and M., 140 – 141.
19   Bruce-Mitford, op. cit., Vol. 1, 1975, 588 – 647.
20   C. and M., 228 – 229.
21   Dr Rupert Bruce-Mitford, for whose kind scrutiny I am grateful, notes the dependence of the argument upon what Bede meant by pecunia, and rightly observes that it could mean wealth and riches, as well as money. We, too, take words like gold and riches to mean money. Bede was familiar with the use of money in his own lifetime, and there seems to me, as to the standard editors of his great work, a strong degree of probability that he was thinking of money when he wrote pecunia in the three passages discussed here. My friend Valerie Fenwick kindly showed me Bede's use, once, and in metaphor, of the word nomisma (C. and M., 238): a vision of the impending death, abroad, of a holy princess is described as the return of a gold coin, aureum nomisma, to its place of origin.
22   Birgit Arrhenius, Review of The Sutton Hoo ship-burial, Vol. 1, in Medieval Archaeology, XXII, 1978, 189 – 195.

failed to dishonour him. If the argument in what follows in the Postscript is accepted, then there was even stronger reason for elevating the coins, the embarrassing pretext for the battle with Aethelfrith, into a commemorative trophy of that battle.

Postscript: spoils of the victory at the Idle river

Two relevant books have appeared since this Northumbrian connexion with the coins was postulated. They prompt a brief epilogue. Brian Hope-Taylor's magnificent volume on *Yeavering* — his prose and archaeological draughtsmanship matching the epic work of excavation — bears the date 1977 on its title-page but was brought out, by HMSO, only after two more years. The Vol. 3 of the big British Museum *Sutton Hoo Ship-Burial* series appeared in 1983, including Rupert Bruce-Mitford's conclusions on the three hanging-bowls.

From 616, when he and his troops killed Aethelfrith of Northumbria in battle (the *Handbook of British Chronology* explains why the summer of 616 is the right date for this event, and not the 617 offered by the *Anglo-Saxon Chronicle*), until his own death — whenever that took place, probably about 624 — Raedwald's power undoubtedly extended over Northumbria; at first in fact, but perhaps towards the end of his life more hypothetically. That is to say, it extended over York and, beyond, over the Cheviots and the complex and predominantly British society of Bernicia Dr Hope-Taylor has so startlingly revealed.

That extensive, paramount power of Raedwald coincided with an Anglo-Saxon political idea known as *bretwaldaship*. It means, probably, 'rule over the whole of Britain'. Without actually using the word *bretwalda*, Bede listed five such Anglo-Saxon rulers, ending with Raedwald of East Anglia and Edwin of Northumbria. It is strange that the word itself appears in writing only two centuries later, in the *Anglo-Saxon Chronicle*. *Bretwaldaship* must have existed as a political notion, and probably as a name, in Raedwald's day. But he and the others gave it political reality not by voting, nor by 'taking turns', but by the personal exercise of power. I mention this because my old friend Dr Bruce-Mitford seems drawn, and committed in his major writings on Sutton Hoo, to the idea that all the glittering, kingly trappings in that ship-burial were the regalia of a *bretwalda*, as distinct from that of a mere hereditary king of the East Anglian Wuffinga dynasty. Raedwald's *bretwaldaship* was unique in East Anglia's history; and so, as Rupert Bruce-Mitford considers, the family felt it could bury all the insignia of *bretwaldaship* with him.[23] The great whetstone-sceptre was a pagan emblem, he says; and, as such, it would be

23 Bruce-Mitford, *The Sutton Hoo ship-burial*, Vol. 2, 1978, 347, 375, etc.

'unacceptable' to Christian successors, who would feel relieved to be rid of it.[24] I wish I found these ideas persuasive.

I find it impossible to imagine Raedwald being buried at Sutton Hoo by Christians eager to be discharged of such pagan barbarities. As we saw, Raedwald's successor as ruler in East Anglia was not converted to Christianity by Edwin until at least three years after Raedwald's death, and then the conversion failed to 'take'. Furthermore, *bretwaldaship* was essentially a political ideal, surviving, perhaps, as a romantic image of heroic British aspiration in the very opaque, unrecorded, days as Rome declined. What we see of Raedwald, in Bede, and in the ship-burial — always supposing, as we have to, that it is his — does not suggest a political idealist; he looks more like an extremely effective pragmatist. My strongest conviction (shaken only by the thought that it does not coincide with Rupert Bruce-Mitford's, who has pondered all these problems for decades, and almost lived them) is that the glorious regalia consigned to that ship was the man's *personal* equipment: for state ceremony, for battle, for recreation, and for Valhalla or wherever he thought he was going. And above all, on this last journey he would take with him his trophies: those coins, in their incredible purse, and the spoils of the resounding victory they led him to, the climax of his remarkable career. His chief trophies I believe to be the whetstone-sceptre and the large hanging-bowl.

The sceptre is exactly what I would imagine Aethelfrith holding as he sat alone on the dais at the apex of the wedge-shaped stadium or grand-stand, in a formal open assembly of his chiefs and priests and elders at Yeavering. The eight unblinking totem-heads (Pl. 1), each slightly different from the others, each looking as old as time, and arranged four round each end of the stone, display all the barbarity of that German ruler who has mastery of his Celtic kingdom by giving them victory and slave-taking in neighbouring British and Pictish territories. That he has crowned it with a proud, regally-antlered bronze stag of Celtic craftsmanship was perhaps a sound gesture of solidarity with his imaginative people. And for Raedwald to take it after his victory beside the river Idle would be as natural as it was for Henry Tudor to wear Richard of York's crown at Bosworth. Not that I suppose Aethelfrith carried the sceptre in battle: merely that it symbolised his power, and Raedwald needed that symbol before allowing Edwin 'crown-colony' status. Whether Raedwald took the large hanging-bowl or graciously accepted it from Edwin we shall not learn. Remarkable enough for the artistry of its external medallions, this bowl contains a small Celtic bronze salmon, mobile on its pedestal as if changing course upstream, an acknowledged king of those turbulent Northumbrian streams: the symbolism is, and was, irresistible.

The rest follows. Rupert Bruce-Mitford expresses with lapidary clarity the way the rest of the fabulous gold and jewelled regalia was fashioned,

24   Bruce-Mitford, *loc. cit.*, 1978, 377.

probably in the Sutton Hoo neighbourhood, by craftsmen of genius 'after being fascinated by the large hanging-bowl, in which Celtic millefiori finds its finest expression, and which the Sutton Hoo goldsmith himself repaired'.[25] Later,[26] Bruce-Mitford thinks the bowl may have been made in a royal Celtic workshop in the Kingdom of Elmet, in the Leeds area. For one moment[27] he seemed on the verge of seeing what I believe to be the crucial significance of the link with Aethelfrith and Edwin's Northumbria. Alas, he was adverting to the link with Edwin's new lordship over 'substantial Celtic elements in the population' in order to develop his theory that the sceptre, with its Celtic stag, was a symbol of *bretwaldaship*. I see that link as the very source of the stag-sceptre. One registers that *Sutton Hoo, Vol. 2*, appeared a year ahead of the Yeavering volume. But *Vol. 3*, with Bruce-Mitford's learned study of the hanging-bowls, appeared five years later, in 1983, suggesting Elmet as the possible Celtic source, and not even considering Northumbria.

Towards the end of his very fine book, Brian Hope-Taylor has a sentence.[28] which gives some credibility to my unambiguous thoughts on 'the Germanic-British element in the Sutton Hoo regalia'. He claims: 'The idea of an East Anglian-Northumbrian political and cultural axis under Raedwald and Edwin is entirely in harmony with the historical facts; and it could account for several points of correspondence betwen the decorative arts of Rendlesham and Lindisfarne.' The reference to Lindisfarne is timely: it brings Iken and St Botolph into focus, and the beginnings of East Anglian Christianity.

25 Bruce-Mitford, *loc. cit.*, 1978, 595. (595) The cast bronze animal head with snout and eyes is an original Celtic fitting, but a Germanic craftsman has replaced enamel eyes by garnets set in gold foil.
26 Bruce-Mitford, *op. cit.*, Vol. 3, 1983, 293.
27 Bruce-Mitford, *op. cit.*, Vol. 2, 1978, 597.
28 Brian Hope-Taylor, *Yeavering*, H.M.S.O., 1977, 321.

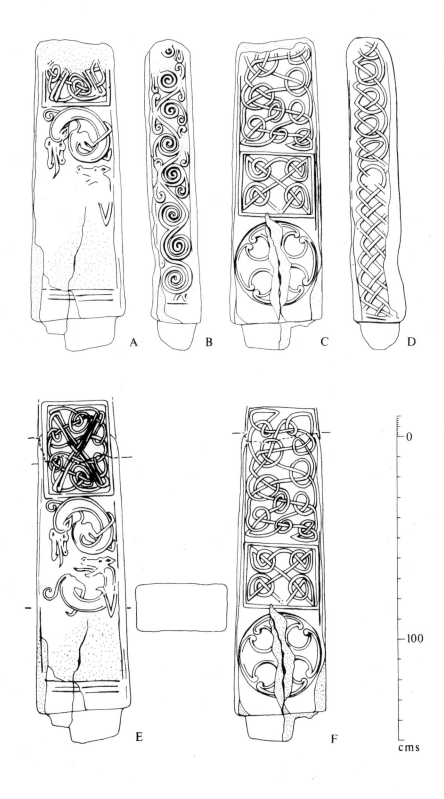

A   B   C   D

E   F

0

100

cms

3

St Botolph, the Iken Cross, and the Coming
of East Anglian Christianity

From the first quarter of the 7th century, when Raedwald and his queen preserved East Anglia and much of eastern England as a bulwark against the Christianity brought from Rome to Canterbury in 597, we move on to the middle decades of the century, when East Anglia received the teaching of Christ in both the Roman and Irish traditional forms. These major variations seem not to have obscured the essentials in this part of England. Elsewhere there was the usual indignation: the Irish and British naturally thought they had preserved the authentic Word, while the Roman and 'European' mission felt themselves to be more directly linked back to St Peter.

In January of 1977, Dr Stanley West, the Director of Suffolk County Council's Archaeological Unit, was on a routine inspection of the ruined nave of Iken church. His practised eye most fortunately noticed, low down in the wall of the western bell-tower where it abuts the west end of the nave, that a small surface of limestone in the masonry bore carving that was palpably Anglo-Saxon. It was a moment M. R. James would have relished. There had lately been some speculation by an archaeologist working at Hadstock, over in north-west Essex, that his remarkable discoveries in the deeply impressive Anglo-Saxon church dedicated to St Botolph there might mean that Hadstock was not only the *Cadenho* it was called in Domesday Book, but was more likely than any other place to be the *Icanho* where St Botolph governed a celebrated monastery. Suffolk people had long believed that Iken was where Botolph had his monastery, for Iken, too, had a church dedicated to him. Now, apart from the similarity between the names Iken and *Icanho*, here was a piece of Anglo-Saxon carving. The stone must be examined, and the ruined nave excavated.

Dr West has described the excitement of that month at Snape.[1] When the carved stone emerged from the tower, it was found to be no less than five and a half feet long, the base of a large free-standing cross. The patterned carving has proved rather confusing to the experts, but Dr West and his team showed clearly that there had been another, much earlier, church beneath at least the north side of the nave, with wooden walls, and possibly going back to the 7th century. I was asked to review the historical evidence, and reported as follows.

The *Anglo-Saxon Chronicle* provides the starting line. Under the year 654

---

1 *Proceedings of the Suffolk Institute of Archaeology and History*, XXXV, 1984, 279—291.

(653 in Text E), the chronicler recorded: 'In this year [King] Anna was slain, and Botwulf began to build the Minster at *Icanho*'. The *Chronicle* occasionally combined two unconnected statements in one sentence, but there is a clear, and significant, connexion between the two parts of this one. In the first big *Sutton Hoo* volume, Rupert Bruce-Mitford considered the relevance of that sentence as a pointer to the location of *Icanho* at Iken, in south-east Suffolk, close to the heart of King Anna's East Anglian kingdom.[2] He also floated the suggestion that *Icanho* minster 'may well have been founded in commemoration of Anna'.

The East Anglian kingdom was created, and then very effectively christened, during the first half of the 7th century. The recorded details are scanty, but circumstantial evidence suggests that both the formation of the kingdom and its adoption of Christianity took place in extremely warlike, very unquiet, conditions. It cannot be supposed that Raedwald, whose rule covered the first quarter of the century, established his supremacy as Bretwalda over the remaining Anglo-Saxon kingdoms without fighting and the exercise of formidable strength. The Sutton Hoo helmet, sword and shield — and the forty-oared ship itself — are impressive symbols of might, apart from the glittering craftsmanship. But, with Raedwald's death in 624/5, the *bretwaldaship* passed to his protégé Edwin of Northumbria. This must have reflected the reduced prestige and power of Raedwald's immediate successors in East Anglia. Then, after Edwin's defeat and death in 632, and the burning of his great wooden hall at Yeavering,[3] the forces of Penda of Mercia rapidly expanded and presented an ugly, indeed terrible, threat to East Anglia. He soon wrested back from East Anglia the lands of Middle Anglia — Leicester and the East Midlands — and put his son Peada in charge. Then he invaded the East Anglian kingdom, and not until Oswiu of Northumbria's victory over Penda at the Winwaed in 654 could the East English begin to feel safe again.

That constant threat of harassment and military incursion by Penda's heathens from the Midlands provided the conditions — coincided with the two formative decades — in which Christianity came into East Anglia. Perhaps we ought not to feel surprised at the adoption of Christianity by the East Anglians in times of alarm and invasion: the earliest Christians of the Roman empire seem to have been strengthened under much more Draconic persecution. The precise dating of events in these years is still open to argument.[4] An acceptable framework seems to bring King Sigeberht, thought to have been Raedwald's step-son[5] and described by Bede as 'very Christian and learned', to rule East Anglia in 630/1. A fugitive in Gaul from Raedwald's hostility, he there accepted Christianity, and, as soon as he

2 R. L. S. Bruce-Mitford, *The Sutton Hoo Ship-burial*, 1, 1975, 707n.
3 B. Hope-Taylor, *Yeavering*, 1977, 277.
4 R. L. S. Bruce-Mitford, *op. cit.*, 1, 1975, 696–698.
5 *op. cit.*, 700.

began to reign, took care that his whole kingdom shared his faith. Anxious to imitate the good institutions he had seen in Gaul, he founded a school. (It was perhaps at Dunwich, but Bede was not specific.) From Canterbury, the Archbishop sent him Bishop Felix, born and ordained in Burgundy, who supported him superbly in these efforts, and brought him teachers and masters from the Canterbury school.[6] Sigeberht personally preferred the kingdom of heaven: he handed his earthly kingdom to his kinsman Ecgric, 'who had previously ruled part of the kingdom' (Middle Anglia? Norfolk?). He himself withdrew into a monastery he had founded: at *Betrichesworde* (Bury St Edmunds), according to the local tradition recorded in the *Liber Eliensis*.[7] After Sigeberht had been there perhaps six years (*multo tempore*), Penda launched his first attack. The East Anglians must have allowed their fighting force to decline fatally during the decade after Raedwald, and now they dragged Sigeberht out in the forlorn hope of stiffening the army's morale. He declined to bear arms, however, carried a wand into battle, and both he and Ecgric were slain and their army beaten by Penda's heathens. A wand, presumably Raedwald's, dissolved in the ship-burial: its presence was deduced from the survival of elegant gold filigree bands and garnet studs.[8]

Before this first of Penda's East Anglian aggressions, *Betrichesworde* (Bury) presumably seemed a safe enough site for a monastery. Another East Anglian monastery was founded during Sigeberht's reign: an ascetic Irish saint, Fursa, established himself in *Cnobheresburg*, a '*castrum*', 'near the sea': probably in the great Roman fort, Burgh Castle, overlooking the Yare estuary north of Lowestoft, but conceivably at Caister-on-Sea.[9] And Bishop Felix himself received the seat of his bishopric in Dunwich 'city', i.e. presumed Roman fort,[10] also on the coast, remote from Penda. Bede spelt this city *DOMMOC*, the *Liber Eliensis, DUNUUOC*. It has recently been argued that *DOMMOC* might have been the Roman fort at Felixstowe, but that argument was fairly well disposed of by Professor Whitelock.[11] Whether *DOMMOC/DUNUUOC* was at Dunwich or Felixstowe, Iken may be seen to fit into a pattern of coastal monastic sites (which, c. 650−60, came to include Bishop Cedd's two Essex establishments at Bradwell-on-Sea and Tilbury).

The period of Felix's successful evangelism as bishop was measured, by

6   B. Colgrave and R. A. B. Mynors (eds.), *Bede's Ecclesiastical History of the English People*, 1969, (hereafter C. and M.), 190, 266−268.
7   E. O. Blake (ed.), *Liber Eliensis*, Camden 3rd Series, XCII, 1962, 11.
8   R. L. S. Bruce-Mitford, *The Sutton Hoo Ship-burial*, 2, 1978, 397 and fig. 279.
9   C. and M., 268−277; and S. Johnson, 'Burgh Castle', *East Anglian Archaeology*, No. 20, 1984.
10 C. and M., 190.
11 D. Whitelock, 'The Pre-Viking Age Church in East Anglia', *Anglo-Saxon England*, I, 1972, 1−22. A final argument for its being at Dunwich was the discovery of the last bishop's seal near Eye priory — linked with Dunwich but not at all with Felixstowe: see Pl. 7 and p. 130.

Bede, as seventeen years: these were 630/1 to 647/8, covering Sigeberht's reign and most of Anna's. It is generally reckoned that Sigeberht was slain by Penda's heathens in 636/7. Professor Whitelock argued[12] that 'Penda was hardly likely to be strong enough to attack the East Angles until after he had defeated Oswald of Northumbria in 641'. But that argument may be reversed. Would he have been strong enough to attack Oswald until after he had defeated East Anglia? At all events, King Anna succeeded Sigeberht probably in 636/7. He succeeded a king slain by Penda, and was himself, as we saw at the beginning of this chapter, slain by Penda in 654, the year the minster at *Icanho* was founded. Felix's bishopric was no kind of pastoral idyll, more a saga: Penda put East Anglia's new Christianity on the anvil: an enduring link was forged between Christianity and patriotism.

There is a record of at least one other incursion, presumably by Penda, and probably c. 651. This is the Nivelles *Additamentum de Foillano*, written within six years of Fursa's death.[13] *Cnobheresburg* was wrecked and apparently extinguished. Fursa's successor as abbot (his half-brother Foillan) was saved from death only by the approach of King Anna. Foillan got his church valuables and books away by ship to France. 'The most Christian King Anna was expelled.' What is meant here by Anna's 'expulsion' is not clear. It may mean that his death at Penda's hands three years later, (again presumably) near Blythburgh, occurred during an attempt to return from exile.

If speculation is permitted, I think Anna, after his 'expulsion', may have lived in exile among the *Magonsaetan* near Ludlow or Shrewsbury in Shropshire, as far away as possible from East Anglia. Dorothy Whitelock[14] admitted the authenticity of a story told by Osbert of Clare of a canon of Bromfield, near Ludlow, who had spoken with people who had seen a vision of Anna's daughter, St Etheldreda, *at a church dedicated to her on the Welsh border*. Professor Whitelock dismissed Osbert's claim that a little wooden church had been built there by King Anna: 'it is impossible that he should found a church on the far side of heathen Mercia'. Well, it would provide an explanation — otherwise lacking — for Osbert's extraordinary story. Furthermore, Bede expressly stated:[15] 'King Penda did not forbid the preaching of the Word, even in his own Mercian kingdom, if any wished to hear it. He merely despised those Christians who did not live up to their faith.' Professor Whitelock accepted the *Icanho*-Shropshire link attested by Aethelheah, Botolph's successor c. 674−90 as abbot of *Icanho*, in an exchange of landed endowments between *Icanho* and the double monastery at Wenlock. It seems perverse to reject as 'impossible' Osbert's circumstantial explanation of an otherwise very improbable link across the whole width of England.

12 *op. cit.*, 6.
13 *ibid.*
14 *op. cit.*, 12 and n.
15 C. and M., 280.

It seems all the more feasible that, c. 651—654, Anna was in the land of the *Magonsaetan* (south Shropshire and Herefordshire) as soon as you look closely into his family history. King Eorcenberht of Kent (ruling 640—664) married one of Anna's daughters, Seaxburgh. (Bede's tribute to Anna was: 'a good man, with good and saintly offspring'.[16]) King Eorcenberht's kinswoman, (probably his brother's daughter) Eormengild, married Merewalh, ruler of the *Magonsaetan*. In short, Anna's daughter, queen of Kent, was closely related, probably aunt, to the wife of the ruler in south Shropshire. What more natural than that Anna should find refuge there? If so, what more likely than that he would found a church there? Nor is it really surprising that Merewalh's daughters vied with Anna's in being saintly. One of them, Mildred, went back to her mother's kingdom as abbess of Minster, between Richborough and Reculver. It has been assumed that, when she died c. 700, her grandfather's nephew Aldwulf (king of East Anglia 662/3—713) dedicated a church in Ipswich to her. After centuries, it became the Town Hall, probably on the site of a 7th-century *vicus regius*, with the Cornhill already marked out as the town's chief *forum*.[17] Finally, no wonder that, when St Mildburg, another of Merewalh's saintly daughters, founded the double monastery at Wenlock, she linked it to the revered memory of Botolph. His successor as abbot of *Icanho* gave her lands that included '97 hides at Wenlock'. It is hard to see how a Suffolk abbot would have Wenlock lands to give unless there were some such personal links as I have suggested. Like the late Professor Whitelock, I have not felt able to accept the story that Botolph was chaplain in a nunnery abroad where abbess Liobsynde of Wenlock had been educated, not that I find it improbable. It seems based on even less verifiable evidence than the Osbert of Clare story I have been examining.

That story is the nearest we approach to an authenticated early statement connecting *Icanho* with Anna — apart from the sentence in the *Anglo-Saxon Chronicle* that sparked off Dr Bruce-Mitford's conjecture that *Icanho* might have been a memorial to Anna. In addition to his kingship during the testing years of Penda's attack, Anna's better known qualifications for remembrance in a new monastic house were the examples of 'goodness' attributed to him by Bede. He and his nobles helped Fursa extend and improve his monastic buildings at *Cnobheresburg*. And through Anna, according to Bede,[18] King Cenwealh of Wessex accepted Christianity. He had made the mistake of marrying Penda's sister and then repudiating her. In consequence, in the later 640s, he spent three years in exile in East Anglia with good King Anna.

Lastly, there was the celebrated saintliness of his daughters, for which some credit is probably due to him: Aethelthryth (or Etheldreda, or

---

16   *op. cit.*, 234. According to the *Liber Eliensis*, Anna had a son, St Jurmin, whose remains, like Anna's, lay at Blythburgh until abbot Leofstan's day, 1044—1065, when Jurmin's were translated to Bury (E. O. Blake, *op. cit*, 12; T. Arnold, Memorials of St Edmund's Abbey, I., 1890, 352). Some of St Botolph's bones went to Bury at the same period: see p. 50, below.

17   N. Scarfe, *The Suffolk Landscape*, 1972, 101.

18   C. and M., 234.

Audrey) who founded Ely, Seaxburgh who succeeded her at Ely as abbess, Aethelberg who became abbess of *Faremoutiers-en-Brie*; and then a step-daughter of his followed Aethelberg there. Commenting on the departure of ladies to nunneries abroad, Professor Whitelock reflected that it 'suggests that there were at that time no nunneries in or near East Anglia: the first may have been . . . Ely, about 673'. May not the activities of Penda have had something to do with the absence of East Anglian nunneries and these retreats to nunneries abroad?

There is respectable testimony[19] that Anna's remains had been enshrined at Blythburgh, presumably near the place of his death, and that those remains were being venerated there in the 12th century. They conceivably rested in the precursor of a small monastery, ruins of which lie immediately north-east of Blythburgh parish church: Ipswich ware found there[20] suggests a real possibility of 7th-century occupation of the site of the later Blythburgh priory. So does the whalebone writing-tablet — carved with interlace — found there and presented in 1902 to the British Museum by the then owner of the Priory.[21] The original presence of Anna's tomb at Blythburgh seems not to preclude the theory that one of Anna's brothers (one, Aethelric, was connected with abbess Hilda of Whitby) helped Botolph establish his monastery at a suitably quiet, remote undeveloped place. Blythburgh in those days is likely to have been already a royal *vill*, and perhaps market — bustling, and anything but quiet!

We turn now to the question of *Icanho*'s identity with Iken, and to Botolph's life and his posthumous physical fortunes. Since Dr Stanley West's excavation in 1977, there seems no shadow of doubt that the *Icanho* minster stood approximately where St Botolph's church at Iken stands today, on its *ho* — which means a spur — jutting out romantically above the lonely Alde estuary. A recent attempt to argue that Icanho was Hadstock (in Essex!) has been thoroughly discounted on etymological and numerous other grounds by Edward Martin.[22] The main toponymous evidence of identity with Iken was put forward in 1924 in a long, learned and — for its date — admirable article in the *Proceedings of the Suffolk Institute of Archaeology*.[23] Claude Morley had drawn the author's attention to a transcript of three skins mostly devoted to a 14th-century Butley priory rent-roll. It gives the rent paid 'in parochia de ykenho' by William Fransebroun. To clinch the identification with Iken, one finds, in the 1327 Subsidy Return, a Roger Fausebroun paying 3s. subsidy in Iken-with-

19   E. O. Blake, *op. cit.*, 18.
20   *Proceedings S.I.A.H.*, XXXIV, 1978, 55.
21   W. Page (ed.), 'Anglo-Saxon Remains' and 'Domesday Survey', in *Victoria County History: Suffolk*, I, 1911, 350−352.
22   E. A. Martin, 'St Botolph and Hadstock: A Reply', *Antiquaries Journal*, LVIII, 1978, 153−159.
23   F. S. Stevenson, 'St Botolph (Botwulf) and Iken', *Proceedings S.I.A.H.*, XVIII, 1924, 30−52.

Chillesford-and-Dunningworth. (A house in Iken, presumably on their site, is still called' Fazeboons.) Since 1924, there has been no sensible room for doubt that *Icanho* and Iken coincided. Yet the recent proponent of Hadstock seems not even to have considered the possibility.[24]

Does Domesday Book record a church at Iken? I find four of every five medieval Suffolk churches clearly referred to in Domesday Book, which however makes no mention of Iken by name. It does, though, register two churches in the adjoining *vill* of Sudbourne[25] which was important as an early administrative centre of the 'Liberty of St Etheldreda' (indicating yet another close link with Anna), and which may very well originally have included Iken within its territory. One of these two churches, with 16 acres, was held in Domesday Book by Gilbert de Wiscand (Wishant) of Robert Malet, who founded, shortly after the making of Domesday Book, Eye priory. Among the gifts to the new priory from one of Malet's tenants (named Roville, but perhaps he had meanwhile supplanted Wishant or was sub-tenant), was the church of St Botolph at Yca.[26] The dedication to St Botolph luckily reduces any confusion with Eyke nearby, whose church seems not to have been dedicated to St Botolph as Iken's still is: it is slightly confusing that among the Roville gifts to the new priory at Eye was the tithe of their demesne at *Clakestorp*, a lost Domesday vill in Loes Hundred and now located as having been in Eyke. The most tantalising aspect of the gift to Eye priory of the church of Botolph at *Yca* is the enigmatic intention expressed in the charter: 'ut sint ibi fratres monastici ordinis serviendum Deo'. If William and Beatrix de Roville wanted the priory of Eye to establish monastic brethren to serve God at St Botolph's, Yca, may they not have had an idea in mind of bringing back into service the remembered former monastery there? If so, nothing is known of their wishes being put into effect.

What do we know about Botolph himself, and does it tell us anything about what might be expected of the former building he made so illustrious at Iken?

The sole, but very impressive, glimpse of Botolph comes in an anonymous *Life of Abbot Ceolfrith* of Wearmouth and Jarrow.[27] In his late twenties, after some years at Ripon with Wilfrid, who was probably the most dynamic English churchman of his remarkable generation, Ceolfrith had come south to Kent to see the form of monastic life there. Then he came to East Anglia to see the version of monasticism conducted by Abbot Botolph, himself universally acclaimed as 'a man of unparalleled life and learning and full of the grace of the Holy Spirit'. This would have been about the year 670, when *Icanho* minster had been going for about sixteen

24 W. Rodwell, 'The Archaeological Investigation of Hadstock Church, Essex: An Interim Report', *Antiquaries Journal*, LVI, P.1, 55−71.
25 W. Page, *op. cit.*, 456, 521.
26 Eye Cartulary, Essex Record Office, D/DByQ 19, f. 64v.
27 C. Plummer (ed.), *Venerabilis Baedae Opera Historica*, 1896.

years. But apart from those phrases in the *Life of Ceolfrith*, we hear nothing more about Botolph. That Bede says nothing is disappointing. The story, is, alas, not finally provable that when Jarrow was founded, c. 681, Bede, aged about eight, went there under Ceolfrith's care, with 22 monks. The plague came among them, 'and no one was left to sing the offices except Ceolfrith and one little boy'. That boy may well have been Bede. Anyway, accidentally or intentionally, Bede omitted all reference to Botolph. Either Ceolfrith omitted to tell Bede about him, or Bede omitted to record it. By the time Bede read the reference in the *Life of Ceolfrith*, Ceolfrith himself was beyond reach, unable to amplify.

Sometime after 1070, four centuries after Botolph lived, a *Life* of him was written by Abbot Folcard of Thorney. And there are brief references to his life in *The Slesvig Breviary*. (Both are printed in Acta Sanctorum.[28]) Both were dismissed by the late Dorothy Whitelock for their 'absurdities',[29] but there are reasons, as we shall see, for Thorney to have preserved some local traditions that may contain a grain of truth. One thing both sources refer to is a 'Scottish' (i.e. Irish, Celtic) connexion (no more than that) in Botolph's background. I mention it because I am inclined to believe that too much has been made of the 'differences' between the Irish and Roman traditions — at least so far as they affected the conversion in East Anglia.

Professor Whitelock admitted there was at least a 'likelihood' of Irish influence in Bishop Felix's background.[30] This makes it the easier to understand Fursa's settling down alongside him, a few miles along the Suffolk coast. I do not find it hard to reconcile, as Professor Whitelock did, the practice at *Icanho* of a religion 'full of the grace of the Holy Spirit' by a man of unparalleled life and learning, with the thought that his experience might have included Irish as well as (undoubted) Roman forms of the faith.

I stress this because, in her account of 'The pre-Viking age church in East Anglia',[31] Professor Whitelock 'concluded' her 'evidence of Celtic influence in the East Anglian church' and, only later (page 9) — as though it were 'of interest' but hardly fundamental — referred to the Celtic training of Bishop Cedd, and Cedd's baptism of Swithhelm, a prince of Essex, at Rendlesham, an East Anglian royal *vicus* only five miles from Iken — 'though the East Anglian church', as she put it, 'was aligned with Canterbury'. This may be making too much of East Anglia's — and for that matter Essex's — 'alignment'. Bede noted that Felix of East Anglia respected the great Aidan of Lindisfarne. We cannot reasonably doubt that Botolph was present with Cedd at Swithhelm's baptism, when King Aethelwald, Anna's brother and probably Botolph's original sponsor at Iken, 'supported Swithhelm as he ascended from the holy font'.[32] Incidentally, Bede's description of this rite

28 *Acta Sanctorum*, IV, 1867, 324–330.
29 D. Whitelock, *op. cit.*, 11n. In dismissing Folcard's *Life*, we lose a credible, not absurd, tradition of Iken's likely appeal to Botolph in 654: 'he chose a spot at *Ikanho*, a desert place infested by demons: on his approach, the devils raised a terrible stench and, wailing loudly, left.' I see those 'devils' as a group of displaced British — Iceni, indeed, fishers in the mud-swamps of the un-banked estuary.
30 *op. cit.*, 5.   31 *op. cit.*, 6.   32 C. and M., 297, 284.

makes one wonder whether the font may not have been set in the floor and shaped like the mid-4th-century Romano-British-Christian font uncovered in West Suffolk at Icklingham.[33] If Bishop Cedd's 'alignment' had been rigidly Celtic, he would hardly have been invited to play his crucial, and successful role of mediator — 'vigilant interpreter for both parties' — when the differences, mainly over the dating of Easter, were finally argued out at the Synod of Whitby in 664.[34] I should be surprised if the outcome were felt to be of the most urgent importance by East Anglians — or East Saxons — quite clearly tolerant of the two distinctive and viable traditions.

As to Cedd's undoubted Northumbrian Celtic background, it seems to have had no effect on the shape of the fabric of his church at Bradwell-on-Sea, so much of it so astonishingly still standing. The Taylors[35] confirm that this remarkable survival from the 7th century bears evidence of the multiple-span arcade between nave and chancel — as at Reculver and St Pancras, Canterbury, in Kent, and with an eastern apse instead of the rectangular chancel the Northumbrians seem to have preferred. For all that has been suggested in this article about Celtic influences in early East Anglian Christianity, it would be surprising, therefore, if the fabric of *Icanho* minster did not follow the lines of its near contemporaries in Kent and Essex. The foundation of an early timber building was revealed in the excavation, but the use of that material would probably not have affected the ritual function and lay-out of the church.

Bede's devotion to his old master, Ceolfrith, and what is known of Ceolfrith's long life of dedication, is impressive indirect testimony to the work of Botolph at *Icanho*. He must have been a model abbot indeed to earn that tribute from Ceolfrith's biographer: in Ceolfrith's exemplary life, and perhaps even in Bede's, Botolph's work here may begin to be measured. Under his successor Aethelheah, c. 674—90, *Icanho*'s influence was at work as far off as Shropshire: we can imagine its impact nearer home.

Abbot Folcard of Thorney's word is accepted that Botolph died at his monastery, and was buried by his disciples, on 17 June, the day on which he is still remembered:[36] saints were naturally commemorated on their death-days — their birthdays in heaven. Ole Worm — Doctor of Medicine at the Copenhagen Academy and Denmark's great 17th-century antiquary — recorded that the three days ending on 17 June, when the feasts of two other saints were celebrated jointly with Botolph's, were formerly known in Denmark as Bodelmess, or Bodelmas.[37] The other two were St Vitus and St Vihelm, a 13th-century abbot in the Roskilde diocese.

33   S. E. West and J. Plouviez, *East Anglian Archaeology* No. 3, 1976, 72—79.
34   C. and M., 298
35   H. M. Taylor and J. Taylor, *Anglo-Saxon Architecture*, I, 1965, 92—93.
36   *Acta Sanctorum, op. cit.*, 328.
37   O. Worm, *Fasti Danici*, Haffn (Copenhagen), 1643, p. 114. It is clear from pp. 88 and 136 of that work that Worm had Botolph in mind, though in this particular calendaring of the Bodelmess Botolph's name is printed as Botilde. It was anyway Botolph's date.

Two centuries after Botolph's death, Danes invaded East Anglia, killing King Edmund in 869, at Bradfield near Bury as we now think, and settling in Norfolk very much more densely than in Suffolk. Their destruction of the monasteries they came to, including *Icanho* (see below) seems only to have strengthened the faith. It is extraordinary that about 2,000 coins have been found commemorating 'Saint Edmund, King' by name, that they mostly came from East Anglian mints, and that this public celebration of his death as a saint was begun before 892, within about twenty years of his death.[38] This massive numismatic commemoration of a Christian martyr so soon after the event is our strongest evidence of the firmness with which Christianity was held and the speed of Christian recovery in Danish East Anglia, strengthened presumably by the tensions of Danish occupation. This late 9th-century recovery of Christianity *may* coincide with the marking of the site of Botolph's *Icanho* with a memorial cross. (The dating of the carving on the length of cross-shaft found at Iken is puzzling the experts:[39] the end of the 9th century seems a possible date, but up to a century later is also thought possible. The precise date does not greatly alter the function of this memorial, merely shifts the time of its erection. A variety of dates can be accommodated by the Anglo-Danish history of the site.)

The Danish King Guthrum, who at least formally accepted Christianity from Alfred in 878, and according to Asser died in 890 and was buried at the royal *vill* of Hadleigh in Suffolk, may have been something of a restraining influence on his pagan fellow-countrymen in these parts. A Christian Danish king presumably revived, for instance, the church at Blythburgh, and perhaps a successor sheltered it through the renewed Viking storms of c. 991–1016. Otherwise, belief in the presence there of King Anna's remains is unlikely to have survived. How was Botolph's *Icanho* affected, and what became of his remains? His posthumous travels add strong confirmation to *Icanho*'s identification with Iken.

The most significant records seem to be these. In the 12th century, the *Liber Eliensis*[40] showed that Sudbourne was owned by the Danish earl Scule in the 930s and 940s, two important decades in terms of the local revival of Christianity. Then, about the year 970, King Edgar and his Queen Alftreth gave the Sudbourne manor to Bishop Aethelwold of Winchester (later Saint Aethelwold) in return for a translation into the English language, by Aethelwold himself, of the Rule of St Benedict (the Rule by which all Benedictine monastic life was conducted — from Monte Cassino to Iken in Botolph's day and to Ely in Aethelwold's day). Aethelwold, receiving Sudbourne from the king, handed it on to St Etheldreda (Ely).

The next sources are later, from the Middle Ages in the *Legenda* of John

---

38   C. E. Blunt, 'The St Edmund Memorial Coinage, *Proceedings S.I.A.H.*, XXXI, 1970, 234–255.

39   R. Cramp, 'The Iken Cross-shaft', *Proceedings S.I.A.H.*, XXXV, 1984, 291–292.

40   E. O. Blake, *op. cit.*, 111.

Capgrave and the Chronicle sometimes called John Brompton's, sometimes called the Jervaulx Chronicle. Both are quoted in the *Acta Sanctorum*.[41] Since there are minor differences, we will cite Capgrave, and note the differences where relevant. From Capgrave we see that, at about the same time as the king's gift of Sudbourne to Bishop Aethelwold, the Bishop got permission from the king to have the remains of saints removed from places destroyed by the Danes to the monasteries that were being built: among these remains were Botolph's at the monastery at *Icanho* 'quod idem S Botulph in vita sua construxerat, et post-modeum per interfectores S Edmundi Regis destructum fuerat' (Brompton). Capgrave described the difficulties presented by St Botolph's bones. 'When, at the order of Bishop Aethelwold, the monk called Ulfkittel, with many others, came to Botolph's tomb, and recognised the precious bones in their shroud, and in their arms tried to raise him to remove him; so firmly was he fixed that no amount of exertion was able to move him.' Moreover, the Saint's head was to be despatched to Ely, the middle of the body to the royal collectors, and 'the rest' (presumably the limbs) to Thorney. (Brompton agrees about the head going to Ely, but switches the destinations of the other parts!)

The first point we notice is that the decision of Bishop Aethelwold to dispose of holy relics from places destroyed by the Danes, including Botolph's at *Icanho*, came at roughly the same time as his grant of Sudbourne from the king, and his own grant of it to Ely. This rough coincidence itself perhaps corroborated the location of *Icanho* within the Manor of Sudbourne c. 970.

Next, there is that specific reference to the destruction of the *Icanho* monastery by the Danes. The whole implication of the authorised redistribution of Botolph's bones is that *Icanho* monastery was not rebuilt, though at least enough still stood in c. 970 to enable his tomb to he found.

Finally, we see that these *intentions* to despatch Botolph's remains in three different directions were, for whatever reasons, miraculous or otherwise, not fulfilled. For there is convincing evidence of changes of plan and further delays.

Notes written in a copy of Marianus Scotus[42] record that King Cnut

41   *Acta Sanctorum, op. cit.*, 324 and 330. Richard Barber drew my attention to a possibly earlier source. Leland, at Tynemouth priory, transcribed a *libellus* of 'resting-places of saints', a lost document of perhaps the late 12th century (*Joannis Lelandi Antiquarii Collectanea cum Thomae Hearnii edit. altera*, Vol. III, 1774, p. 408). Its details of the partitioning of Botolph's remains tallied with Capgrave's not Brompton's. All three appear to have been misinformed on this matter, as we see later. A word or two of independent evidence might have been expected in the *annales* of Thorney abbey, 961—1421, compiled on B.L., Cotton Nero C. VII, fols. 79—83 — another reference I owe to Richard Barber. But there the only hagiolatrous details calendared for the century after the year 961 were the feast of St Dunstan (on 9 April 988, a month early!) and the 'invention' (discovery), in 1001, of the corpse of St Ives. It is odd that only these two were on that calendar, and frustrating that Botolph was not.

42   Oxford, Bodleian Library, MS Bodley 297. T. Arnold (ed.), *Memorials of St Edmund's Abbey*, I, 1890, 352.

authorised the removal of St Botolph's bones from *Grundisburgh* to St Edmund's abbey at Bury, newly founded by the king in 1020. The notes go on to record that this removal was finally accomplished one very dark night in Edward the Confessor's reign by Abbot Leofstan (1044 – 1065), 'a column of light dispelling the darkness above the feretory' — not a difficult effect to stage.

F. S. Stevenson, who quoted these notes from the margin of Marianus Scotus in his article on St Botolph[43] was clearly baffled, and could think of no convincing explanation of the presence of Botolph's remains at Grundisburgh. Yet the explanation is surely this. Grundisburgh and Burgh St Botolph are now separate adjoining parishes. The *Oxford Dictionary of English Place-names* explains Grundisburgh as 'the burg, or fort, at Grund' and adds that Grund 'very likely' was the original Old English name of the place, meaning as it did 'the foundation of an old building-site'. Presumably the name Grundisburgh originally referred to the ancient Belgic or British buildings in the massive Belgic camp behind and beneath St Botolph's church in that part of Grundisburgh now merely called Burgh. The name expanded to Grundisburgh when the *burh*, the strong-point, was brought into civil use. This impressive defensive site gives, I think, the clue to the presence of St Botolph's bones there (i.e. in what was a part of the whole Grundisburgh) in Cnut's day. The fact that the *Life* of Botolph was written by an abbot of Thorney (Folcard) in the 11th century suggests that they got their share all right. But it is by no means clear that Ely or Westminster ever received the portions Edgar allotted to them. The translation of at least some remains from Grundisburgh to Bury under Cnut's authority (though accomplished in the time of the Confessor) shows clearly that they had not been distributed as Edgar instructed. *Some* part of the saint reached Ely, and was damaged (E. O. Blake, *op. cit.*, 222).

But between Edgar's orders, c. 970, and Cnut's establishment of Bury abbey in c. 1020, there were renewed ferocious Viking raids in the neighbourhood, notably in 991 and 1010. Edmund's own mummified corpse was removed from Bury during that bleak time and taken for refuge to St Paul's churchyard in London. The hallowed relics of Botolph were, as I understand all this evidence, brought back from that exposed spur above the estuary at Iken to the relative security of the ramparted position above the valley at Burgh. In short, the recorded details about the use of Burgh/Grundisburgh as a temporary, sheltered, inland repository for Botolph's bones, and their final transfer from there, go a long way towards confirming Iken as the site of *Icanho*.

A generation ago in his essay on 'The East Anglian Kings in the Seventh Century',[44] Sir Frank Stenton wrote:

> It is remarkable that under these kings, whose reigns were short and sometimes disastrous, Christianity should have become rooted in East Anglia

43   F. S. Stevenson, *op. cit.*, 41.
44   P. Clemoes (ed.), *The Anglo-Saxons: Studies Presented to Bruce Dickins*, 1959, 49 – 50.

so firmly that it was unaffected by the fortunes of local rulers. There is no hint in Bede or any other early historian that the East Anglians ever relapsed into heathenism in times of trouble. The outstanding figures in the recorded history of East Anglia during these years were not the kings, but the men who established Christianity under their protection — Felix, who made his bishop's seat at Dunwich a centre for religious instruction, Fursa, the Irish ascetic of Burgh Castle, Botulf of Icanho, whose fame as an organiser of monastic life spread throughout England.

The richness of the royal ship and its treasures at Sutton Hoo has inevitably deflected attention from these remarkable churchmen, and towards the rulers of East Anglia at the end of the pagan period. Stenton's dictum may do less than justice to one or two of the early East Anglian kings: to Sigeberht for instance, and Anna, and would certainly not apply to Aldwulf, who ruled from 662/3 to 713 and who was a correspondent of the celebrated Boniface. A new appraisal of the earliest East Anglian churchmen was unquestionably overdue. Dr West's remarkable discovery of the Iken cross has concentrated our attention usefully on St Botolph, and perhaps enabled us to establish more firmly the circumstances of his exemplary life of the spirit on that spur overlooking the broad estuary at Iken.

Plate 1 Sutton Hoo. One of eight mysterious Germanic Heads carved (four at each end) in the whetstone-sceptre: weight 5 lb, almost 2 ft long, and surmounted by an antlered stag's head of Celtic bronze-work: see p. 36.

Plate 2 Sutton Hoo. The large hanging-bowl. Three rings are fixed to the bowl by 'otter-head' hooks with medallions of exquisite Celtic decoration (detail, Pl. 6). Mobile bronze salmon lurks within: see p. 36.

Plate 3 Sutton Hoo. Celtic bronze fish, with traces of tin and paint decoration, pivots on pedestal: base set with millefiori and scrolls of blue glass: see p. 36.

Plates 4 and 5 Sutton Hoo. 1939: uncovering the purse (upside down) with coins, the great gold buckle, and gold mounts from the sword harness. (Photo. Margaret Guido.) Purse-lid sumptuous: gold frame: the plaques elaborate cloisonné work, gold cells housing carved garnets, millefiori and glass inlays. So it was a grand ceremonial purse (see p. 32). The facing pair of horses (top centre) belong to same stud as pairs actually buried with limbs interlaced at Beckum. Westphalia. Pattern of man between two beasts matched at Torslunda, E. Scandinavia.

Plate 6 Sutton Hoo. Beautifully preserved Celtic pattern on roundel of hanging-bowl (Pl. 2): mainly rich red enamel, with bronze 'hair-spring' coils: inner ring and hub inset with millefiori and five dark-blue glass rings. Cast bronze boar's head, snout upwards, is Celtic, into which Germanic craftsman has set garnet eye-replacements. Cf. eyes on seal-die, Pl. 7.

Plate 7 Bronze seal-die of bishop Aethelwald, presumably the bishop Aethelwald who was last of the Anglo-Saxon bishops of Dunwich, c. 845 to 869, when the Danes slew King Edmund: see pp. 26 and 130. Its impression reads SIG EDILVVALDI EP. The nine wolves'-heads, originally with garnet eyes, are distant connections of the creature in Pl. 6.

Plate 8 S. Eadmundus, rex Angliae, sharing a column with S. Susanna of Babylon in the choir at St Sernin's basilica, Toulouse (p. 56).

Plate 9 The prolific Bury monk-versifier, John Lydgate, presented his credulous, devout *Life of St Edmund* to the young Henry VI when he stayed as guest of the abbot in 1433. Now in the British Library (BL Harl. 2278), its illustrations have the charm of a children's book. Here (fol. 67v), on the left, the king's head is retrieved from the wolf, and, below, is rejoined to the body. There were no rabbits in England in 869 — they were a later introduction. By 1433 they were bred in warrens all around Bury.

Plates 10 and 11 Folio 9 of Lydgate's *St Edmund* (Harl. 2278) shows the author praying to the martyr. Behind him a secular figure in blue sits holding a staff. The marble screen linking the four 3-lb candles that were alight night and day was probably provided from Edward I's grants in 1285 and 1296 (Pat. 13 Ed.I, m. 13, and 24 Ed.I, m. 18). His closest counsellor, Henry de Lacy, gave two of the gold crosses on the 'roof-ridge' of the golden shrine, one with a carbuncle (sapphire), which prompted

Lydgate to address the saint as 'charboncle of martirs alle, o hevenly gemme, saphir of stablenesse'. The small square panel presumably enabled the guardians of the shrine to check the presence and condition of the saint. Fol. 117 shows the 'lid' raised, as it seems to have been during the fire of 1465 (see p. 69). These 15th-century book-illustrations are not drawn with the accuracy of blue-prints, but they were drawn for a king who had knelt at Edmund's shrine, and must give a fairly close impression of it.

Plate 12 The late Anglo-Saxon stone crucifix formerly surmounting the east gable of Kedington church (see p. 75). Some years ago it was brought into the chancel, to prevent further weathering.

Plate 13 Bradfield Combust church. Wall-painting, c. 1393, of St George, mounted, with his own cross on his armour and his horse's trappings, and Lord Roos's peacock-feather crest on his helmet: p. 80.

Plate 14 The Bury Bible, Corpus Christi College, Cambridge, MS. C.2. Master Hugo's idea of an attack on Jerusalem as the prophet Jeremiah described it. The high animation distinguishes it, and compares well with the ivory, opposite.

Plate 15 The New York Metropolitan Museum of Art's ivory cross: front centre-piece. Moses, leading the Jews out of captivity, raises the brazen serpent on a cleft stick, prophetic of Christ's cross (see p. 86). It is hard to imagine that anything could be expressed with greater virtuosity than this small central medallion, with figures clinging on to, and tumbling all about, the framing roundel.

Plate 16 The Bury Bible. The detail of the knights defending
Jerusalem compares closely with that of the soldiers in Pl. 17.

Plate 17 The Metropolitan Museum of Art's ivory cross: detail. The soldiers guarding the tomb have collapsed at the sight of the angel. The cords holding the censer above them demonstrate the fineness as well as the liveliness of the sculpture.

Plate 18 The front of the walrus ivory cross, complete but for its base and its hanging figure of Christ. The missing Christ may very well not be the poignant ivory in Oslo's Museum of Applied Art. Arrangements to keep the two extraordinary works together have foundered. Even without the Christ figure, this cross is the outstanding masterpiece of English art in The Cloisters at the north point of Manhatten. Adam and Eve squat at the bottom of a 'Tree of Life'. The seven pieces of walrus-ivory have been so cunningly combined that the curve of the tusks makes the tree itself seem to sway.

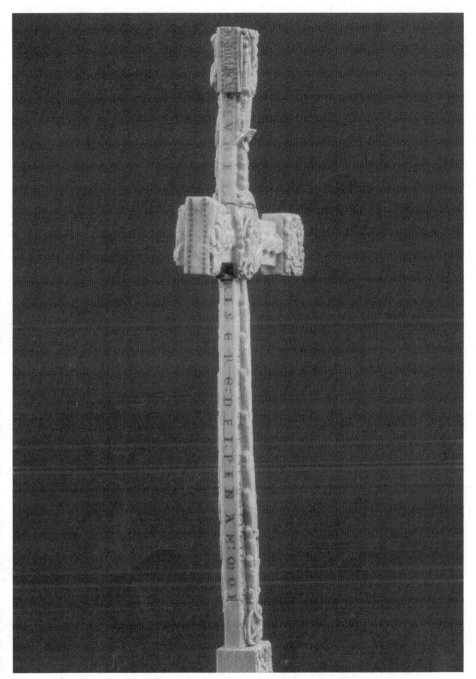

Plate 19 This cross was designed to be seen all round, not just from the front. The boldly carved message down the side reads: 'JUDEI RISERE DEI PENAM MOR[TIS]: the Jews laugh at the death-agony of God': see pp. 84–5.

Plate 20 Rear centrepiece. The Lamb of God is goaded by the lance of the Synagogue, whose eyes are closed in blindness (and whose folded sleeve looks, in the Plate, like two extra prongs of the lance). See pp. 95–6.

Plate 21 At the top, the Ascension; in the middle, the High Priest arguing with Pilate – 'Write not "King of the Jews" '; below, the significant outcome, beside the Hand of God, "Rex Confessorum, King of the Confessors" is written instead.

Plate 22 The Deposition and Lamentation: 'They shall weep for him as for an only begotten son' (see pp. 93–4). This double scene, with crowds, is another miniature miracle. In detail, there is the tenderness of Nicodemus releasing Christ's hand with the pincers. The whole picture seems to ache with grief.

Plate 23 The Ashfield Cross. It stands 10 ft 6 in high, 'wheel-headed', apparently late Anglo-Saxon, and with inscrutable inscription. See p. 17, and *Proceedings*, Sufk. Inst. of Arch., XX, 1928, pp. 280−6. The damaging metal clamps were in position in 1928.

Plate 24 The sea-marsh site of the first Leiston abbey: see p. 141.

Plate 25 Fife-and-Drum Cottages, the former Murrills manor-house, Yoxford, and now vanished: see p. 153.

ST EDMUND AND WEST SUFFOLK

4

St Edmund's Corpse: Defeat into Victory

In Britain in 1939 and 1940, whether we were flying Spitfires or working the new Radar chain or were, as in my case, a schoolboy on a cliff-top facing Brittany, with an 8 mm English Hotchkiss machine-gun last used in the Boer War and so without ammunition, we instinctively recoiled from imagining the possibility of overwhelming invasion. The Poles, the French and most of civilised Europe were being invaded and defeated by Hitler's Panzers and Stukas, but they were different. They lived alongside Germany. People in Europe were probably more adjusted to such experiences. We seldom think — why should we? — of those long centuries of our earlier history when invasion, and defeat, were all too often within living memory.

Unable to resist the Danish marauders who slew him, King Edmund of the East Angles made amends after his death by providing one of the most effective symbols of English resistance to the invader ever recorded in our history. King Alfred and the West Countrymen were able to hold the Danes and bring them to terms, and to Christianity. It is this revival of both Christianity and English patriotism, against the renewed incursions of raiding Northmen, that explains Edmund's prodigious medieval fame. Over sixty English churches were dedicated to him. The first historian of Iceland, Ari, used 'Edmund's slaughter' as the episode from which to measure the date of an event '250 years after'.[1]

Such posthumous power naturally, or supernaturally, made Edmund's body, and the shrine that housed it, objects of great veneration and awe. Today in Padua, in the basilica of St Anthony, who was in life no more than an inspired preacher, one may witness a continuous surge-past of the faithful, uttering anxious prayers as they press their hands against the walls of his tomb. Imagine the dread of those who stood before Edmund's shrine nearly a thousand years ago, in 1014, when King Cnut's father, Sweyn Forkbeard, had threatened destruction or a heavy ransom to the saint's little town, and had himself been struck dead.[2] East Anglians saw the death-bolts of the saint at work, and voted him money from their ploughlands. Sweyn's son had the same idea, replacing Edmund's secular guardians by a Benedictine monastery and confirming its control over the town. In 1044 Edmund

---

1 G. N. Garmonsway, *The Anglo-Saxon Chronicle*, 1953, p. xix. See *Islendingabók*, transl. by H. Hermannson, *The Book of the Icelanders*, Islandica 20.
2 During the Middle Ages two pictures of this dramatic scene were displayed near Edmund's shrine beyond the high altar of the abbey: M. R. James, *The Abbey of St Edmund at Bury*, Camb. Ant. Soc., 1895, p. 137.

was given all royal customs over the land of everyone in the area that till 1974 was West Suffolk. Not long after Hastings, the formidable Norman king confirmed Edmund in all his liberties and immunities. The saint had not only vanquished the Danes: he had held his own with William the Conqueror.

King Edward I, no less formidable than William, proposed in 1294 to tax the saint's town, a thing unheard of in 'the Liberty'. When he, of all people, relented, word got about that his bodyguard had heard him bellowing in the night, and rushed into his bedchamber to hear him shouting that 'Edmund was making another Sweyn of him'. (For Edward's amends, see pl. 10.)

Such stories reveal the peculiar sanctity of Edmund's shrine, not only with simple superstitious people, but with the most practised potentates. The presence of Edmund's body within that shrine was essential to the maintenance of the fortunes of the abbey, the town, and the whole Liberty of St Edmund. Its removal from the shrine, except to secure it from the Vikings, would have been unthinkable in those days. Yet testimony to its positive presence in the shrine is something we should examine. For, by the fifteenth century, a skeleton, or at any rate some bones, in the basilica of St Sernin in Toulouse had been labelled 'corpus beati Aymundi confessoris Regis Anglie' and later showed itself no ordinary relic.

By about 1580, perhaps much earlier, 'Aymund' had become 'S Eadmundus Rex Angliae', and ranged among the nine 'protectors' of the town, who were painted in fresco on the great hexagonal columns on either side of St Sernin's choir: he is found on the Epistle side, with St Susanna of Babylon (Pl. 8).[3] In 1631, he repaid all this attention by being invoked at the right moment and ending an outbreak of the plague at Toulouse. Perhaps the most miraculous of all this skeleton's achievements was to survive, or be thought to have survived, the Revolution — as dangerous a time for holy relics in France as our Protestant Reformation was for medieval effigies. In 1901, the Roman Catholic cathedral of Westminster was building, and the Archbishop of Toulouse was persuaded to part with the skeleton. In July it reached Newhaven, and was housed by the duke of Norfolk at Arundel until Westminster should be ready for it. A letter from M. R. James in *The Times*,[4] and one from Sir Ernest Clarke in *The Bury Post*,[5] seem to have persuaded Cardinal Vaughan against taking it in. Whether French or Anglo-Saxon by birth, those old bones have found an unexpected last resting-place in Sussex.

3 *Congrès Archéologique de France, XCIIe session, tenue à Toulouse en 1929*, Paris, 1930, p. 55, In 1968, paintings of, apparently, two centuries earlier were alleged to have been found beneath those of the late 16th century. They did not include the underpainting of the St Aymond column.

4 2 August 1901.

5 3 September 1901. I am indebted to Mr W. G. Arnott for lending me his offprint of this letter. A full report of Cardinal Vaughan's public acceptance of Sir Ernest Clarke's evidence appeared in *The Times*, 10 September, 1901.

There are those who seriously believe the Toulouse skeleton to be that of the last pre-Danish king of East Anglia. They believe it was stolen from the shrine at Bury in 1216, and removed to France by the French prince Louis,[6] in league with the anarchical English barons in that year after they had broken the Concord of Runnymede.[7] It is not impossible. So we look at the English evidence, which is luckily at its most illuminating in the decade or so before 1216, when Jocelin of Brakelond was writing. But we will start at the beginning.

The first need is to establish the condition of the king's corpse at the time of his death, and the circumstances of its first burial. Whether he was over-powered in his hall at *Haegelisdun*, or more robustly fought and was slain in battle, we need not deny him the wounded body and severed head specified by Abbo.[8] Abbo's version of the miraculous finding of the head may contain a grain of truth. When Edmund's forlorn followers searched Haegelisdun Wood for the head they were guided to it, according to Abbo, by shouts of 'here' and found it between the paws of a wolf. We need not believe, as medieval people did, that the shouts came from Edmund's own lips, or that the wolf had any but disloyal intentions. When the wolf had 'withdrawn', those entrusted with the job 'applied all their skill and ability to fitting the head on to the body *pro tempore*, and committed them, joined in this way, to a suitable tomb. Over it they built a primitive chapel, where the body rested for many years.'[9] Pl. 9 shows how the event was pictured in 1433.

Sometime during the first half of the tenth century,[10] when the Danes had been brought to terms by Wessex, Edmund's body was translated to Bedricesworth, one of his family's 'vills', and where his predecessor Sigberht had founded a monastery early in the seventh century.[11] When Edmund's body was brought here, it was guarded first by voluntary devotees, then by a college of half-a-dozen seculars.[12] The desire to have them replaced by regular monks probably explains Abbo's emphasis on the remarkably incorrupt condition of the corpse. He said it might be assumed that in the years

---

6 See below, pp. 63–67. The Rev. Richard Yates, in his *Monastic History of St Edmund's Bury*, 1805, p. 147, noticed that this belief had been expressed already by Pierre de Caseneuve in 1644: see below, note 53.

7 A. L. Poole, *From Domesday Book to Magna Carta*, 1951, p. 477.

8 Thomas Arnold, ed., *Memorials of St Edmund's Abbey*, I, 1890, pp. 15–16 (hereafter cited as Memorials); Garmonsway, *op. cit.*, pp. 70–71. Cf. *Proceedings, Suffolk Inst. Arch.*, XXXI, 1969, p. 220. It is nowadays conjectured that Haegelisdun and Haegelisdun Wood may be located in Bradfield St Clare, only five miles from Bury. A King's Hall Manor in adjacent Rougham belonged to Bury abbey before the Conquest. More confirmation is needed.

9 *Memorials*, I, pp. 18–19. The words *pro tempore* imply that a more permanent connexion was made later; see below, note 27.

10 See *Proceedings, Suffolk Inst. Arch.*, XXXI, 1969, p. 222.

11 E. O. Blake, ed., *Liber Eliensis*, 1962, p. 11. It was presumably the first St Mary's (minster) church that was moved to its present site to make room for the new north transept of the abbey church by Godfrey the Sacrist, c. 1115. See A. B. Whittingham, *Arch. Jour.*, CVIII, 1952, p. 173.

12 *Memorials*, I, p. 30.

since Edmund's death the body would have putrified; but, on the contrary, there was no trace of his wounds, or scars, only a tenuous red crease, like a scarlet thread, round his neck.[13] Abbo referred to a woman, called Oswen, who had opened the tomb regularly on the anniversary of the Lord's Supper, and carefully attended to the corpse.[14] The point he was making was that incorruptibility of the flesh was a miraculous consequence of the young king's carnal purity in life. Abbo was an emissary of the great Benedictine house of Fleury on the upper Loire, sent over at the request of the monks of Ramsey to 'raise the tone' of religious life in England, including the tightening of the Benedictine rules of celibacy and chastity. Towards the end of his account of Edmund's 'passion', Abbo came to the point: 'The Catholic Fathers, in the rolls of their religion . . . teach that men who preserve their chastity till death and endure persecution even to martyrdom are compensated on earth, after death, with incorruption of the flesh . . . the natural attribute of angels.'[15]

Abbo made two other points about this valuable corpse. The first was that Theodred, bishop of London (942 – 951),[16] who led the renewal of Christianity in Danish East Anglia, himself checked the saint's condition: 'handled the body, washed it, clothed it afresh in the best clothes and replaced it in a wooden coffin'.[17] This shows that Edmund's value as an English patriotic and anti-heathen symbol was clearly recognised by the bishop. Secondly, Abbo recorded the story of a headstrong young magnate who demanded to have the coffin opened up so that he could see Edmund for himself, and who was alleged to have gone out of his mind at the moment of looking. Does this story suggest the preparation of an ultimate

13   *Ibid.*, pp. 19 – 20.
14   Her trimmings from his nails and hair were still preserved in the abbey and reported present by Henry VIII's Commissioners. From their Report Weever, in his *Funerall Monuments*, 1631, disconcertingly mistranslated 'crinis' (hair) as 'a sinew'.
15   *Ibid.*, p. 24. At Fleury, now known as St Benoît sur Loire, after Benedict, a prominent 12th-century capital at the junction of the north transept with the nave is carved with a representation of St Benedict's resolute resistance to a damsel introduced to him by the Devil: the naked saint is shown stepping gingerly into a thornbush.
16   From the location of the private estates bequeathed in his will, it seems likely he was a Suffolk man.
17   C. F. Battiscombe, *The Relics of St Cuthbert*, Oxford, 1956, pp. 44 – 46, draws attention to the remarkable similarity between the two cults — of St Edmund at Bury and St Cuthbert at Durham. Referring to this passage of Abbo, he writes: 'Since the preservation of a mummy depended primarily on the extent to which it could be kept free from contact with air and moisture, stories of grooming "incorrupt" bodies or washing them . . . must be treated with the greatest reserve.' He adds: 'It would be hard to think of any pious attention calculated to destroy a mummy more quickly than washing it, even supposing that there could have been a mummy of St Edmund to wash!' There can be no doubt at all that *an* embalmed body was present in St Edmund's shrine at this stage; and no strong reason for supposing it could not have been Edmund's: see below, note 27. In the discussion following my reading of this paper on 26 February 1970 at a research seminar of the University of East Anglia's Centre of East Anglian studies, the late Dr Calvin Wells pointed out the fallacy in Battiscombe's belief that air is inimical to mummies. At the same time he expressed reservations about the probable efficiency of embalmers in ninth-century East Anglia.

safeguard in case anything should happen to that body? It was already attracting rich gifts; and theft, at least by unbelievers, could not be ruled out. An attempt had already been made on the treasures. Nor could the good condition of the corpse be forever guaranteed. Unless we believe in miracles of this primitive kind, we are bound to assume that those early devotees of Edmund were very gifted embalmers: this story of Abbo and his successors must be reckoned *prima facie* evidence. And we must assume that repair-work was occasionally necessary; indeed that some element of deception was implicit in this 'miracle' of incorruptibility. Unless we believe that such skill in embalming was beyond Edmund's court, there seems no serious reason to suppose that the body guarded in the shrine at Bedricesworth was a substitute for Edmund's. The variety of prodigious technical accomplishments exposed at Sutton Hoo, from an earlier age, as well as Sutton Hoo's evidence of links with the Near East, should make us cautious before assuming that embalming skills were beyond the capacity of the servants of Edmund's household or the craftsmen of his kingdom.[18]

From this time of 'the tenth-century Reformation', St Edmund's collegiate church at *Bedricesworth* began to acquire its great possessions. Bishop Theodred himself left estates to the Saint.[19] In 945, the Saint's namesake, King Edmund, granted him great privileges over the immediate neighbourhood.[20] The king's son Eadwig gave Beccles and Elmswell to the Saint,[21] and so on. During the new savage Viking onslaughts the chief guardian of the shrine, Aylwin, whose parents were patrons of St Etheldreda, personally conducted Edmund's body to the greater security of St Gregory's church in St Paul's churchyard, in London for the three years 1010−13.[22] It was after this period of crisis that Cnut took the hint from Abbo, and from his own father's sudden death: he replaced the secular priests by a monastery of Benedictine celibates. A new monastic church was built under the supervision of Bishop Aelfwine, c. 1022.[23] When Danegeld was levied, the people of Bury were to pay their geld to the use of Edmund's monastery. Bedricesworth's change of name to Bury about this time, reflects the need to fortify the place in the teeth of the Viking raids: *burh*

18   C. F. Battiscombe, *op. cit.*, p. 60n., cites Dom H. Leclercq in the *Dictionnaire Chrétienne et de Liturgie*, who in turn cites Rufinus of Aquileia and St John Chrysostom, both testifying to the efficacy of myrrh as a preservative of the body and a preventive of corruption. He notes that the mixture of myrrh and aloes, which Nicodemus and Joseph of Arimathea brought to embalm Jesus with, became the normal Christian prescription in subsequent centuries. According to John XIX, 39, they used 'about an hundred pounds weight'. Tight bandages coagulated with the ointment and formed a second skin. However indirect they may have been, links between East Anglia and the Near East in the time of Edmund's seventh-century forebears are unquestionably demonstrated in the Sutton Hoo silver, as Ernst Kitzinger at once recognised (*Antiquity*, March 1940, pp. 40−63).
19   C. R. Hart, *Early Charters of Eastern England*, 1966, pp. 53−4.
20   *Ibid.*, pp. 54−8.
21   *Ibid.*, p. 248.
22   *Memorials*, I, pp. 40−45.
23   Hart, *op. cit.*, p. 64.

implies a defended town. It remained for Edward the Confessor, in 1044, to grant St Edmund even more lavish privileges over the whole liberty, and for William the Conqueror to confirm them.

Yet, in the time of Edward the Confessor, a woman cured of dumbness at the shrine complained that it was neglected and covered with cobwebs.[24] Abbot Leofstan (1044 – 65) was stung into holding a public inspection of the body. Old Aylwin, himself now one of Edmund's monks, his eyesight growing dim, was asked to attend. He felt the body and found it in as good order as it had been on its return from London, a cross that St Alphege had coveted still lying on the breast. A marvellous fragrant odour of sanctity[25] pervaded the church, and two extraordinary episodes followed. Some of the details were recorded by Archdeacon Hermann at the end of the century; some by Abbot Samson a whole century later. First the Saint's clothes were removed, apparently so that the body might be properly reddened with blood and riddled with wounds.[26] Then, to test whether the Saint's head and body really were miraculously reunited, Abbot Leofstan took hold of the head, told a young monk called Turstan to hold on to the feet, and pulled. Turstan was pulled towards the abbot![27] One might suppose that to have been pre-arranged were it not recorded by Hermann that the abbot's hands were thereafter paralysed and his speech and sight temporarily affected. His unseemly forwardness and exertion with the holy king, virgin and martyr, had brought on a stroke.[28] At the end of the next century, Abbot Samson referred to his predecessor as doubting Thomas, and when he himself came to inspect Edmund, though a friend of Richard the Lionheart, was nervous enough to mutter: 'Turn not to my perdition my boldness in touching thee: thou knowest my devotion and my purpose.'

It must be admitted that those two acts of Leofstan, taken together, do raise doubts whether the body in his care really was that of the young king, arrow-riddled and beheaded by the Danes two centuries earlier. The most persuasive reason for accepting its authenticity is the testimony of Aylwin, whose devotion and whose authority on the subject can hardly be doubted.

24 *Memorials*, I, p. 52.
25 Battiscombe, *op. cit.*, pp. 59 – 60, notes the frequency with which 'an odour of heavenly sweetness' was enjoyed on such medieval occasions, and admits that this 'terebinthic' odour is an added indication of embalming if other signs of embalming are also present.
26 *Memorials*, I, p. 53. 'Exuitur itaque sanctus sancti martyrii vestibus partim rubeis rubore sanguinis, partim perforatis ictibus telorum crebris, sed tamen reponendis, saluti credentium profuturis'. The absence of wounds may be explained by the creation of a new outer skin in the embalming process. In interpreting this passage I have followed H. E. Butler, Professor of Latin in the University of London (*Chronicle of Jocelin of Brakelond*, ed., 1949, p. xviii). Perhaps a more probable meaning is that only the clothes were blood-stained and gashed.
27 This episode leaves no doubt that there was a body in Edmund's shrine; presumably one whose skull and vertebrae had been firmly wired together before embalming, if this *was* the venerated king. Grave doubts about the likelihood that this corpse was that of the king were expressed at the seminar referred to in n. 17 above. *Memorials*, I, p. 134.
28 When he and Aylwin died, they shared a tomb with the woman Oswen (see above, p. 58) at the very feet of Edmund: James, *op. cit.*, p. 136.

If we can accept the authenticity of Edmund's body in the Confessor's reign, then the balance of probability is in favour of its having remained in its shrine at Bury until the Dissolution of his abbey. So far as the Toulouse bones are concerned, the suggestion has not yet been made that they were removed from Bury in Anglo-Saxon times.

Eleventh-century people were not all silly, unquestioning believers of anything the monks cared to 'stage'. Hermann, writing soon after Abbot Baldwin's death in 1098, mentioned rumours that were put about by William Rufus' unconventional court to the effect that Edmund's body was not truly incorrupt; people were bold enough to say they thought the riches lavished on the shrine might be better spent on the army. Hermann naturally expressed his opinion that they would regret such impious thoughts.[29]

That was being said in 1095, when the great apsidal east end of Baldwin's new abbey church was finished and ready for the translation of the Saint's body from the old church built under Cnut. A direct result of the rumours was that Rufus declined to sanction the new building's dedication to the Saint at that time, though he agreed to the translation. Hermann recorded how Herbert, bishop of East Anglia, tried to exert his authority and take part in the translation. But the Saint's liberty was maintained and the ceremonies were performed by Bishop Walkelin of Winchester and Ranulf Flambard, the king's chaplain. Abbot Samson, writing a century later, added much detail to Hermann's contemporary account. He seems to have used the work of Prior 'John of C.', who probably went on from Hermann's time into the first half of the twelfth century, introducing a rather objective view of a monk called Hermann who made familiar play with some relics of Edmund to embellish his otherwise commended sermons.[30]

The translation of the saint took place in the presence of an enormous multitude. (Two other East Anglian saints were translated with him to the new sanctuary: St Jurmin, probably King Anna's son, brought from Blythburgh, and at least some of St Botolph.) There was a drought in East Anglia at the time of the translation. Bishop Walkelin commanded that Edmund's body should be carried outside the church. Walkelin was not bishop of St Swithin's diocese for nothing. Happily for Edmund's reputation he timed the demonstration well, and the drought was duly ended.

The most circumstantial piece of medieval testimony lies in the *Chronicle* of Jocelin of Brakelond, written at the beginning of John's reign.[31] Jocelin showed how the Judges of the Exchequer dared not approach the shrine to strip part of its precious metal to help ransom Richard I, 'for the fury of St Edmund can strike at a distance, much more those who

29   *Memorials*, I, pp. 86–7.
30   *Loc. cit.*, pp. lv, 156–160, 168–175.
31   *Chronicle*, ed. H.E. Butler, 1949, pp. 97, 106–116.

approach to strip him of his shirt'. If judges were frightened, monks were, presumably, more so. Jocelin went on to write: 'In the year of grace 1198, the glorious martyr Edmund wished, by scaring our convent, to teach us that his body should be treated with greater care.' One June night, the guardians of the shrine fell asleep, a candle slipped, and the whole area of the shrine was ablaze; when it was extinguished, 'the silver panels came away from the wood, which was reduced to the thinness of my finger'. They sent for the goldsmith that night to avoid scandal. Yet next morning the pilgrims were inquisitive, 'for lying rumours had spread that the Saint's head had been singed'. Samson made plans to celebrate Edmund's feast (which fell five months later, on 20 November) by placing the shrine on a loftier marble plinth, 'for greater security and glory', and restoring the front of the shrine. in pure gold. The three days following the feast were declared a public fast, and on the third day the feretory containing the body was placed on the high altar while the work on the new plinth was done. Jocelin describes the silk[32] and linen cloths that were bound round the coffin, and the coffin itself, 'with iron rings at the end like a Norse chest', standing in a wooden trough to protect the coffin from the stone. A gold figure of St Michael, a foot long, covered up the hole in the coffin-lid through which in ancient times the guardians used presumably to check the presence and condition of the body. (Has he been replaced by a mounted St George in Pl. 10?)

Two nights later, Samson inspected the body himself, with his Sacrist and Walter the Physician: twelve strong monks, white-robed, took off the panels and, with difficulty, the lid, which was held down with sixteen long nails. Many linen and silk[33] wrappings were removed, and when the outlines of the body appeared, Samson said he dared not go further and see the sacred body unclothed. He touched the eyes, the nose, which he pronounced very large and prominent, the breast, the arms, the fingers, the toes. Another twelve, including Jocelin himself ('Jocellus the Cellarer'), then crowded forward to see, and John of Diss, and the vestry servers, were sitting watching from above in the roof. The rest slept, and were in tears next morning when they heard what they had missed. Samson clearly did not want another public spectacle of the kind Abbot Leofstan had allowed. All seems to have gone well. The panelled shrine was then set up on its grander, safer plinth, and the guardians by whose negligence the fire had started, were replaced by new ones with new rules for stricter vigilance.

32   See following note.
33   Since nothing of this has survived, little can usefully be surmised. An up-to-date discussion of the silks found when St Cuthbert was uncovered in 1827 may be read in Battiscombe's symposium on *The Relics of St Cuthbert* cited above: Gerard Brett, discussing the 'Rider' silk from that shrine, describes a considerable silk industry south of the Caspian in the 10th century, centred on Tabaristan and exporting from Bokhara. Various other silks at Durham derived from Byzantium. At present there seems to be no general study of the early distribution of silk in the West.

Now, can we envisage that in 1216, only eighteen years later, some monks of St Edmund (presumably at least a dozen), were able to find the courage, the means, and the total secrecy, to smuggle this awe-inspiring body out of the monastery, into the hands of the French prince Louis, 'Le Lion', who was with the leading English baronial rebels that year? This is the theory held by those who believe St Edmund's bones were in St Sernin's, Toulouse, by 1450. They rely on a short passage in an anonymous medieval French history of the Dukes of Normandy, apparently by a contemporary chronicler in Flanders or Artois.[34] It gives a remarkable detailed narrative of the civil war in England, in which the barons, not content with Magna Carta, had offered John's crown to Louis (the son of King Philippe Auguste, whom he succeeded in 1223 as Louis VIII). The passage quoted described the breakdown of peace-negotiations in June 1217, after loyal old William the Marshal, at Lincoln, had knocked out half the total number of knights in the rebel army. It continues: 'Then Louis sent the viscount of Melun o grant chevalerie vers St Edmont, por tenser la tierre' — 'towards St Edmund, to contest the country': the trouble with *tenser* is that it can also mean 'protect'. It goes on to say that 'they made their sortie, then pillaged[35] the town of St Edmund, acquired much booty from the land, and returned to London'.[36] The abbey is not mentioned, still less the shrine. One difficulty in accepting the authenticity of this whole passage is its firm placing in June/July 1217. Roger of Wendover, also a contemporary, described very circumstantially, in the *Chronica Majora*, Melun's death in London a whole year earlier, in the summer of 1216. (Edmont, according to the distinguished nineteenth-century editor of the *Histoire*, appears in the manuscript as Odmont!)

There are more serious difficulties than mere discrepancies of text. In August 1213, the Bury monks unanimously elected Hugh of Northwold as their abbot in succession to Samson, but they did it in a manner that seemed to challenge John's royal customary rights in the business. John's alarming displeasure was signalled unmistakably, and the monks quickly divided into two parties of almost equal numbers. Half stood by Hugh and their own decisions; half, led by the odious sacrist, responded to the king's cause. A most unedifying but instructive struggle ended almost two years later on 10 June 1215, at Windsor, with John's acceptance of Hugh — five days before his concord with the barons at Runnymede.

Now these two years were chronicled in vivid but sober detail, by a member of Hugh's party, in the *Cronica de Electione Hugonis*[37] (usually abbreviated to 'the *Electio Hugonis*': it is described at some length in chapter 8). The relevance of the *Electio* to the fate of Edmund's shrine is fairly

---

34   F. Michel, ed., *Histoire des Ducs de Normandie*, 1840, p. iii.
35   *Barroiierent*. The use of *baroier* in this chapter is actually cited in F. Godefroy, *Dictionnaire de L'Ancienne Langue Française*, I, 1881, p. 589.
36   Michel, *op. cit.*, p. 198.
37   Ed. R. M. Thomson, Oxford, 1974.

obvious. It describes the close connexion between the monkish supporters and opponents of Hugh and the corresponding barons and prelates as they aligned themselves against, or in favour of, the customary rights and liberties of the king.

After Runnymede, Robert fitzWalter led the barons against John, and Roger Bigot was among the barons: it was fitzWalter who offered the English throne to Louis (whose wife, Blanche, had at least some claim) if he would join them. Yet, a year earlier, in June 1214, the *Electio* shows both fitzWalter and Bigot in the chapter-house at Bury, trying to bring Hugh's supporters round to the king's point of view! Bigot, a familiar figure at the abbey, addressed Hugh's loyal supporter, the cellarer, in this apparently very familiar way: '*Frater Karissime*, although it is up to all of us to preserve the blessed martyr's liberties intact and unharmed . . . it is especially incumbent on me, as *his standard-bearer by hereditary right*, and on Robert fitzWalter, here present and on his men and faithful followers.'[38]

How hereditary Roger's standard-bearing for St Edmund was is hard to determine. In Samson's day, when the earl of Clare pretended it was *his* duty to carry it, Samson replied: 'Earl Roger Bigot maintains that he holds himself to be seized of the duty of carrying St Edmund's standard, for he carried it when the earl of Leicester was captured and the Flemings destroyed.' This was in 1173, in the battle fought at Fornham, just outside Bury's north gate. Roger carried Edmund's banner on the old king's winning side: his father, earl Hugh, fought on Leicester's side. Perhaps Roger's performance in 1173 was the inauguration of this hereditary office. Jordan Fantosme, whose Chronicle gives the fullest and most vivid contemporary description of the battle, confirmed 'dan Rogier le Bigot's' eagerness to win his spurs (lines 1029, 1078) and that he performed great deeds that day. All Jordan says of St Edmund's standard is that the earl of Arundel was with the company that had the standard at its head. However, as Jordan reports, or invents, dialogue that seems fairly authentic between Arundel, Humphrey de Bohun and 'dan' Roger — three of the five heroes of the day — uttered just before they advanced, they were probably known to have fought in the same company. This does something to endorse Roger's claim, later, that he had carried the standard; and certainly nothing to contradict it.[39]

It seems to have been as natural and as frequent for fathers and sons to be on opposing sides in these struggles as it was in the Hanoverian court manoeuvres. Roger's own son was part of John's royal household in Poitou, turning the king *against* Hugh's acceptance as abbot. William the Marshal, the old warrior-statesman — a tough blend of Wellington and Mountbatten — staunchly loyal to the crown, was also present in Bury chapter-house that day when Roger Bigot spoke for John's rights. But William the

---

38   *Loc. cit.*, pp. 86—89, and p. 117 below.
39   H. E. Butler, ed., *The Chronicle of Jocelin of Brakelond*, 1949, 57—58; R. C. Johnston, ed. *Jordan Fantosme's Chronicle*, Oxford, 1981, lines 1008—1095. Cf. p 136 below.

Marshal's son fought on the barons' side for Louis. Devotion to Edmund's liberties was bound up with the safety of his shrine. It seemed to me necessary to demonstrate the close involvement of king and barons in the life of Edmund's abbey. The ease and frequency of communication between both factions in the abbey and both factions in the politics of the realm is one of the revelations of the *Electio* and is illustrated more fully in chapter 8. The divided allegiance between members of the leading families would add to the difficulty of hushing up any such sensational scandal as the removal of Edmund's body by a party of Louis' men — ostensibly anyway on the same side as Roger Bigot — not to mention the involvement of Archbishop Stephen Langton or of the abbot of St Edmund himself. After fourteen more years at Bury, Abbot Hugh went to Ely as bishop for twenty-five years. When he died in 1254, at the foot of his effigy was carved the martyrdom of Edmund, and by his right side the sainted king is praying.

The English chroniclers described this war of 1216−17 in considerable detail. As monks they might have been expected to note a ransacking of St Edmund's town, still more his abbey and shrine. They do not. They chronicle ferocious excursions by John and his separate forces through the baronial territory early in 1216, which included the capture of Colchester keep, the biggest object of its kind in Europe. A most significant witness is Ralph of Coggeshall, who was chronicler (as well as abbot and a remarkable builder) of the Cistercian abbey at Little Coggeshall. There he was close enough to the affairs of Bury to devote a well-informed paragraph to Samson's examination of 1198 of the 'incorrupt and supple' body of Edmund 'in the presence of eighteen monks'. He recorded that at Christmas 1215, Tilty abbey had been violently entered during Mass and many stores ('*apothecas*') broken into and goods ('*institorum deposita*') taken. Similarly his own abbey had been entered on 1 January, and twenty-two horses taken.[40] These outrages were blamed on John's retainers rather than on himself, and notably on a character called Buc de Brabant. Ralph described how they then rushed off via Bury St Edmunds to Ely.

Father Bryan Houghton has postulated a 'fifth column' within the abbey, smuggling the corpse out secretly to Louis and the barons.[41] He has adduced not a word of contemporary evidence for such double treachery — to both their abbey and to John — nor any comprehensible motive. Louis and the barons were all under the pope's solemn excommunication.[42] The royalists

---

40 Joseph Stevenson, ed., *Radulphi de Coggeshall Chronicon Anglicanum*, Rolls Series, 1875, p. 177. Cf. *V.C.H. Essex*, II, pp. 134, 125.

41 The Very Rev. B. R. S. Houghton, formerly Roman Catholic parish priest of Bury St Edmunds, very kindly supplied me with a copy of his unpublished monograph, dated 20 February 1965. His book, *St Edmund, King and Martyr*, was published in 1970 by Terence Dalton at Lavenham, Suffolk. Father Houghton told me (letter of 6 March 1970) he then attached great importance to the spelling *Eadmundus* on the medieval underpainting at S Sernin (note 3, above). Curiously enough, no spelling, indeed no underpainting, had been revealed when I visited St Sernin's in August, 1970.

42 Poole, *op. cit.*, p. 478.

fought in the name of the Church, and wore the badge of crusaders.[43] Abbot Ralph of Coggeshall, interested enough to record Samson's inspection of Edmund's body, gives no hint at all of any baronial interference with the Saint or his abbey. Head of a Cistercian house, he would have no interest in 'hushing up' such a sensational loss by the Benedictines, rather the reverse.

In 1216, Louis' baronial supporters controlled Pleshey and Hedingham and proceeded against a number of other East Anglian castles. Orford was one.[44] Norwich they found deserted, and garrisoned it.[45] They besieged Cambridge, took its castle, and marched on, pillaging, through Norfolk and Suffolk. They extorted ransoms from Yarmouth, Dunwich and Ipswich. Then, after ravaging Colchester and thereabout they returned to London. There the viscount of Melun fell ill and died. Roger of Wendover, who recorded this, is as silent as Ralph of Coggeshall about that 'pillaging of St Edmund's town' a year later with which Melun was credited by the French history of the Dukes of Normandy. Wendover was a monk of St Albans, whose own troubles with the barons he described minutely. At Redbourn nearby, the reliquary of St Amphibalus' church was plundered by Louis' henchmen. Indeed this is the one well-attested plunder of relics of the whole war.[46] Roger would surely have at least mentioned the rape of the famous reliquary of his fellow Benedictines at Bury, less than sixty miles away?

If, despite the absence of English confirmation, the French chronicler was right about Melun and St Edmunds, then he did establish an indirect link between St Edmund and Toulouse. In return for 10,000 marks, Louis agreed, at the Treaty of Kingston,[47] never to support English rebels again, was absolved, and returned to France. Two years later, in 1219, he himself went crusader and took part in the siege of Toulouse whose people were Manichean heretics. We are asked to believe that he acquired the mummy from Melun (who completely mistrusted him) and that then, two or three years after his excursion into East Anglia, Louis had gone campaigning in the 'Midi' with a mummified English saint in his baggage; that the heretical Tolosians now acquired the relics by sallying out and ransacking his camp, which was on the far bank of the Garonne: alternatively that he based himself on St Sernin's, which was then a separate *bourg* to the north of the *cité*, and personally made the abbey a present of Edmund's body.[48] It is not impossible. It seems highly improbable. What would seem at least no more improbable is that during the Hundred Years War the Tolosians were

43   Poole, *op. cit.*, p. 478.
44   W. Stubbs, ed., *Memoriale Walteri de Coventria*, II, 1873, p. 235.
45   H. R. Luard, ed., *Chronica Majora*, Rolls Series, II, 1874, p. 663.
46   *Op. cit.*, III, 1876, pp. 16–17, Apparently Amphibalus' own relics had been translated from Redbourn to St Alban's abbey in 1178: Sir Henry Chauncey, *Historical Antiquities of Hertfordshire*, II, 1926, p. 397.
47   In August 1970, a very confused notice displayed by the clergy of St Sernin's for the information of visitors, referred to 'the relics of St Edmund, King of England, formerly interred at Kingston in England'.
48   See below, n. 53.

engaged in displaying some invented relics of a popular English patriot-saint, either to advertise their attitude to the war, or merely to tease English merchants and travellers in the town. Or that Louis himself was the inventor.[49]

St Edmund's fame was essentially north-west European. Nevertheless, had they acquired his celebrated body in 1219, the monks of St Sernin would have known whose bones they were supposed to be (and would have come under very heavy pressure to return them: they were by no means short of relics). Lucca cathedral had had an altar to St Edmund since 1071.[50] Yet in 1517 there was certainly uncertainty at Toulouse about these bones. That year, a fine black-letter history of the town appeared in French.[51] As Sir Ernest Clarke, noticed,[52] it lists all the saints whose remains reposed in Toulouse, starting with the apostles, James the Less, Simon, Jude and Barnabas. Twenty-fifth down the list comes what is described as 'le corps de saint aymond confesseur du roi dangleterre', i.e. saint aymond, *confessor of the king of England!* *Du roi* must be a 1517 misprint for *et roi*, and reflects, I think, the uncertainty of Aymond's identity. The old word 'confessor', traditionally spoken with the emphasis on the first syllable (we *should* say Edward the Cónfessor), indicates an important category of saints: those who unflinchingly testify (confess) to their beliefs, without being called on to die as martyrs (martyr is from the Greek work meaning, similarly, witness). Next in the list came 'saint honeste, confesseur et disciple de saint saturnin', who certainly *was* both confessor and a disciple of Saturnin, or Sernin, first bishop of Toulouse. It was only after Aymond's effectiveness with the plague in 1631 that a local scholar, Pierre de Caseneuve, boldly identified him with the king of East Anglia.[53] Before that it can have been no clearer to the people of Toulouse than it is to us today whose bones are represented by that strange label: 'Aymond confessor of the King of England'.

Before my first visit to Toulouse in 1970, I had not fully understood the

---

49 Father Houghton's book, p. 62, refers to 'the possibility' that Edmund's Feast Day, 20 November, had been celebrated at Toulouse long before the 17th century. If so, it would indicate that the Toulouse relics were alleged at the time of their acquisition to be those of the East Anglian saint. It was a date widely advertised in the Calendars of the Feasts of Saints.

50 *Memorials*, I, pp. 68, 137.

51 *Les gestes des tholosais*, premierement escriptz en langaige Latin par duscret at lettre maistre Nichole Bertrandi advocat . . . et apres translates en francoy.

52 *The Bury Post*, 3 September 1901.

53 Pierre de Caseneuve, *Histoire de la Vie et des Miracles de S Edmund, Roy D'Estangle*, Tolose, 1644. This was a *pièce d'occasion*, undertaken during the horrors of the Plague in 1631, when the town vowed to elevate the relics of 'this great martyr'. In 1644, the Archbishop of Toulouse performed the elevation 'before the eyes of this town'. The book is an industrious, indiscrimate selection from many medieval sources of the life and miracles of the East Anglian king. On the crucial subject of the translation from Bury to Toulouse it says merely: 'On croit que — it is thought that — ce fût le Roy Louys huitième, pere de S Louys, qui en fit un present a cette venerable Eglise . . . Nous lisons que — we read that — all the Princes who besieged the town of Tolose were lodged in the Abbey of S Sernin.'

enormous importance of St Sernin's as a pilgrimage church on the main route to — almost comparable with — the great church of St James at Compostela. It is thought, for instance, that the early 12th-century sculptor of the porte Miégeville at Sernin's worked at Compostela on the Las Platerias gate. This function of St Sernin's as a great pilgrimage church is to the point: it establishes a motive for the collection of the widest possible range and variety of relics, and renders their authenticity all the more questionable. In 1434, the number of pilgrims from England licensed to visit Compostela was 2,460.

Even if St Sernin's had claimed unequivocally in the fifteenth century that they had Edmund's bones, that would hardly amount to proof that they had them. The monks at Bury at that time claimed to have some of the coals St Lawrence was roasted on: there is a very wide gap between belief and proof. Much nearer this time, two opportunities for the removal of Edmund from Bury did occur: the risings of the town against the abbey in 1327 and 1379 − 81. In the first of these riots the townsmen attacked and burnt many of the monastic buildings. They were rebelling against the irksome monastic hold over the town, and naturally made for the muniments and records that established that hold. They also made off with priceless gold and silver vessels from the treasury and rich vestments.[54] In a letter seeking the sympathy and advice of the Mayor and Aldermen of London, the Alderman and Commonalty of Bury were careful to blame the monks for starting the violence and 'great mischance which has befalled our town'. They continued: 'The whole commonalty was roused, the abbey was burnt, but by God's grace the church was saved.'[55] In the exchange of vituperation that led next year to the abbot's abduction to London and Flanders, presumably so that he could not testify in the Crown's case against them, no accusations were made, on either side, of any tampering with Edmund's shrine.

Similarly, in 1381, the main object of the attention of John Wrawe, John Tollemache and the Bury rebels was the contents of the abbey's muniment room, the old charters and agreements that gave legal sanction to the town's subordination. The Prior, the Keeper of the abbey's court-rolls, and a third man were summarily beheaded by the mob, who made the monks bring the offending documents to the Guildhall. They also made them hand over a great gold chalice and a gorgeously bejewelled crucifix, worth 300 marks, as a pledge that the monastery would accept an abbot committed to the town's liberation. Then the king recovered control, the Bury townsmen returned

54 The 'Depredations' are detailed in *Memorials*, II, pp. 330−4. The Pleas of the Crown in the case are printed in *The Pinchbeck Register*, ed. Hervey, 1925, I, pp. 95−271. It is important to note that Samson's arrangements for the continuous guarding of the body of St Edmund, night and day, by two monks, were among the regulations for the abbey that were confirmed by the Pope in August 1256: see Rolls Series, *Papal Registers*, I, 1893, p. 334.

55 See V. B. Redstone, 'Some Mercenaries of Henry, Earl of Lancaster', *Trans. R. Hist. Soc.*, 3rd ser., VII, 1913, p. 116, a transcript from Memoranda Roll, A.1 membr.vi (8) dorso, City of London Corporation Records.

the documents and the treasures, and faced a bill for 2,000 marks for damages. All this was described by John Gosford, the abbey's almoner, an eye-witness.[56] Again, though both abbey and church were invaded, there was not the least suggestion that Edmund's shrine was violated. If it had been, there would certainly have been venomous recrimination from the opposing party.

One catches a last vivid glimpse of the shrine in the glare of the great fire of 20 January 1465.[57] It was a still, sunny day, and some plumbers left a brazier alight on the west tower of the abbey church while they went down to eat their lunch. A breeze got up, the roof-timbers caught, and suddenly great flames appeared inside the church. An eye-witness described the course of the fire, and M. R. James has printed the description in his *Abbey Church of St Edmund at Bury*.[58] The bells clanged out a warning, and the townspeople ran from all quarters to help. From the west front the fire spread eastwards along the roof. The central tower and spire, with its delicate lantern tracery, collapsed and the flames, uncontrollable, leapt and darted on, reducing everything to a huge heap of charred embers. As they approached the shrine they burnt through the rope suspending the wooden cover, which caught alight but fell into place on the sarcophagus and enclosed the martyr as in an oven (*clibanus*), 'so that he was unscathed'. Daring men broke some windows, rushed into the church throwing water on the flames, and seeing that the shrine was intact raised a shout of joy to those outside. The fire veered north, and destroyed the Lady Chapel before it died down.

No record is known of any formal 'verification' of the Saint's condition after this oven-warming. This does not mean that none took place: it would be surprising, indeed, if none did. Similarly at the Dissolution of the abbey in 1539, there is no mention of Edmund's body by the Commissioners in their report to Thomas Cromwell, Henry VIII's vicar-general. Their two letters from Bury to Cromwell[59] were written for particular reasons: any reference to Edmund's remains, vitally important though they had been in the formative years and hey-day of the abbey, would have been irrelevant now. Nobody was seriously thinking of trying to make a Sweyn of Henry VIII. One letter, referred to Edmund's 'riche shryne whiche was very

56   Edgar Powell, *The Rising in East Anglia in 1381*, Cambridge, 1896, pp. 14 − 21, 142 − 3.
57   A vivid illustration of the open shrine in 1433, from B.L. Harl. MS. 2278, is reproduced as Plate 11. Drawn with unusually realistic detail, much of it confirmed by other written sources, it nevertheless illustrated Lydgate's account of the translation of Edmund's body from the 'rotounde' chapel in 1095, and cannot be regarded as conclusive evidence that the mummy was displayed so flagrantly, or at all, in 1433. The detail in Plate 10 is naturally more convincing. Professor Peter Lasko's first response to the elaborate goldwork in 10 was that it might represent an *early* thirteenth-century refacing: but 11 suggested to him immediately work of Edward I's time.
58   *Loc. cit.*, above, in note 2.
59   T. Wright, ed., *The Suppression of the Monasteries*, Camden Soc., 1843, pp. 85, 144; also James, *op. cit.*, pp. 169 − 171.

comberous to deface', was devoted exclusively to the subject of the value of
the loot to be had in Bury. If the matter of Edmund's body had been mentioned, it would have been in Dr John Ap Rice's letter, but Dr Ap Rice did
not trouble to give the names of those whose 'skulls and bones' he did refer
to: St Petronilla's for instance, or St Botolph's, which were treasured in the
abbey and occasionally carried about the fields for purposes of encouraging
the rain.[60] The fact that such details were not reported to Cromwell means
that they were beneath his notice, not that such items were not found. Dr
Ap Rice did tell Cromwell he firmly believed that the monks of Bury 'had
confedered and compacted bifore our commyng'. If they retained the
reverence for their patron we might reasonably expect, they took the oppor-
tunity to bury him quietly, unobserved.

In 1634, William Hawkins, master of Hadleigh Grammar School,
published some ingenious and delightful Latin verses. Describing a lawsuit
at Bury, he shows that he had searched everywhere among the ruins and the
nettles there for the place where Edmund's bones lay.[61] He never found it.
The site was not remembered. But the story provides a significant piece of
evidence. An intelligent schoolmaster-poet, living in west Suffolk one century after the Dissolution, naturally assumed that Edmund's body had in
the end been interred in the town whose great distinction it had largely
shaped for at least six centuries.

The last word on the Toulouse relics has yet to be written. When I first
put this study together for the St Edmund Commemorative Volume of the
Proceedings of the Suffolk Institute of Archaeology in 1969, the 16th duke
of Norfolk, in whose chapel at Arundel Castle they reposed (see p. 56
above), was against subjecting them to carbon dating tests. His Grace the
present duke has, in 1984, willingly referred the matter to the Vicar-General
of the Archdiocese of Westminster. With the co-operation of the duke, the
monsignor, the Home Office and the County Archaeological Unit of Suffolk, and allowing for all proper formalities and safeguards, we now seem
to have a chance to determine at least the age of these relics to within a
bracket of about 160 years. If the tests showed clearly that the relics dated
from c. 789 − 949, then there would be good reason to examine the story of
Louis and the siege of Toulouse again from the Toulouse end, with the

---

60   John Weever, *Ancient Funerall Monuments*, 1631, p. 724.
61   *Corolla Varia*, Cambridge, 1634. This point was first noticed by Sir Ernest Clarke, of
     Bury, whose studies advanced our understanding of St Edmund and Bury considerably at
     the start of the present century. Hawkins's work is fully described in Pigot's *Hadleigh*,
     1860, pp. 176 − 86. These lines come in a passage entitled *Devastalia*:

> Pergit & indagans magnivestigia Templi,
> Pro tam Daedaleâ fabricatis arte columnis,
> Pro tot Nobilium Mitratorúmque sepulchris,
> Urticas reperit. Quaerit super omnia, Regis
> Ossibus *Edmundi* quisnam locus. Ossa colentúm
> Tot votis ambita diu, tot ditia donis
> (Ipsum Ubi vix restat) nusquam sunt . . .

assistance of the Association des Amis de la Basilique Saint-Sernin. If they show a different date, we must continue to assume, with William Hawkins, the Caroline master of Hadleigh Grammar School, that at the dissolution of his abbey St Edmund was interred either within his great doomed church or outside among the hundreds of his brethren in their blissful cemetery, between the eastern apses and the little confluent rivers. The body in the shrine had lost its alarming magic and all its patriotic meaning.

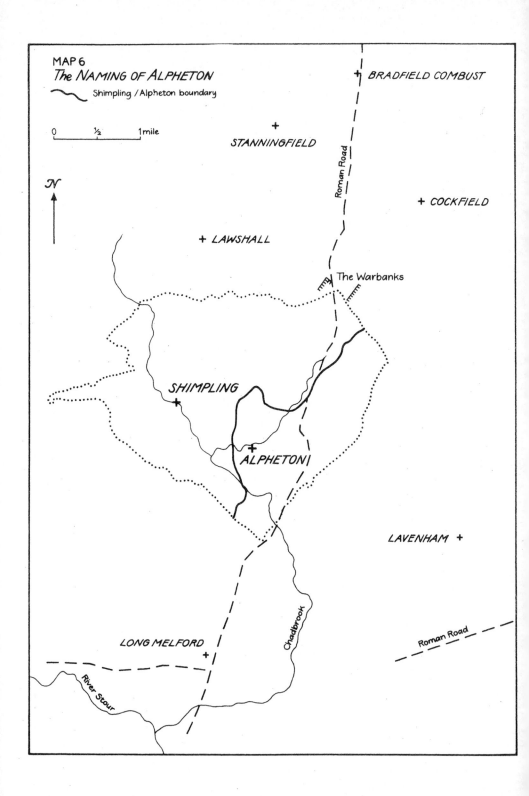

MAP 6
The NAMING OF ALPHETON

〜〜〜 Shimpling / Alpheton boundary

0   ½   1mile

N

BRADFIELD COMBUST

STANNINGFIELD

Roman Road

COCKFIELD

LAWSHALL

The Warbanks

SHIMPLING

ALPHETON

LAVENHAM

LONG MELFORD

Chadbrook

Roman Road

River Stour

5

The Naming of Alpheton:
Two Landed Anglo-Saxon Ladies in Domesday Book

Alpheton's name is familiar to travellers from Bury St Edmunds to Long Melford, which Alpheton adjoins. Most of its houses stand near the main road, leaving the Hall and church of the one-manor parish idyllic and remote. The name is pronounced, curiously, Al-feet'n, and for once we can form some idea how, and when, it was acquired.

E. Ekwall's invaluable *Concise Oxford Dictionary of English Place-names*[1] gives 1204 as the earliest record of the spelling of Alpheton: *Alfledeton*. In fact there is a slightly earlier one, c. 1186−1191[2] virtually identical: *Alfledetun*. The big majority of Suffolk's place-names appear already in 1086 in Domesday Book and seem much earlier. So there is a likelihood that here — unusually for Suffolk — it is a late estate-name from the period 1086−1186. Ekwall shows that the meaning is 'Aelflēd's *tun*', that is, her 'estate' (Aelfled, pronounced Elfleed, was a female name). There is a good candidate for the identity of the Aelfled in question.

The map shows that Alpheton was probably carved out of the parish and manor of Shimpling, a very large manor, as we shall see. Shimpling is separated by one parish (Lawshall) from Stanningfield. Stanningfield had become, between 1066 and 1086, part of the very interesting fief of Ralf Bainard. Domesday Book[3] shows that in Stanningfield 'Elflet' (i.e. Aelfled), described as 'a freewoman', held under St Edmund's abbey at Bury, in the time of King Edward (i.e. until 1066), 1 carucate of land. In 1086, Bainard held it by exchange with Bury abbey. There were also 5 acres of meadow, a mill, &c.; and three freemen had been under commendation to the said Elflet, which shows she was a woman of rank, to whom homage was due.

This late Anglo-Saxon landed lady is likely to have been the 'Alflet' who was Roger of Poitou's predecessor over in Bosmere Hundred, a dozen miles east of Stanningfield. The younger son of Roger de Montgomeri, Roger of Poitou already held vast estates. Domesday Book[4] shows that Alflet, under commendation to Harold, had held in 1066 two carucates as a manor in Stonham, woodland for 60 swine, and the third part of a church; also, in Willisham, 2 carucates as a manor, 5 acres of meadow, and a church endowed (well) with 32 acres. In his admirable edition of the

1   4th edn., 1960.
2   In R. H. C. Davis (ed.), *Kalendar of Abbot Samson*, 1954, 66.
3   Fol. 415b.
4   Fol. 351.

Domesday Survey of Essex,[5] J. H. Round thought the Alflet who was Roger of Poitou's predecessor in a house in Colchester in King Edward's day 'cannot be identified in any Essex manor'. If Round had glanced, as he sometimes did, over into Suffolk, he would have noticed at once that Alflet was Roger of Poitou's predecessor in Suffolk manors at Stonham and Willisham. In Stanningfield, a mere two miles from Alpheton (Aelfled's *tun*), though Elflet was not precisely the predecessor of Ralf Bainard, another of the Conqueror's tenants-in-chief, she was a tenant of some rank: her position as St Edmund's tenant, before her eviction by Bainard, perhaps implied that she was actually living at Stanningfield?

It is illuminating to read a passage from the great J. H. Round's introduction to the Domesday Survey in the Essex Victoria County History:[6]

One of the points of difference in the distribution of land before and after the Conquest is the wide extent of the estates held by women on the eve of that event as compared with those which they are entered as holding at the time of the Domesday Survey . . . An instance in point is afforded, in the case of Essex,[7] by the broad lands of Ailid, 'a certain freewoman', from which the fief of Ralf Bainard was largely formed. In this county she had been his predecessor at Wimbish and at Little Dunmow, as at Henham, at Ashdon, and probably at Pentlow, all of them valuable manors. In Norfolk, at Fincham, Barton, the Shouldhams, Tottenhill, Boughton, Bradenham, Merton and Wilby, Ailid had been his predecessor. In Suffolk, she had held 'under the glorious king Edward', the great manors of Shimpling and Kedington.

That tribute to Edward the Confessor in the Norman text is surprising. And only five paragraphs further on,[8] the same phrase was repeated: 'Losam (Loose Hall, Hitcham, on the Wattisham boundary) Lefstan holds as he held under the glorious king Edward'. The loyalty to the Confessor felt by the undisplaced English tenant, Lefstan, was natural, but was it shared by the scribe? Lefstan had experienced the general dispossession at his old manor at Great Bricett, adjoining Wattisham, where Ralf fitzBrien had already given 54 acres of Bricett to 'a certain church' — presumably the great church of St Leonard de Noblac (just west of Limoges) to which he attached the priory he founded at Bricett in 1110.

Naturally, the Domesday scribe overlooked, and so did J. H. Round, Ailid's late husband's direct descent from the truly glorious ealdorman Brihtnoth, hero of the battle against those earlier Northmen at Maldon in 991. It is now possible to reconstruct this distinguished family-tree. E. O.

5 *Victoria County History*, Vol. I., 577n.
6 *Op. cit.*, I., 347.
7 For another Suffolk instance, cf. the displacement of Ulveva at Kelsale: Scarfe, *The Suffolk Landscape*, 1972, 168—172. The last chapter of Christine Fell's *Women in Anglo-Saxon England*, 1984, deals with the question in a general way.
8 Shimpling entry: fol. 415b. The Loose Hall entry, 416b. The *V.C.H.* translation of the Loose Hall entry omits 'as a manor' — a very rare slip in that translation. The Bricett entry is on fol. 417. Loose Hall is shown on Map 3, near Hitcham.

Blake[9] neatly showed how Brihtnoth's daughter, Leofflaed, left her own daughter, Leofwaru, the Suffolk estate of Wetheringsett on condition that she married Lustwine. She did, and Wetheringsett passed to their son, Thurstan, who bequeathed it mostly to Ely. Thurstan in his will, c. 1043 – 1045,[10] not only left Wetheringsett to Ely (except lands to go to the village church), but he left Kedington for her lifetime to *his wife*, Aethelgyth (and thereafter to his two chaplains and to the priest Aelwig). So Aethelgyth, widow of Brihtnoth's great-grandson Thurstan, is the 'Ailad' who held the 5-carucate Domesday manor of Kedington, with its church, which still bears a simple carved stone crucifix from her day. She is also the 'Ailith' who held the 6½ carucate manor of Shimpling, from which Alpheton, *Aelfled's tun*, seems to have been carved soon after.[11]

We do not, and probably can never, know which, if any, of her considerable domains she preferred as a home, a place to live. Her husband's bequest there to his chaplains points to Kedington as a favourite haunt of his. From their extent, and their pleasant situation, the probability is that Kedington and Shimpling were high on her list. That Ralf Bainard's Norman fief was constructed from estates of two wealthy Anglo-Saxon women whose lands lay as close as Aethelgyth's Shimpling and Aelfled's Stanningfield inevitably suggests some relationship between the two women themselves: a neighbourly friendship at least, the shared calamity of Hastings and their subsequent adversity; and perhaps even some degree of kinship. Surely there, somewhere, lies the explanation how Alpheton, when it came to birth beside Ailith's old domain of Shimpling, was given Aelfled's name. It can hardly, I think, be mere coincidence. At least we feel we know a little about her.

I believe there may be one last glimpse of her in the remarkable third section of Abbot Baldwin's 'Feudal Book', which gives the personal names of all the freemen and sokemen where Domesday Book was content to give numbers; and which may have been compiled a decade later. For St Edmund's great manor of Rougham, adjoining the town to the east, Domesday recorded the enormous number of 90 freemen, most of them small holders. Here, among the best endowed, with 51 acres, rendering 4 shillings and 8 pence, Baldwin's book listed 'Aeilfled, widow, with her adopted daughter'.[12] Here, with more modest tenure and perhaps correspondingly more security, she fades from the records — except, perhaps, in the name of Alpheton.

9   *Liber Eliensis*, 1962, 423.
10   D. Whitelock (ed.), *Anglo-Saxon Wills*, 1930, XXXI.
11   Fols. 413b, 415b. The Kedington cross appears on Plate 12.
12   D. C. Douglas (ed.), *Feudal Documents from St Edmund's Abbey*, 1932, 30. R. H. C. Davis's edition of the *Kalendar of Abbot Samson*, which contains the earliest reference to *Alfledetun*, c. 1186 – 91, includes a transcript of a grant, in c. 1200, of a toft of 2 acres in Westley, immediately west of Bury, 'lying between the land of Geoffrey the Clerk and the land of Aileve, the daughter of Alflede': *op. cit.*, 112. Aileve is not quite Ailith, but Alflede seems to have been an uncommon enough name in the neighbourhood to make one wonder if here is not another glimpse of the same family, some four generations after their appearance in Domesday Book.

6

Labelling the Bradfields: Monks, Knights, Combustion, and the Memorial to a Pilgrim

Bradfield is likely to be among the earliest Old English place-names in Suffolk, as we saw in chapter 1. Its literal translation is simple: 'a wide *feld*', feld meaning 'open country: land free from wood: a plain'.[1] Even without the adjective *brād, feld* implied a broader, more open clearing than a glade, which had its own word, *lēah*, as in nearby Brockley. The implications of such *-feld* names, distributed as they are across the heavy clays of Suffolk, are less simple: the *-feld* element, as we saw on pp. 17—19, must refer to wholesale clearance of woodland for farming (perhaps with coppicing in the peripheral uncleared woods). These agricultural activities must have characterised the area, and may well have continued in it, when the English settled and named it accordingly. The combined dimensions of the three adjoining parishes known as Bradfield today are 'broad' enough to justify that adjective — some 2 x 3 miles — though one supposes the tree-clearings to have lain at the heart of the total area marked out by the perimeter boundary of the estate-parishes amalgamated by that place-name. In fact, Bradfield was only one of a cluster of three such cleared areas: immediately south lay the even larger Cockfield, 'Cohha's *feld*', 3 x 3 miles; and west, and also adjoining, Stanningfield, originally spelt *Stanfeld*, meaning stony-*feld*, of more modest dimension; but the whole neighbourhood must have created the impression of open swathes of pastoral or arable farming, in the ancient woodland. See Map 3, p. 19 above.

What may well explain these large-scale tree-cleared farmlands postulated by the place-names is the firm but fragmentary evidence of a Romano-British villa-site beside a small lake just beyond the northern edge of Bradfield (OS 1:50,000, Sheet 155,901613). It was at one time an important villa, to judge by the surviving 15-ft high conical grave-mount, Eastlow Hill, opened in 1844 by the Rev. Professor J. H. Henslow, and then standing near three smaller mounds.[2] Eastlow Hill lurks in boscage close beside the north-south Roman 'Peddars Way', which was used to form the west boundary of the northernmost Bradfield estate: to the south it was also made the impressively straight boundary between Cockfield and Stanningfield. Bradfield's stretch of the Peddars Way was probably the *Stanstrete* beside which 6 acres of arable were identified in an agreement of 1206.[3] But a minor and parallel north-south Romano-British estate road has been confirmed

1 Ekwall, *Dictionary of England Place-names.*
2 *Proceedings of the Suffolk Institute of Archaeology*, IV, 1874, 257—281.
3 R. H. C. Davis (ed.), *Kalendar of Abbot Samson*, 1954, 102.

running through Bradfield St George and St Clare[4] — St Clare Hall being sited almost upon it (see map 3). The disuse of the villa by no means argues the end of the Romano-British farming here; though, from the place-name point of view, the continuance of the farming would have involved the abandonment of the British language of the minority, and the adoption, however halting, of Anglo-Saxon speech. This has always been part of the story of the occupation of another people's land.

So there are some grounds for thinking of a possible Romano-British Anglo-Saxon overlap in this group of -*felds*. And this strengthens the case for looking at -*feld* place-names as potential indicators of similar primary Anglo-Saxon settlement.[5]

From the 6th to the early 11th century, half a millennium, there is a dauntingly long silence from all sources of Bradfield's archaeology and history. However, the development of three parish names, and identities, within the original broad *feld*, is traceable from late Anglo-Saxon times to the 14th century; since when the names have not changed, even if the identities have. The earliest steps are still slightly hypothetical. One of the three, now Bradfield Combust, was never among the possessions of St Edmund's abbey, and we will consider it last. The other two, now Bradfield St Clare and Bradfield St George, were given to the monks as two quite separate gifts before the Norman Conquest. We will try to discern their early recorded development through their names.

The two handsome gifts of Bradfield estates were made to St Edmund in the first half of the 11th century. The original charters do not survive, nor do copies, but there seems no reason to mistrust the Lists of Benefactors the abbey preserved: they attributed the grant of one of their Bradfield possessions to Ulfketel, c. 1005—1009, and the other to the East Anglian bishop, Aelfric III, c. 1039—1043.[6] It is not indicated which benefactor gave which Bradfield estate, but the motives behind the gifts may be seen.

A. J. Robertson, in her *Anglo-Saxon Charters*,[7] had 'little doubt' that the Ulfketel making extremely valuable grants c. 1005 to St Edmund's shrine and its community of secular priests was Ulfketel Snilling, the stalwart defender of Danish East Anglia — very much in the spirit of St Edmund himself — against the warlike new Danish invaders. *Snillingr* means valiant, and his valour got East Anglia known as Ulfkill's Land all over the Norse world.[8] The gift could have been a thank-offering for the Danish withdrawal in 1005. If so, it was premature. They came back, routed him at Ringmere (Norfolk, 1010), and slew him at Ashingdon (Essex, 1016), when Cnut's army overcame Edmund Ironside's. Cnut commemorated Ulfketel at Ashingdon: his own name may well commemorate him in the large cluster

4 P.S.I.A., *op. cit.*, XXXIII, 311—313.
5 See ch. 1., p. 5 and its fn. 11, and pp. 13—26.
6 C. R. Hart, *The Early Charters of Eastern England*, 1966, 62 and 248.
7 1939, 392.
8 Stenton, *Anglo-Saxon England*, 1947, 375.

of Ilketshall parishes grouped with Bungay (see chapter 1, p. 28 above). Cnut went on to found a Benedictine abbey to house St Edmund's mummified corpse more honourably at Bury. In that new abbey, Ulfketel, Edmund's benefactor and fellow-defender of the kingdom against the Northmen, would certainly have long been remembered with pride, much as Brihtnoth was remembered at Ely (*Liber Eliensis*, Blake ed., p. 136), where his remains are now assumed to be secreted in the south wall of Bishop West's chantry-chapel.

Meanwhile, Domesday Book has recorded the three Bradfields in terms that enable us to identify them today. St Edmund's two holdings were the present parishes of St George and St Clare, though thus far only the former is recorded as having a church. It was a 3-carucate manor with three freemen tenants and a separate 1-carucate farm of nine freemen. Its elongated dimensions, 1½ x ½ mile, presumably applied then to the ploughed lands within the peripheral woodland (some of which still survives as coppice: see map 3). A century later, c. 1186−1191, this was listed in the *Kalendar of Abbot Samson*[9] by name — as both Juliane Bradefelde and Bradefelde Sancti Georgii. This means that the manor had been held by a lady, Juliana (otherwise unrecorded), during the previous century, and that her name was already being supplanted as an estate- and parish-label by that of the patron saint — a development common in Suffolk but not in Essex.[10] Samson's *Kalendar* names a few of the smallholders in this Bradfield: Adam the huntsman and Godwin the carpenter fit naturally into the picture of Bradfield St George in King John's day, and for centuries.

It is surprising to find that, despite appearances, Bradfield St Clare has kept one of its *secular* labels, St Clare, to this day — as if it were an Essex parish. In Domesday Book[11] one of its tenant farms (2½ carucates) was held by 10 freemen, another (1½ carucates) was held by Roricus, and the third (½ carucate) by Falcus (*sic*). Presumably this Folco's family made good: a century later (1186−1191) Samson's *Kalendar* labelled this Bradfield 'Bradefelde Folconis' (p. 16), and p. 17 showed how 'in Bradefelde, Folco holds 1½ knights' fees of the abbot'. A decade later, still in Samson's day, Jocelin of Brakelond[12] recorded that 'In the year of grace 1200, a list was made of the knights of St Edmund and of their feudal holdings, from which their predecessors were enfeoffed': and that 'Gilbert of St Clare holds two knights', in Bradfield (1½) and in Wattisfield (½).[13]

Enquiring into the naming of Alpheton (chapter 5), we discovered civilian, indeed women, tenants of the king being replaced by Norman (male) magnates. (This subject is touched on in Christine Fell's recent book,

9   Davis, *op. cit.*, 16−17.
10 See J. H. Round, 'The Origin of Essex Parishes', in *Family Origins*, 1930, 266−274.
11 Fols. 362b−363.
12 H. E. Butler (ed.), *The Chronicle of Jocelin of Brakelond*, 1949, 120.
13 Chronicle, *op. cit.*, 121.

Women in Anglo-Saxon England, 1984, 89; more evidence remains to be dug out of Domesday Book.) Looking at Bradfield St Clare, we see a more familiar form of the Norman assertion of control, with the knightly St Clare family displacing Folco's. The St Clares seem to have been established within the feudal zone of St Edmund's Liberty since before 1135.[14] Here is the explanation of Bradfield St Clare's function by c. 1200. The St Clares were knights, and presumably took their name from St Claire-sur-Epte (on the frontier of Normandy), which in turn took its name from either the first bishop of Nantes, who lived c. 280, or from St Clair, priest and martyr, c. 894, a Rochester man. Naturally, the Suffolk place-name can originally have had nothing to do with the St Clare who was a female devotee of St Francis: she died only in 1253, and was canonised two years later. The secular label Bradfeud Sencler appeared in the Norwich Valuation in 1254. Would the St Clare family have adopted St Francis's disciple as patron saint of their parish church? The earliest physical feature of the present church of St Clare is a carved coffin-lid of the 13th century. Presumably it covered the corpse of a St Clare or one of his fellow knights. These St Clares would have looked to a much earlier St Clair as their family patron.

Bradfield Combust's story is relatively straightforward. It never belonged to the abbey. By 1086, the count of Mortain had taken a holding of a mere 20 acres in Bradfield;[15] but, combined with two neighbouring smallholdings, in Whelnetham ('*hamm* — meadow — distinguished by its swans') and Stanningfield, it made up a whole carucate. It was, not surprisingly, known as Little Bradfield until it became Bradfield Combust in the 14th century. How and when did the Combustion occur?

It used to be asserted, e.g. by W. A. Copinger, in his *Manors of Suffolk*[16] that the burning here took place in 1327, when the Bury St Edmunds business community took advantage of the general disorder at the end of Edward II's reign, and ransacked the abbey's treasury and muniments to get their hands on those charters felt to be intolerably oppressive. But from the enquiry that followed the depredations, it is clear beyond doubt that the Bradfield Hall 'combusted' in 1327 was the hall of that name standing within the precinct of the abbey and beside the river, east of the church.[17] That Edward II himself stayed in that Bradfield Hall may have contributed to its combustibility. Historically-minded monks like Jocelin of Brakelond seem to have thought of it as the eponymous messuage, with adjoining garden, that was 'once the abode of Bederic, after whom this town took its original name, *Bedericsworth*'.[18] The present-day interest of this connexion in Jocelin's mind with the earliest days of the abbey lies in the recent evidence,

14   D. C. Douglas (ed.), *Feudal Documents from the Abbey of Bury St Edmunds*, 1932, lxxxvi – lxxxvii.
15   Domesday Book, fol. 291.
16   1910, VI, 255.
17   Lord F. Hervey (ed.), *Pinchbeck Register*, 1925, I, 106 – 109.
18   Chronicle, *op. cit.*, 102.

not yet fully substantiated, that King Edmund's martyrdom at 'Haegelisdun' may have occurred in Bradfield, and that the chapel 'at the little place of Sutton nearby' where his embalmed corpse first lay before being removed to 'Bedericsworth' is represented by Sutton Hall, through which the boundary was made between Bradfield St Clare and Cockfield.

So when did Bradfield Combust acquire its distinguishing affix? Little Bradfield had come to the Lords Roos (or Ros) in the 14th century. Their earliest surviving court roll (WSRO: E. 7/17/1) refers still to the parson of Bradefeld *Parva*, Little Bradfield, in 1333, six years after the great disturbance. But Peter Northeast has found, and kindly given me, a reference to *Brundbradefeld* as early as the Feet of Fines of 15 Edward II (July 1321 to July 1322). On 14 April 1322, the lord Badlesmere through whose daughter the Rooses inherited Little Bradfield was hanged as a traitor. The burning was conceivably related to that misadventure, but it remains highly possible that still earlier references may emerge to explain this most dramatic of the Bradfield labels. (Two most mysterious labels, Hoketon Bradefeld, perhaps related to a former *Hoketon* in Cavendish, and Stowen Bradefeld, appeared briefly in the 13th century and resist explanation.)

The Roos lords of Bradfield Combust were based principally in the North, and buried grandly in Rievaulx abbey. Nevertheless, on the north wall of the nave of Bradfield Combust church is a faded but superbly painted figure of St George, as mounted crusader, dated c. 1400 by the experts.[19] John, 5th lord Roos, married in 1382, came of age in 1386, and, seven years later, died without progeny, of malaria at Paphos in Cyprus on his way back from pilgrimage to Jerusalem. On this wall at Bradfield Combust, St George is painted, armed and mounted, spearing the dragon with his left hand, and brandishing a great sword with his right. On his helm he wears the proud peacock feathers of the Roos heraldic crest. It identified him unmistakably.[20] This precisely contemporary picture of St George at Bradfield specifically commemorates the young 5th lord Roos, and may be reckoned a most unusual funeral monument. It also celebrated the knightly, as distinct from the monkish, side of life in medieval Bradfield. (Pl. 13)

19 Pevsner, *The Buildings of England: Suffolk*, 1974, 107.
20 My friend John Blatchly clinched the identification: in *The Book of Family Crests* (1838, Washbourne), Pl. 73, no. 9, shows 'a peacock in his pride' as the crest of various North Country branches of the Roos family. G.E.C.'s *Complete Peerage*, XI, 1949, p. 102, attests 'pilgrimage' and not 'Crusade', though Roos's old commander, Arundel, had planned to go crusading in 1389. Association with Arundel would not have endeared Roos to Richard II, and the Holy Land may have offered a 'healthier' prospect than Richard's England. A contemporary averred that Roos died 'to the great loss of all England: *totius Angliae grandi damno*'. Arundel was executed four years later.

7

The Walrus-ivory Cross
in the Metropolitan Museum of Art:
the Masterpiece of Master Hugo[1] at Bury?

In 1964, the late Sir Kenneth (afterwards Lord) Clark, knowing my interest in the history of Bury St Edmunds, kindly sent me a copy of the New York Metropolitan Museum's publication of its recently acquired masterpiece, a walrus-ivory cross designed and carved with great virtuosity. The publication was entitled 'The Bury St Edmunds Cross',[2] and its author, Thomas P. F. Hoving, associate curator at the Museum (and later its Director) gave some persuasive reasons for linking the cross with St Edmunds abbey at Bury. For Hoving, the dating evidence indicated the decade 1181 — 1190, which covered the famous election of the subsacrist, Samson, to the abbacy and ended in the massacre of fifty-seven Jews in the town. But he mentioned the possibility, 'which deserves further examination', that 'most of the carvings' (there are no fewer than 108 figures on the cross) were done 'around 1150, and the inscriptions added under the direction of Samson' (the cross bears over 60 inscriptions in Greek and Latin, apart from one in old Hebrew). Later articles[3] assumed the later date, and with that the cross continued to be labelled. I felt it was time to examine the earlier one, not least because Professor Peter Lasko had lately suggested a very much earlier one.[4]

1 The first problem is the name of this great medieval artist, which was probably Master Hugh: we have it only in Latin. *Electio Hugonis* becomes 'the Election of Hugh', but *manu magistri Hugonis* has generally become 'by the hand of Master Hugo'. Perhaps this is because he was early seen to be 'incomparable' and was therefore probably not English! His versatility somehow suggests the Italian Renaissance. I was relieved to see that Lawrence Stone, in his own remarkable work *Sculpture in Britain: the Middle Ages* (Pelican History of Art), 2nd edn., 1972, with the Bury cross on the frontispiece, refers to him as Master Hugh. Unluckily, there are so many other Hughs in the story of Bury alone: I feel, perhaps weakly, that on balance it might be less confusing to go on with Hugo. M. R. James (*The Abbey Church of St Edmund at Bury*, Cambridge, 1895, 128) was 'inclined to conjecture' that Abbot Anselm, 1121 — 48, who had been abbot of St. Saba in Rome, brought Hugo with him from Italy.
2 Metropolitan Museum of Art, *Bull.*, XXII, No. 10 (1964), pp. 317 — 340. I am primarily indebted to Lord Clark for arousing my interest in this great masterpiece of sculpture. I am also indebted to Professor George Zarnecki, Dr Rosalie B. Green and Professor Peter Lasko for reading early drafts of this article. Since it was first published, a re-appraisal by Thomas Hoving at a seminar in London (July 1974) showed how his recent study of Oslo Museum's Christ led him to substantial agreement with my thesis. See p. 94 below.
3 C. M. Kauffmann, 'The Bury Bible', *Jour. Warburg and Courtauld Insts.* XXIX (1966); Sabrina Longland, in the Metropolitan Museum's *Bulletin* XXVI (1968), and *Jour.* II (1969); and in *Connoisseur* CLXXII (1969), pp. 163f; John Beckwith, *Ivory Carvings in Early Medieval England* (1972), articles 104 and 105. I must thank the Librarian of Corpus Christi College, Cambridge, for enabling me to study the Bury Bible.
4 *Ars Sacra, 800 — 1200* (1972), pp. 167 — 168. In 1984, he still clung to that early date. In a

81

In his letter to me in 1964 Lord Clark wrote:

'I think the connection with Bury is convincing. But as you will see, this is established by comparison with the Bury Bible, which would put it back to Abbot Anselm [1119 — 1148]; the connection with Samson which he seeks to prove via the Jews goes too much against stylistic evidence for my taste.'

I had my own reasons for thinking that, if the Bury connexion were truly convincing, then certainly what one knew of the history of St Edmund's abbey in the 12th century pointed to a date nearer to the end of Anselm's abbacy and to the Bury Bible than to the 1180s. However, my ignorance of all but the most elementary 'history of style' of the period made me hesitant about presenting some related details of the life of that great Benedictine house. I assemble them here, for they may enable scholars who continue to accept the cross's Bury provenance to think again about its date. I confess I am not as reluctant as I was twenty years or more ago to express opinions about style and its history.

Without going into the intricacies of 'dampfold' and suchlike, there must be something to be said for attending to very marked general similarities. For instance, compare the breathtaking vigour of the aggressive knights in the Bury Bible with the 'Moses and the Brazen Serpent' centrepiece of the Cross (Pls. 14, 15). And then there is an obvious and precise comparison between the defending knights of Jerusalem in the Bury Bible and the soldiers sleeping at Christ's tomb (Pls. 16, 17). Then one remembers the appallingly vigorous writhing of a featureless moneylender being dragged down to Hell on a piece of stone from which all intricacies of carving have, alas, been eroded by the weather. It reposes in Moyses Hall Museum in Bury, and has been assumed to come from the west front of the abbey, perhaps in Hugo's day: it is shown as Fig. 3 in Professor Zarnecki's article on 'Romanesque Objects at Bury' in *Apollo*, June, 1967. These certainly dispose one to the idea that the Cross could be one of Hugo's masterpieces.

---

new, and very closely argued, article in *Zeitschrift für Kunstgeschichte*, I., 1985, pp. 39 — 64, München, Ursula Nilgen makes a fair and sensible plea for scholars to stop automatically linking the Cross by name with Bury, 'if only because to call it, so soon, "The Bury St Edmunds Cross" seems to block research'. But at the end of her article, Nilgen seems content to abandon the cross to limbo, to leave it with no setting at all, except that its sculptor must have been of English origin and have made the continental influences his own (p. 63). For disappointingly vague reasons, of patronage and of style, she proposes to associate him with Thomas Becket's intellectual entourage, and to phase the masterpiece in to 'the fairly broad circle of the Channel style, on the English side'. Leaving the link with Bury where it stands may be a good exercise, but one hopes for more cogent alternatives than Ursula Nilgen finds she is able to muster here; preferably, of course, as potentially persuasive as the almost unnervingly circumstantial case that has now been compiled for Bury. As we have seen in chapter 2, there are still those who are reluctant to accept the weight of evidence that Raedwald is the likely candidate for the burial-ship monument at Sutton Hoo. In all such questions, we are — inevitably — dealing only with probabilities: they may be reduced to possibilities, but only by powerful and specific counter-arguments. I am grateful to Ian Waters for his help with some difficult German translation problems.

Revising my 1974 article a decade later, I had just written that paragraph when I found I had overlooked the publication of what I believe will come to be regarded as essentially the definitive re-assessment: Dr Elizabeth Parker's 'Master Hugo as Sculptor: A Source for the Style of the Bury Bible'.[5] Reading her title, I hoped it implied that my attribution of the Cross to Hugo had at last been accepted. I was not disappointed, and was delighted to read: 'It is perhaps time to reassess an assignment of the cross to Bury St Edmunds. Although much evidence would not seem to support its place at Bury, the stylistic parallels to Hugo's Bible must be the determining factor. *These seem difficult to deny*. It is not only in similar details already noted by scholars that the comparison holds, *but in the look of the works as a whole* [my italics: N.S.]. Both abound with supple little figures brimming with life . . . energy is everywhere generated.' Dr Parker is no ordinary art historian: her comprehension of the known artistic background, and her direct, trenchant observation, seem to me to clinch these fundamental questions of both attribution and location.

However, Dr Parker's avowed concern was with 'the stylistic source of the Bury Bible'. Mine is with the general historical understanding of the peculiar subject matter of the carvings: surely they contain positive, irrefutable evidence as to when the cross was made and where it was intended to stand? Let me briefly review the dates that style-historians have so far produced for this cross. The first c. 1050, by Wiltrud Mersmann, was swiftly dismissed by Thomas Hoving in the original Metropolitan Museum publication cited above. Hoving's own date, c. 1181 − 90, he justified in these words: 'The cross is . . . a virtual seminar in the style of the late twelfth century, for in the figures one can detect the inexorable and fascinating change from a Romanesque to a decidedly early Gothic point of view.' In the articles already cited, neither Michael Kauffman nor Sabrina Longland nor John Beckwith challenged Hoving's date, though I have found few art-historians who did not (privately) think it too late. Then, in Peter Lasko's book, which he described in his preface as 'on the whole an unrepentant history of style', we are given stylistic reasons for thinking 'a date of c. 1100 − 1120 very possible'.[6] (Such wild fluctuations by art-historians, from the 1050s to the 1180s and then back to 1100s or 1110s are breathtaking: S. R. Bassett, reviewing (in *Archives*, Oct. 1985) *The Golden Age of Anglo-Saxon Art*, described the dating of the major ivories as 'still impressionistic'. Lasko thought:

> The cross certainly shows, here and there, slight beginnings of the 'dampfold' style that was to dominate English art from about 1135 onwards, when the Bury Bible was illuminated by the painter Hugo, but it hardly represents a fully developed form of it.[7]

5 *Gesta* XX/1, 1981, pp. 99 − 109, The International Center of Medieval Art, The Cloisters, Fort Tryon Park, N.Y., 10040. Her judgment is further refined, jointly with C. R. Little, in the Catalogue of the 1984 exhibition of the cross in Venice and Milan.
6 Lasko, *op. cit.*, p. 293, n. 43.
7 *Op. cit.*, p. 167. By 'the painter Hugo' Lasko must mean 'Hugo *as* painter', for Hugo's

Plainly, such a judgement rests precariously on the assumption that, at a certain time, in this case c. 1135, all English artists, at least all those composing groups of clothed human figures, whether in manuscript illustration, wood, stone, or ivory carving, or bronze casting, were more intent on exploiting a trick of style than on expressing the mood of a subject. This is a big assumption, particularly with the master-artists, who presumably felt free to borrow or originate, to develop or 'soft pedal' or rest a particular 'style' at will and as the subject and the medium dictated. Art-historians are not always themselves artists and where they are dependent on stylistic development as a substitute for dating evidence risk assuming a comparable dependence in the mind of the artist.

My friend Peter Lasko forced me to say this by his implied contrast between the incipient 'dampfold', as he sees it, in the cross, and the developed form established (he implies) by Hugo's Bible. For there seemed to me a possibility, I put it no higher, that Hugo executed both the Bible *and* the cross, and in that order! Perhaps I might go a little further and say that *if* Hoving's evidence is accepted, of the connexion between the cross and St Edmund's abbey at Bury, then the possibility of Hugo's authorship becomes a strong one. (Publishing that in 1974, I pitched my claims at 'a possibility' because I felt the need to respect the view of John Beckwith, who in 1972 had published the standard work on *Ivory Carving in Medieval England* and was, in correspondence, contemptuously dismissive of both Hoving's long article in *The Metropolitan Museum Bulletin* and mine. In 1981, Dr Parker quoted my assertion of the 'possibility', though I supposed I had gone on to make it a strong probability; and with her own expertise she splendidly confirmed and endorsed my own views. It is perhaps instructive that two historians, bemused by the same ivory cross, can come, by such different paths of deduction, to the same conclusion.)

Blunt speaking about style is unavoidable. For one aspect of style has led Lasko to suggest a date, c. 1100−1120, which seems, on more basic counts, to make nonsense of the whole conception of this cross. To the non-specialist, the extraordinary artistic beauty of the cross lies in the overall design — in the relation of the various parts to the whole, the vitality and rhythm, even the relation of the figures to the whole dimension of surrounding space — and finally, but fundamentally, in the treatment of the very remarkable subject-matter.

It was this subject-matter that led Hoving to connect the cross with Bury and to give it (unnecessarily, as I show) so late a date, and especially the subject-matter, the messages, of the carved inscriptions. First, there are the most prominent of the inscriptions, those carved in capital letters down the sides of the whole main-post of the cross: 'The synagogue falls after stupid,

---

contemporaries adjudged bronze-casting his greatest accomplishment: see below. He was manifestly a major artist, ready to try his hand in more than two materials and two dimensions.

criminal effort', and 'The Jews laugh at the death-agony of God' — *JUDEI RISERE*, etc.: see Plate 19. Then there is the very strange wording of the placard projecting over the hand of God (Plate 21), in which, in Greek, 'Jesus of Nazareth, King of the Confessors' replaces the usual title 'King of the Jews'. Again, the implication seems to be strongly anti-Jewish; as if the donor of the cross could not stomach the idea of Christ as king of that people. ('Confessor' meant 'believer in Christ as Messiah'.) Not only is this rare substitution of Confessors for Jews matched in a surviving Gospel of Mark from Bury abbey (Pembroke College, Cambridge, MS 72), but there is an identical mistake in the spelling of the Greek form for Confessors (EXOM [O] LISSON instead of EXOMOLOGESION).[8] That is perhaps Hoving's most clinching argument for the cross's Bury origin.

Another remarkable parallel, between the capital-letter inscription (about the Curse of Ham) on the cross and the text of a verse arranged by Samson for the decoration of the monk's choir at Bury, is cited by Hoving as additional evidence for linking the cross not only with Bury, but also with the time of Samson. But, of course, an inscription on an *earlier* cross at Bury with which Samson was familiar might equally explain his versification of that particular story about Ham's Curse.

I need not recite here Hoving's very full account of the anti-Jewish elements that led him to conclude: 'The cross may not be the only medieval monument that carries on a polemic against the Jews, but it is not matched in vehemence.' He did not exaggerate. Its anti-Jewish feeling is certainly strong enough to warrant the deduction that that feeling provides an essential clue to both the place and time (perhaps even the very occasion) of the cross's conception and execution. And that seems to rule out the possibility of Peter Lasko's preferred dates (c 1100—1120). Lasko rightly remarks: 'That the anti-semitic content of these inscriptions points exclusively to Abbot Samson of Bury St Edmunds (1182—1211: Hoving, *op. cit.*) is not convincing.'[9] But he is not at liberty to assume that anti-semitism found any expression in England in the first two decades of the 12th century, let alone the sort of explosively vehement expression seen in this cross. Hoving's generalisation is similarly misguided: 'It is against this poor, alien people and their synagogue, harried and persecuted through the centuries, that the text of the cross directs itself with wrath.'[10]

Even the briefest reference to H. G. Richardson's book on *The English Jewry under Angevin Kings* (1960) would have corrected the misconception that the unimaginable suffering of the Jews in our own century makes us prone to. Richardson re-affirmed that there is no suggestion that Jews were settled in England before 1066, and he showed that, under the conqueror, a Jewish community from Rouen was established in London: that 'French the

8   Hoving, *op. cit.*, p. 338.
9   Lasko, *op. cit.*, pp. 292—3, n. 41.
10   Hoving, *op. cit.*, p. 328.

Jews in England remained until their expulsion in 1290'; and that 'this Frenchness the English Jews shared with the English nobles.'[11] What he is saying is that, far from being 'a poor, alien people', they were seen as part of the new alien governing establishment, however much they might be divided by religion from the other ruling Normans. Richardson also shows that there is no evidence of the Jewish community's being settled outside London until after 1130,[12] and that there, under Henry I's long rule (1100−1135), they enjoyed real privileges and liberties, and the king's protection.[13]

Perhaps equally relevant to Lasko's suggested dating is Richardson's evidence on the traditional hostility with which Christian churchmen naturally regarded Jews. Early in the 1090s, the Norman abbot of Westminster based a written 'Disputation' between Christian and Jew on discussions he himself had had with a learned Jew, and he makes the Jew ask why they should be treated like dogs, since it was agreed that the Mosaic law should be observed. Another 'Disputation', borrowing heavily from this one, but written late in, or soon after, Henry I's reign, omits that reference to Jewish ill-usage, and for Richardson this exemplifies the improved relations secured, however temporarily, under Henry I.[14] In short, in England, the years 1100−1135 are the years most unlikely in the 12th century to have provided the circumstances of so considerably antijudaic a great work of art.

Finally, Richardson shows the Jews spreading out from London *under Stephen into parts he controlled*, such as Norwich and Cambridge. It seems to me that this is the period (1135−1154) in which anti-Jewish sentiments began to develop. It is certainly the time at which Bury St Edmunds begins to fit into the picture.

I think those who have studied the cross might agree that the most dramatic and significant of its carved scenes are set at the centre, the intersection, of the cross: at the back (Plate 20), the poignant figure of the Lamb of God; at the front (Plate 15), most telling of all, and so lively as to be almost in motion, the lifting up on a cleft stick (symbolic, prophetic of Christ's cross, according to St John's Gospel, 3.14) of a brazen serpent by Moses in the wilderness, so that those murmuring Israelites who had been bitten by real serpents might look on it and be cured (Numbers, 21.8−9).

The unquestionable importance of this superb centrepiece would cast doubt on the proposition that the Oslo Museum's Christ was conceived for this crucifix if his head masked it.[15] (On the contrary, the severe tilt of the

11 *Op. cit.*, pp. 3−5.
12 *Ibid.*, pp. 8−9: nor have later writers shown reason to think otherwise, e.g. V. D. Lipman, *The Jews of Medieval Norwich* (1967).
13 *Ibid.*, pp. 109−112.
14 *Ibid.*, pp. 24−25.
15 M. Blindheim, 'En romansk Kristus-figur av hvalross-tann', *Årbuk*, 1968/9, Kunstindustrimuseet i Oslo, Oslo (1969); also Metropolitan Museum of Art, *The Year 1200, Catalogue* (1970). It was then agreed that this Christ and cross remain together, 1 year in Oslo and 3 in New York, for the next 12 years. They are now separate again.

head down on the right collarbone may mark the sculptor's intention to leave a view of the whole dramatic action of the centrepiece, with Moses flinging his message scroll quite clear.) For me, the natural interpretation of the powerful centrepiece starts with Moses, the most prominent figure, brandishing out from the cross, for all to see, his ominous, frightening message to the Israelites that proved all too truly prophetic: 'Thus thy life shall be in suspense before thee, and thou shalt [fear, day and night, and shalt] have none assurance of thy life.'

Whoever designed this cross was, surprisingly enough, addressing the Jews, trying to persuade them to save themselves from their enemies by understanding the truth about Christ's death. The message of this beautiful crucifix was, as usual, an urgent plea for a certain kind of understanding. The quotations betray much bitterness against the Jews for their part in slaughtering the Lamb of God, yet lead into this central message of hope for them. But how was it supposed that they would read it?

Jocelin of Brakelond's *Chronicle*, begun in 1198, during the year of his first appointment as cellarer to St Edmund's abbey,[16] was written as a record of Abbot Samson's rule and of his encroachment on the rights of the convent, especially the rights of the cellarer,[17] though the intensity of Jocelin's feelings produced such a vivid portrait of Samson that many modern writers, including Hoving, refer to the *Chronicle* as 'a biography'.[18] Hoving expresses disappointment at Jocelin's 'somewhat brusque' references to Samson in the role of subsacrist and master of the works, yet Jocelin does record that, at the time of the ransoming of King Richard, Samson as abbot gave all his attention to the making of a very precious gold and silver cresting to St Edmund's shrine, from which prominent place it could hardly be removed.[19] I feel that Jocelin's *Chronicle* gives so full a picture of the abbey in his day that, had this cross been made during it, its creator, a major artist, and his achievement are most unlikely to have gone unmentioned. As to the Bury cross, Hoving quoted, without seeing its full significance, the reference by Jocelin that, above all, seems to me to make sense of the cross's extra-ordinary messages. One of Samson's first acts on becoming abbot, in 1182, was to dismiss the sacrist, William Wiardel. Jocelin explains why: 'The sacrist, William, was called the father and patron of the Jews; for they enjoyed his protection, and could come and go as they pleased, and went hither and thither throughout the monastery, *wandering past the altars* and round the feretory, even while masses were being sung . . .'[20]

16 Over the matter of the time at which Jocelin first began writing his *Chronicle* I disagree slightly with Mr R. H. C. Davis, to whom we are indebted for the important discovery that Jocelin held this office, second only to that of prior: R. H. C. Davis, ed., *The Kalendar of Abbot Samson*, Camden Soc. (1954), pp. li—lvii. See ch. 8, below.

17 This thesis I first propounded to the Suff. Inst. Arch. in a lecture in April 1963.

18 Hoving, *op. cit.*, p. 336.

19 H. E. Butler, ed., *The Chronicle of Jocelin of Brakelond* (1949), p. 97.

20 Hoving, *op. cit.*, p. 336. Jocelin's explicit and unambiguous statement is fundamental to the case that the Cross, with this Christian message and warning, was designed for the

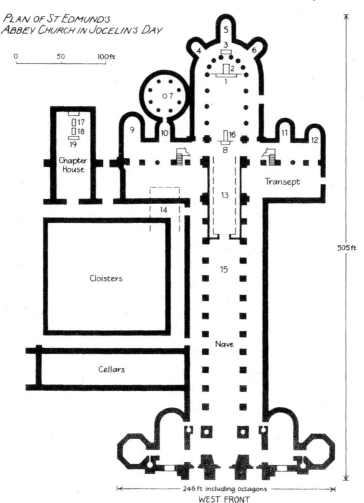

With acknowledgments to M.R. James and A.B. Whittingham

PLAN OF ST EDMUND'S
ABBEY CHURCH IN JOCELIN'S DAY

0   50   100 ft

Chapter House

Transept

505 ft

Cloisters

Cellars

Nave

|← 246 ft including octagons →|
WEST FRONT

1	High Altar	7	'Rotunde' Chapel of St Edmund	13	Monks' Choir
2	Shrine of St Edmund	8	Choir-altar: probable position of the Bury Cross	14	Site of 7th-century Minster of St Mary
3	Altar of St Thomas and Shrines of St Botulph and St Jermin	9	St Martin's Chapel	15	Altar of Holy Cross
4	St Saba's Chapel	10	St Mary's Chapel	16	Abbot Baldwin's Tomb
5	St Nicasius' Chapel	11	St John's Chapel	17	Abbot Ording's Tomb
6	St Peter's Chapel	12	St Nicholas' Chapel	18	Abbot Samson's Tomb
				19	Lectern

I assume that 'the Bury cross' was a small altar cross, and stood in a church frequented by Jews; for its central purpose seems to be to address a warning to them and a passionate appeal to them and all unbelievers to embrace Christianity. There cannot have been many such churches. It is to me of prime significance that, in a monastic church already linked, by Hoving, to this cross, on stylistic grounds, there is such remarkably explicit evidence that here the Jews would have been able to read its message; though not, presumably and significantly, after 1182.

At Bury, the altar most likely to have been dignified by this smallscale masterpiece is that of the monks' own choir, which seems sometimes to have been known as 'the small altar'.[21] This seems nevertheless to have been the main altar in the choir (see plan opposite). There was a low wall behind it, and I think the ivory cross may have been stood upon that. The great abbot Baldwin's tomb lay just beyond this wall. If 'the small altar' was a second altar in the choir, then the cross may have stood on that. There was already a rood, heavily adorned with gold and silver by Archbishop Stigand, above the high altar[22] east of the monks' choir. The monks' choir itself was given a new enclosure by Samson when he was subsacrist: he had pictures painted on its walls and composed elegaic verses for them.[23] The textual coincidence between cross and murals, cited by Hoving to suggest that the sculptor knew the paintings, could equally have worked the other way round, with Samson quoting a text he knew from daily familiarity with the cross on the altar of his own choir. Other reasons for thinking it belonged here, rather than at a side altar of the main nave altar, are its exquisite quality and its relatively small size: just under 2 feet high, and barely 14 inches in width. I see it standing so as to be visible from each side and from behind, as well as from the front, on a low screen behind the monks'

---

monks' choir at Bury. It is astonishing, in the face of Jocelin's statement, to read Ursula Nilgen's footnote 7 (p. 45): 'Norman Scarfe's conclusion — that the Jews, who according to written sources were able to move freely at certain times in the abbey and observe the Cross, and were thus able to reflect on its message — is of course untenable, *erscheint allerdings unhaltbar*. Normally,' she adds, 'neither Jew nor Christian was able to approach such a valuable cross.' I do not see how my conclusion is *unhaltbar* so far as the monks' choir at Bury goes: Jocelin tells us that that is how things were in his choir. That cannot be disputed. But I wonder how *haltbar* Ursula Nilgen's broad generalization is, about the 'normal' inaccessibility of crosses on choir altars? Even if she is right, we are not dealing necessarily with the normal, but (fairly obviously) with the particular and the unusual. If she is right about this (see footnote 4 above), she is certainly making it difficult to establish a setting for this cross anywhere else but in the choir at Bury.

21　M. R. James, *The Abbey Church of St Edmund at Bury*, Cambridge, 1895, pp. 133, 180. I am grateful to Mr Arthur B. Whittingham for his clarification of 'choir altar' and 'small altar in the choir'. Mr Whittingham, the leading authority on the detailed plan of the great abbey, agrees with me that the reredos-cum-parapet behind the monks' choir is the likeliest position for Hugo's cross. Dr Elizabeth Parker seems to think the cross stood on the altar itself, but then it would have been impossible to see details back and front.

22　Butler, *op. cit.*, pp. 5, 108. It was one of Bury's contributions towards the enormous ransom of Richard I. The ivory cross may have been another: see below, p. 98.

23　*Ibid.*, p. 9.

choir altar. We know from the surviving peg-holes on the cross that a separate small figure of Christ, probably the one at Oslo, originally hung from it. I believe, too, that there may have been separate small figures of Mary and John on either side. My reason for thinking this is that, from the *Gesta Sacristarum* much is implied about the sculture of the cross in the monks' choir. For we read that, between the years 1148 — 1156, it was carved incomparably by the hand of Master Hugo: '*Crucem in choro et Mariam et Iohannem per manus magistri Hugonis incomparabiliter fecit insculpi.*'[24]

The stylistic possibilities of 'the Bury cross' being Hugo's work will doubtless be argued out by more expert style-historians than me. I am content to rest my case on the very remarkable comparisons already made by Hoving and Parker between the cross and the other surviving masterpiece by Hugo, 'the Bury Bible'. That has now been dated to c. 1135 on all available evidence, including that of style.[25] His cross he made between 1148 — 56. Meanwhile, perhaps c. 1140, he made the great double bronze doors for the west front of the abbey church: 'As in other works Hugo surpassed everyone else, in the making of these doors he surpassed himself.'[26] The doors have vanished, presumably at the Dissolution. If we assume that this ivory cross is his, and that he did both the Bible and it, may not the passing of between thirteen and twenty-one years and the experience of working in such very different materials (walrus-ivory is harder than elephant-ivory, and the scale of the carving almost microscopic) have by themselves brought about incalculable changes (including gain, or loss, of power) in the great artist's techniques? In analysing the Bury Bible, Michael Kauffmann wrote: 'It is no longer possible to evaluate how far the difficulties in tracing the stylistic origins of the Bury Bible are due to Master Hugo's inventive genius . . .' My feeling is that such a high degree of potential inventiveness is equally likely to invalidate deductions about any major differences of treatment that may be found between the Bible and the considerably later cross.

Meanwhile, if I stop thinking about a hypothetical progressive development of the 'dampfold draperies' trick, and compare the right arm of Amos in Hugo's Bury Bible (Hoving, Plate 22) with that of Moses on the central disc of the cross (Hoving, Plate 24: here, Plate 15), I see Moses as the freer, more emancipated, more assured piece of modelling. Above all, I see these two figures as being extremely close in style, as Hoving, the Metropolitan Museum's expert, did. Whereas I see Amos as an earlier work by the *same* artist, Hoving saw it as an earlier work, influencing a different artist

24   T. Arnold, ed., *Memorials of St Edmund's Abbey*, II (1892), p. 289. The scale of such a group composition would have been almost identical with the 14th-century wall-painting which serves as a reredos to the main altar in Brent Eleigh parish church, 12 miles south of Bury. The 'Rattlesden' St John, dated by Lasko to c. 1180, clearly formed part of a comparable group (see *Proc. Suff. Inst. Arch.* XXXII (1973), p. 269, pl. XXX).

25   Kauffman, *op. cit.*

26   Arnold, *loc. cit.*

working in the same abbey half a century later. And it is reasonable to suppose the *missing* figure of the hanging Christ would have been carved more ambitiously than that of Christ in the miniature Deposition (Plate 22); just as the few surviving large-scale pictures in the Bury Bible show greater virtuosity than the smaller ones, like that of Amos. This point certainly promotes acceptance of the Oslo Museum Christ.

I recognise the force of Professor Lasko's comparison between details of the Bury cross and late 11th-century and early 12th-century Lotharingian works in the same medium: the central ivory panel (? c. 1101/7), for instance, in the book-cover of the Gospels of Bishop Notger of Liège.[27] Before I turn to look closely at the story of anti-Jewish feeling in Bury round about the years 1148—56, which seems to me to help to clinch my own argument, let me consider, briefly, ways in which a superb Bury artist, working in the 1130s and 1140s, might have absorbed some of the plastic ideas Professor Lasko finds running parallel in England and Lower Lotharingia (particularly in Liège), and which might have provided Hugo with a working model.

An obvious means of contact was Baldwin, possibly the greatest of Bury's abbots (1065—1098). Between St Denis and Bury, he was prior of Liberau, in Upper Lotharingia.[28] In furnishing the apsidal eastern chapels of his great new abbey-church at Bury,[29] he is more than likely to have used works of art brought with him or sent as mementoes of the region of his earlier monastic rule. Then, a successor as abbot of Bury, for about five years during the first two decades of the 12th century, was Albold. He had previously been prior of Meaux, on the Marne.[30] The dedication of the easternmost apsidal chapel at Bury to his patron, St Nicaise, suggests Albold's devotion to that saint, and that he would therefore have been familiar with Nicaise's famous foundation at Reims, in Champagne, which was also presumably within the artistic orbit of Liège.[31] In the early 5th century, bishop Nicaise of Reims was martyred as he tried to obtain terms for his people from the barbarian invaders. His statue, with scalpless head, amazingly escaped General von Heeringen's barbarous attack on the cathedral in 1914.

I turn back to Bury and the extraordinary subject-matter of the ivory cross. The main indication that the Jews may have been unpopular at Bury

---

27 Lasko, *op. cit.*, plate 170.
28 *Dict. Nat. Biog.*, *sub* Baldwin.
29 A. B. Whittingham, *Arch. Jour.* CVIII (1952), p. 170 and R. Gilyard-Beer 'The Eastern Arm of the Abbey Church at Bury St Edmunds', *Proc. Suff. Inst. Arch.*, XXXI (1969), pp. 256—262.
30 R. M. Thomson, *The Chronicle of the Election of Hugh*, Oxford, 1974, xxvi, called Albold 'prior of St Nicaise, Meulan'. A note in a copy of Marianus Scotus (MS Bodley, 297, p. 413) described Albold as prior of St Nicasius, Meldensis, i.e. Meaux. The Roman name for Meulan was Mellentum.
31 The possible debt of St Edmund's 'pilgrimage-church' transepts to Albold and Saint-Remi (not the cathedral) at Reims is suggested by Gilyard-Beer, *op. cit.*

in the days *before* Samson's abbacy is given by Jocelin of Brakelond. As
cellarer, one of the three chief obedientiaries, he was all too familiar with
the estates and debts of the abbey. Jocelin's *Chronicle* opens in 1173, with
his own start at the abbey. Abbot Hugh was getting old. He was a good
monk, but a feeble abbot, and no use at managing the abbey's money
affairs. St Benedict's *Rule* was strictly obeyed, and God was honoured in
the regular services of the monks' choir. But this rich abbey was deep in
debt.

Twenty years earlier, in the time of abbot Ording, a fire had burnt the
refectory, dormitory, chapter-house and infirmary, and the abbot's hall —
all of which had already been newly rebuilt once since the beginning of the
century.[32] Now their repair (Mr Whittingham thinks 'mainly re-roofing')
was quickly put in hand and completed under Helyas, the sacrist for whom
Master Hugo made the new cross for the monks' choir. Abbot Hugh followed Ording as abbot in 1157, so there is every probability that he started
in debt, with so much building-work to be paid for. By the time Jocelin arrived, as a novice, sixteen years later, the abbey's affairs were in a very poor
way.

Borrowing was the only solution that abbot Hugh could think of. Every
half-year, Jocelin says,[33] one or two hundred pounds were added to the
debt. (I suppose a multiplier of about a hundred is not now too much to give
some idea of this in modern money.)

I saw a bond given to William fitzIsabel[34] for £1,040, but have no idea what it
was for. I saw another bond that was given to Isaac, the son of Rabbi Joce,[35]
for £400, but I don't know why. And I saw another given to Benedict[36] the Jew
of Norwich for £880 . . . *We had owed Benedict another debt for fourteen
years.* In all we owed him £1,200, not counting all the greatly increased
interest . . . Then the cellarer, without telling the rest of the monks, owed £60
to Jurnet,[37] Benedict's brother.

Part of Jurnet's home, the Stone House in King Street, still survives in
Norwich.[38] In Bury, Hatter Street, quite close to the abbey, was then known
as Heathenman's Street. The Jews were protected by the king, and when a
Jew died the king could, and sometimes did, claim all his wealth. Christians
who owed money to Jews could actually gain by the Jews' death, for the
king did not usually claim from *them* all the debt that they had owed to the
Jews. Financial indebtedness to the Jews undoubtedly underlay much of
their 'unpopularity', which certainly culminated in slaughter in 1190, but

32   Whittingham, *op. cit.*, p. 176.
33   Jocelin of Brakelond, *op. cit.*, pp. 2 — 6. My italics.
34   He seems to have been a Christian usurer: Lipman, *op. cit.*, p. 98.
35   Richardson, *op. cit.*, pp. 2, 11, 239. Josce was the distinguished rabbi of the London
     synagogue in Henry I's reign.
36   Lipman, *op. cit.*, pp. 95 — 102.
37   *Ibid.*, pp. 27 — 32, Ch. VI (pp. 95 — 112), p. 150.
38   *Ibid.*, pp. 111 — 112.

which was fluctuating ominously in East Anglian towns in the 1140s and 1150s.

Jocelin's references to the Norwich Jews are very much to the point. Jurnet of Norwich was one of the richest Jews in England. In 1144, a Norwich boy of 12 called William was either killed by accident or else murdered, in circumstances that would nowadays lead us to suspect pederasty. It now seems questionable whether the boy's death was caused by a Jew, but the relevance of the story to the Bury cross is that people in East Anglia, at the time of the making of Hugo's cross for the monks' choir, were ready to believe that the boy died of crucifixion at Jewish hands. The evidence relating to the episode was thoroughly examined and published by Augustus Jessopp and M. R. James in their book, *St William of Norwich*, in 1896, and there has been a more recent look at it in a book called *Saint at Stake* by M. D. Anderson. The case is also thoroughly examined and summarised by V. D. Lipman.[39] Apart from the abbey's debts to Norwich Jews, its involvement, and the involvement of Bury and Suffolk people, in the cult of St William is clearly recorded.

On Whit-Saturday, 1152, a Bury woman bent double from infancy went to Norwich as instructed by St William in a dream, and got as close to the saint's tomb as the throne would allow: there she prayed, and an hour later was cured.[40] At a time unrecorded, a Lincolnshire man who (provoked) slew his brother and two nephews with a pitchfork, travelled the saintly shrines of England with his right arm clasped in a ring made from the pitchfork. At Bury, the ring snapped and the arm became acutely painful, whereupon St Edmund, in the usual dream, recommended a visit to St William, who did the trick. Contemporaries, marvelling at the unjealous collaboration of the two saints, reflected that: 'the one withstood the heathen [Danes] raging against the law of Christ, the other endured the Jews, renewing, as it were, in him the death of Christ'.[41]

Here are signs of quite enough anti-Jewish sentiment to warrant the conception of the themes of that ivory crucifix. The translation of the boy William's corpse from a place near the monks' cemetery gate at Norwich to the chapter-house in 1150, and from the chapter-house to the south side of the high altar in 1152, and from there to the Martyrs' Chapel north of the high altar in 1154, must be reckoned something of a register of anti-Jewish emotions, first in Norwich itself, of course, but also in the neighbouring East Anglian monastic and mercantile centre of Bury, where the Jews flourished, to their increasing peril, in their own street.

On a very prominent scroll between the shrouded Christ and the skulls of Golgotha, in the tablet showing the Deposition and Lamentation (Plate 22), the inscription is taken from Zechariah: 'They shall weep for him as for

39   *Ibid.*, pp. 50−57.
40   Augustus Jessopp and M. R. James, *St William of Norwich*, Cambridge, 1896, p. 205.
41   *Ibid.*, pp. 236−241.

an only-begotten son.' Here the Jewish sorrows are anticipated, and a local contemporary reference to St William may well have been implied and understood: he, too, was an only-begotten son.

St Edmund's abbey certainly seems to have supplied the conditions for the carving of this extraordinary crucifix, and belief in the boy William's crucifixion may have supplied the occasion. The 'incomparable' qualities of the design suggest that Hugo's was the hand that made it.

Postscript

At the end of his lively, uninhibited (he had resigned), very informative book about the re-appearance and purchase (from a character called Ante Topić Mimara) of the ivory cross after World War II, Thomas Hoving, the former Director of the Metropolitan Museum in New York, wrote an Epilogue entitled 'Scholars, Rivals and Spies'. He dealt with me in a single paragraph early on, certainly not among the Rivals. I quote it because he left the distinct impression that to one of his 'vital' questions I had no reply! Here is the paragraph:[42]

> In 1974, Norman Scarfe published an article in which he concluded, convincingly, that the cross and its figure of Christ had been carved during the tenure of Abbot Ording by Master Hugo.[43] To Scarfe, the 'small' inscriptions had been written not to condemn the Jews, but to convert them to Christianity. He argued that, during the time of Ording, before the abbey had fallen into debt to the Jews, conversion of the local Jews rather than expulsion and eradication would have been the desired Christian goal. I agree entirely with Scarfe's theory, except for two vital points: only Samson could have conceived the scurrilous verses in the large inscriptions; only he could have ordered the insertion into the Lamb medallion of his own image. To my arguments Norman Scarfe replied that Samson's couplet on Cham which had accompanied the painting in the choir could just as easily have been inspired by the earlier inscriptions on the ivory cross. I had no riposte. But when I asked him who he thought the monk with the raised fist could be other than Samson, Norman Scarfe had no reply.

I had, of course, and here it comes. If it was not instantaneous, that is because I respected his high-powered, almost reckless intelligence and imagination and because the only possible reply — that he was indulging a fantasy — suggests a degree of disrespect I dislike having to express. But he puts the question point blank in his book, and what I have to say in answer is, I fear, equally blunt.

42 Thomas Hoving, *King of the Confessors*, New York, 1981, pp. 332–333.
43 He didn't trouble to list this article in his rather scrappy 'basic bibliography'. The Suffolk Institute of Archaeology's *Proceedings* probably do seem obscure and provincial from Metropolitan New York.

Earlier in his book,[44] he described how he was looking into the background, c. 1135—1156, of Master Hugo and abbot Ording, and came upon Jocelin's account of the election of abbot Samson in 1182. Jocelin (see chapter 8, following) was writing, c. 1200, as cellarer of the abbey, not only assessing Samson's strength in rescuing the abbey from debt and muddle, but putting on record Samson's aggressive encroachments on, in particular, the cellarer's rights. It was in this peculiar circumstance of Samson's aggression that Jocelin recalled the dream of one of his brethren (not a 'confessor' as Hoving calls him) in which Samson appeared standing with raised fists, spoiling for a fight: 'quasi pugillem ad duellum faciendum'.[45]

This dream was recorded by Jocelin, from his memory of events about twenty years earlier, in a document about what he had come to regard as Samson's iniquitous aggrandisement. He showed it to one or two cronies, but he would have kept it hidden securely in his office, for the eyes of his successors as cellarer, to remind them of their customary rights. In a later generation it was copied into the book that still bears the shelf-mark C.28 from the abbey's library. Samson was the very last person whose eyes would read it. In any case, I cannot begin to see how Samson, who as abbot was a friend of Richard I and a considerable grandee, would want himself immortalised as some sort of bruiser.

But nor can I begin to see how Tom Hoving could anyway see this 'floating' figure, as he rightly described it, as any kind of boxer. All we are shown is his left hand, and it is surely not tightly clenched, but rather waving? (Pl. 20: Lamb Medallion) If it really is clenched, then it is someone 'shaking a fist' and not someone squaring up for a bout of pugillism. Nor do I see the figure as a monk: Samson's (premature) baldness might have been some sort of a clue, but this figure is hooded, and the hood differs in no way from those worn by secular figures on this cross, mostly Jews.

Tom Hoving, thinking perhaps of the figures of conventional 'donors', and his sharp eye noticing that the figure had been carved as part of a separate piece of ivory let into this focal point of the rear of the cross, allowed his obsessive hunch about the cloister-monk's dream to lure him away from the realities of scholarship. If he looks at this centrepiece again, I hope he can see what I see.

In the first place, the inserted carving, his floating boxer, is part of the original design — both in terms of overall balance within the roundel and in terms of detail. The face and hands in the carving are the work of the sculptor of the whole masterpiece, who — because of a slip in carving or of a shortcoming in the ivory material — had to make this (in the literal sense) prestigious insertion. Tom Hoving admits he had to perform minor surgery on it before he was certain that it really was something let into the heart of the cross.

44   Op. cit., p. 318.
45   Butler, op. cit., p. 20.

More important, more persuasive and over-riding than these shades of aesthetic judgement and 'hunch', must be the relation of this strange floating hooded creature, with the long nose and fleshy lips, to the extraordinary overall counter-judaism of the entire cross. Here the explanation seems straightforward and fairly simple. Everyone agrees that there is impressive unity in the design of the cross, commensurate with the power of the formidable sermon on the scrolls. In this brilliant central roundel, the Lamb of God is not only three-dimensional in itself, but looking as if it is about to step forward right out of the cross at the same time as it looks back towards the archangel. Round the top of the roundel's elaborate frame is the message '*Johannes: et ego flebam multum*' — and I wept much'. There John stands, broken, weeping bitterly beside the lamb. The archangel (who also seems to be partly in, and partly stepping out of, the roundel) bears the lapidary reply from John's *Book of Revelation*, collated from verses 5 and 12 in chapter 5: 'Behold. Weep not. Worthy is the lamb that was slain', &c. And because there is throughout these carefuly chosen texts the usual reference back and forth between Old and New Testaments, this injunction from St John's *Revelation* is matched in the splendid, almost Michaelangelesque, outer framework of the roundel by the recumbent prophet Jeremiah's terse: '*Eradamus eum de terra viventium*', in chapter 11, verse 19: 'Let us cut him off, erase him, from the land of the living.' Old Jeremiah somehow saw himself as 'a lamb or an ox brought to the slaughter, not knowing that Israel and Judah had vowed to erase him', and he therefore appealed to the Lord of Hosts: 'Let me see thy vengeance on them.'

Caught in the enfilade of all this (one can hardly say crossfire), the strange hooded figure floats in limbo behind the message-scroll of *Revelation* and is presumably himself being relegated from the land of the living by that scroll. If (as I am sorry to doubt) he is really shaking a closed fist, then perhaps he is an Israelite resenting the imputation of Jeremiah that Israel and Judah had vowed to cut off the Lamb in this way. I do not see Samson anywhere in this powerful scene, nor can I imagine how he can possibly have wanted to be portrayed contributing a show of fisticuffs to it.

The remainder of Tom Hoving's Epilogue is a not unsympathetic, but cheerful, description of the way the British Museum, the Victoria and Albert Museum and the Cleveland Museum of Art (in Ohio) lacked the means or the will to acquire this incomparable work of medieval sculpture. The Metropolitan Museum lacked neither, and Hoving, reeling with excitement and pride, found himself being sent to collect it.

The book ends with Hoving's final attempt, in 1978, to get the extremely unattractive Yugoslav dealer, Mr Ante Topić Mimara, to tell him where he found the cross.

' "Was it in Yugoslavia?" I asked softly.
"Never! I would never have taken anything out of my beloved country."
"Hungary?" I quickly asked.
"No." But his eyes flickered.'

The sequel to that interview came in a letter from Tom Hoving in December, 1981, with a signed copy of his book. He told me the book had been condensed that month in the Readers Digest. Some days afterwards, a Hungarian living in the States called to say he had held the ivory cross in his hands in 1930. He named the church in Hungary, and told Hoving that the local story was that an English knight in the service of Richard Lionheart brought the cross to the church on his return from the Holy Land. He died there, and the cross stayed in that church until, in 1945, a Croatian who was a Tito partisan 'liberated' the cross just before the Russian army advanced into Hungary. 'If anything comes of this intriguing tale, I shall let you know.' I heard no more.

This story has much more of probability than the appearance of Abbot Samson above the Lamb of God. Samson himself was on good terms with Richard the Lionheart. On 20 November (the anniversary of Edmund's martyrdom) 1189, the new king came to Edmund's shrine before setting forth on crusade. On Palm Sunday following, fifty-seven Jews were slaughtered in Bury, and Samson got the king's permission to expel the survivors on condition that they kept their goods and the value of their houses and lands. The Bury cross had done nothing for the Bury Jews. It was now superfluous.

On the same page on which Jocelin mentioned, rather coolly, the expulsion,[46] he actually referred to 'the treasure of our church being carried to London for the ransom of King Richard'. A few pages later[47] he recorded that 'When news reached London of the capture of King Richard and his imprisonment in Germany, and the barons were meeting to take advice, the abbot leapt out in front of them all, saying he was ready, secretly or otherwise, to go in search of his lord the king, or of some reliable information.' When Richard was found, in Dürrenstein castle, beside the Danube, between Vienna and Linz, Samson went to him with many gifts.[48]

Then, to raise the enormous ransom, more treasures went off to London. Describing new buildings and repairs at Bury, Jocelin noted[49] that the abbot, 'seeing that the silver retable behind the high altar and many other precious ornaments had gone towards the ransom of King Richard, was unwilling to renew the retable and other similar treasures which, in similar emergencies, might be taken away: he decided to concentrate on making an exceptionally precious ridge-crest for Edmund's shrine, 'for no one would dare to lay a hand on that'. There it is, in Pls. 10 and 11.

46   Ibid., p. 46.
47   Ibid., p. 54.
48   Ibid., p. 55.
49   Ibid., pp. 96 – 97.

I have little doubt that the ivory cross left Bury in 1192—1194. With so much treasure to have to give up, the monks probably sent it off without much compunction, for all its beauty as carving. It is interesting to speculate what value would be set on it in terms of ransom-money. It would fetch most from a purchaser who felt most strongly the need to convert the Jews. Or had it already gone with some knight along the banks of the Danube, in the hope of finding Richard the Lionheart and bringing him a valuable souvenir of St Edmund's Day, 1189? That would most neatly explain the cross's mysterious journey into central Europe on its way to the Metropolitan Museum.

Professor Lawrence Stone, author of the classic standard work on *Sculpture in Britain: The Middle Ages*, kindly wrote in 1977 to say: 'Your analysis of the political and ideological background, which indicates a date in the 1150s, I find extremely convincing. You must be right about this, which strengthens the case for Master Hugo.' Lawrence Stone's one anxiety was that such microscopic detail would have been hard on the eyes of an old man. I cannot see that Master Hugo need have been very ancient: his known great works seem to date from the Bury Bible, c. 1135, through the bronze west doors of the abbey, c. 1140, to the cross c. 1148—56. He also cast a bell.[50] He may have made a seal showing abbot Ording in 1148[51] and probably did much else we have no hint of. If he was thirty when he attained the sureness and mastery to illustrate the Bury Bible, there seems a reasonable chance that at fifty-one his eyesight was still keen enough to guide the hand that performed such carving. The miracle is that he, or anyone, could conceive it.

50 M. R. James, *op. cit.*, p. 199.
51 R. M. Thomson, 'Early Romanesque Book Illustration in England: the Dates of the Pierpont Morgan Vita S. Edmundi and the Bury Bible', *Viator*, II, 1971, 221—223.

8

Chronicles of Bury Abbey:
The Chronicle of Jocelin of Brakelond

In 1842, Thomas Carlyle got hold of a dilapidated horse and rode from Chelsea into East Anglia in pursuit of material for his work on Oliver Cromwell. He rode through Bury St Edmunds, on the way to stay with friends in the nearby rectory of Troston, and his interest was temporarily deflected from Cromwell by the sight of the ruins of Bury abbey and by the text — lately published and a copy of it probably in the library at Troston — of a chronicle written by one of the Bury monks in the time of Richard I and John.[1] Carlyle was stuck with Cromwell, couldn't, as he put it, get 'one word to stand on paper with regard to Oliver'. He turned in escape from the impossible Oliver to the condition of contemporary England which at least *seemed* more tractable: the Chartists, the Poor Law Amendment Act! In the first seven weeks of 1843 he dashed off his most effective book, *Past and Present*, the entire middle section of which was his own peculiar version, in his strange headlong English, of the theme he thought he found in that Bury chronicler, Jocelin of Brakelond.

After six centuries of oblivion, Jocelin acquired fame across Europe.[2] Resurrection should hold few surprises for the Christian, yet it may be doubted whether the Jocelin who was writing that chronicle in Bury over the three or four years from 1198 would have been able to identify himself with the Jocelin of Carlyle's narrative *tour-de-force*. Carlyle flattered himself — with much imaginative patter and song-and-dance, and capital letters all over the text — that he got straight to the reality of the past. He was awfully rude about more academic historians, whom he addressed mockingly as *Dryasdust*.[3] Yet, for all his realism, he has managed to turn Jocelin's story upside-down. In conformity with his instinct that the contemporary need was for a Hero to put things right in Chartist England, he represented the abbot of Bury, the central figure in Jocelin's Chronicle, as that kind of hero. It may be that Carlyle read only the earlier part of the chronicle, where the abbot, Samson (who came from Tottington in the heathland of south-west Norfolk) appears as a strong man indeed, most prophetically and suggestively christened. In the early years of his abbacy,

---

1 J. A. Froude, *Carlyle's Life in London*, I, 1891, pp. 294–308.

2 J. G. Rokewode (ed.), *Cronica Jocelini de Brakelonda*, Camden Society, 1840.

3 In 1864, his Chronicle inspired a paper entitled 'Samson von Tottington', read before the Vienna Academy and published in their *Sitzungsberichte* for that year. I imagine this was not just to celebrate Abbot Samson's visit to Richard I at Dürrenstein a few miles along the Danube.

his labours in recovering the abbey from appalling mismanagement and debt were heroic, and Jocelin, whose novice-master Samson had once been, admired and praised him for it.

But Jocelin went further, and towards the end, at the stage where his narrative broke off, he was thoroughly disillusioned by Abbot Samson's encroachments on the convent's traditional rights — on their 'liberties'. Samson's high-handedness caused increasing discord in the abbey, and even uproar.[4] It was Jocelin's concern for the convent's liberties, not his admiration for the abbot, that moved him to sit down and write his chronicle. Nothing of this disillusion was suggested by Carlyle, who was content to describe Jocelin as Samson's Boswell, a simple-minded foil, 'a learned grown man, yet with the heart as of a good child; *whose whole life indeed has been that of a child*'.[5] There is truth in this description, for Jocelin had an open heart, and responded fairly naturally to Christ's teaching on the subject.[6] But in 1954, in his brilliantly detective and expository edition of *The Kalendar of Abbot Samson* for the Camden Society, Professor R. H. C. Davis showed conclusively that Jocelin was not just a cloister-monk with a gift for vivid description and incipient biographical tendencies: he was no less a personage than the cellarer of the abbey.[7]

Under the abbot, whose duties were to a large extent external, like those of a medieval bishop, the leading officials of the abbey were the prior (more or less equivalent to the dean of a cathedral), and then the cellarer and the sacrist. Jocelin, describing himself in his chronicle, always refers, in the 3rd person, to Jocellus, an obvious (since Ralph Davis explained all!) compound of the words 'Jocelin' and 'cellarer' — *cellerarius*. Jocelin himself described the cellarer as *'pater secundus'* in the convent, meaning 'second only to the prior'. A great deal of the 'chronicle' is devoted to the business of the cellarer. My view is that it was written largely, indeed primarily, to inform future cellarers of their customary rights and functions at Bury, and I share Ralph Davis's view that Jocelin's proper sense of modesty and humility as a Benedictine monk led him to introduce a pseudonym to represent himself in his role as cellarer, when he occasionally assumed a leading part in the administration of the abbey.

It is not easy to define the respective responsibilities of cellarer and sacrist to St Edmund's abbey.[8] Very broadly, the cellarer's business was to keep the convent well supplied with provisions and revenues. The first meaning of 'cellar' is store-house, normally, as at Bury, barn-like buildings above

---

4 H. E. Butler, ed., *The Chronicle of Jocelin of Brakelond*, 1949, p. 118. This, the latest edition of a major medieval text (B.L. Harl. 1005, folios 121—163) badly needs revision.

5 Carlyle, *op. cit.*, p. 103.

6 *Matthew*, 18, 3. Except ye become as little children, ye shall not enter into the kingdom of heaven.

7 R. H. C. Davis, *op. cit.*, li—lvii.

8 These complexities, so far as they concern the borough of St Edmund, were described, and as far as possible resolved, in M. D. Lobel, *The Borough of Bury St Edmunds*, Oxford, 1935, Ch. II, pt. I: 'Government by the cellarer and sacrist'.

ground: the present-day interpretation, a wine-store underground, is a secondary (if important) development. So far as the borough was concerned, the cellarer's function was that of lord of the manor, with the management of the demesne farm and lands, while the sacrist actually appointed the two Bailiffs (acting rather as twin mayors) and ran the town. If the cellarer's internal responsibility was provisions, the sacrist's was all maintenance and building-construction — the fabric of a great abbey. The endemic rivalry between the two 'departments' had very serious consequences, as we see in both the chronicles. One of the debts we owe Jocelin is that he enables us to glimpse all this in action. Much of the action was abbot Samson's, which may distort the picture for the dedicated constitutionalist. It has the advantage of being credible.

My view that Jocelin's motive in writing *was* largely a mixture of personal and constitutional, to set straight the rights and recent wrongs of his own 'department', the cellary, is shared by Ralph Davis, who anyway first suggested it and greatly encouraged my own study of it. It is also shared by Dr Rodney Thomson, of Tasmania, whose valuable edition of the *Electio Hugonis* has added vastly to the confidence and understanding with which we can now read that chronicle. Since his edition appeared, he has written to me to concur that his introduction to the *Electio*[10] wrongly emphasises the purely 'biographical' intention of Jocelin in his *Chronicle*.

In illustrating this view of Jocelin's intention in writing, I must try to give a clear idea of Jocelin's confusingly discontinuous tenure of the cellarer's office, though my reading of it differs in scarcely any detail, and certainly not in substance, from Ralph Davis's.[11] I set this out with almost monkish diffidence, for Jocelin seldom recorded dates for events familiar enough in his cloister during their very unserene lifetime. The fact that he uses any dates at all — 1197 for example — shows that he was writing at least a year or two later.

I believe Jocelin began to write his *Chronicle* about the time, 1197—1198, of his first association and identification with the cellarer's office. From that vantage-point his memory ranged back a quarter of a century to 1173 when, as a Bury boy (Brakelond was the old north quarter of the town), he had begun his novitiate at the abbey. His writing of those days has the vividness of childhood recollected, but it is easy to see that he was really concerned to describe the miserable inefficiency of abbot Hugh's administration. I paraphrase:

Abbot Hugh was growing old. He was a good monk but a feeble abbot and no use at managing the abbey's estates and money-matters. St

9   Butler, *op. cit.*, pp. 28—29.
10   R. M. Thomson, ed., *The Chronicle of the Election of Hugh*, Oxford, 1974, xiii ('Jocelin's well-known biography'), and xxii ('a masterly portrayal of a remarkable abbot over nearly twenty years of his life, and the choice of material for inclusion in it was largely determined by its relevance to this theme').
11   Davis, *op. cit.*, li—lvii.

Benedict's rule was strictly obeyed, and God was honoured in the regular services of the monks' choir[12] but this rich abbey was deep in debt. Twenty years earlier, a fire had destroyed the refectory, dormitory, chapter-house and infirmary, and the abbot's hall, all of which had not long been new-built. They were all rebuilt at once, by a sacrist called Helyas. (For Helyas, Master Hugo carved the ivory cross: so in ch. 7). When abbot Hugh became abbot in 1157, he probably started in debt, with all the new building to be paid for. By the time Jocelin arrived, as novice, the abbey's affairs were dismal. Borrowing more money was abbot Hugh's only solution. Every half-year, one or two hundred pounds were added to the debt.

I wonder if the next details could have been recorded without access to official records, which he could easily gain from 1197, but which he would certainly not have had as a novice. These detailed figures of debts to the Jews occur in the second column of the very first folio of Jocelin's book. They help to persuade me that he did not begin writing until about 1198. 'I saw a bond given to William fitzIsabel for £1,040. I saw another bond given to Isaac, the son of Rabbi Joce, but I don't know what for. And I saw another given to Benedict the Jew of Norwich for £880 . . . We had owed Benedict another debt for fourteen years. In all we owed him £1,200, not counting all the greatly increased interest. . . . Then the cellarer, without telling the convent, borrowed another £60 from Jurnet, Benedict's brother.' And so on.

These first few lines of Jocelin's *Chronicle* are concerned with the financial problems of his community. Certainly, he was preparing the way for his description of Hugh's successor, Samson, and Samson's masterly handling of those problems. During his first year, Jocelin asked Master Samson, his novice-master, about all this borrowing and debt. 'Why don't you speak out against it? You fear God more than you fear men, and have nothing to lose. You have no desire for office.' Jocelin was writing this about sixteen years after Samson had been elected abbot, and you hear the note of irony. Samson replied: 'My son, a child recently burnt is afraid of fire. Abbot Hugh jailed me and banished me to Castle Acre; and others were banished, including the prior, because we spoke up for the common good of our church, and against the abbot's will. This is the hour of darkness, when flatterers prevail. We must pretend to see nothing. May the Lord see and judge.'[13] Jocelin had a good initiation in the difficulty of keeping that most important Benedictine vow: obedience.

Reading about abbot Hugh, whom we have known, alas, in public and private life, makes one feel almost as sententious as Carlyle. He died from a

12 This testimony was perhaps overlooked by a fine Benedictine scholar's reading of Jocelin: Dom David Knowles, *The Monastic Order in England*, Cambridge, 1940, p. 309. There he confessed that Jocelin's chronicle 'defies and eludes any process of analysis or synthesis', and expressed unhappiness at Jocelin's worldly interest in so many business affairs. Jocelin would have agreed!

13 Butler, *op. cit.*, p. 4—5.

dislocated kneecap, and no one wept. Jocelin describes how the monks now set about praying for a suitable new abbot. Three times a week they lay full-length on the floor of their choir in the hope of pleasing God; and they started to discuss the kind of abbot they wanted. Jocelin shows how little our characters change over the centuries. He once saw Samson sitting and listening to a group of monks during their blood-letting — which took place every spring and autumn. After being bled, their routine was eased for about three days.

'At such times, the monks would reveal the secrets of their hearts', said Jocelin. 'I saw Samson sitting and smiling, without a word, and noting the words of each monk. And I heard him repeat some of their opinions twenty years later, when he was abbot.'[14]

There follows a detailed description of Samson's election, which is not only highly dramatic reading — and of course writing — but it is indispensable background for any appreciation of the *Election of Hugh*, an almost equally dramatic chronicle of the election of Samson's successor. Ruthlessly paraphrased, Jocelin continued:[15]

'At last in February 1182, king Henry II sent to Bury for the prior and twelve monks to appear before him at Bishop's Waltham, his castle near Winchester, to elect a new abbot. Excited, all the monks assembled in the chapter-house at Bury. The prior chose twelve to go with him, and everyone approved. Six others were then picked, as good judges, to select three candidates for abbot and write down their names. The three names were put in a sealed box to be taken to Bishop's Waltham for the king to choose from. The group set out on foot.

'Samson brought up the rear. As sub-sacrist he carried the money for their expenses, and also the official letters for the king, hung in a case round his neck, as though he was their only servant. Catching up his long habit over his arms, he followed the rest at a distance.[16]

'After many days and difficulties (for it was February), they arrived at King Henry's castle. Henry II was probably well-disposed towards St Edmund's abbey, for it was there that his chief rival for the throne, Eustace of Blois, died suddenly in 1153, leaving the way clear. Eustace had been intent on robbing Edmund's abbey, a pretty perilous activity, as Cnut's father, and later Edward I, demonstrated.

'The great king Henry received the thirteen kindly and asked for the names of the three from their monastery. They opened the case, broke the seal, and found the three names, with Samson's on top. The prior and others of higher rank than Samson blushed because their names were not among the three. The king said he did not know these three, and he asked for three more names from Bury and three from other monasteries, to make

14   *Ibid.*, p. 14.
15   *Ibid.*, pp. 16 – 18.
16   *Ibid.*, p. 19.

nine in all. Slowly, seven names were eliminated and two were left — the prior and Samson.

'The bishop of Winchester asked them about these two men, and said "Tell me openly, do you wish to have Samson?" The majority answered clearly, "We want Samson." Then the king spoke: "I will do what you want, but watch out. For, by the eyes of God, if you're making a mistake I shall be upon you."[17]

'Samson, elected, fell at the king's feet and kissed them. He swiftly rose, and swiftly moved to the altar with the others from Bury, singing Psalm 51, "Have mercy upon me, O God, according to thy loving kindness." His head was held high and the expression on his face never changed. When the king saw this, he said to those standing nearby, "By God's eyes this man we've elected thinks himself worthy to be in charge of his abbey." '

Jocelin's description of the new abbot's reception at Bury — the processions, the crowds and the torrential bells — and of his person are perhaps well enough known. Nor do I want to recite here the efficient ways in which he made his clean sweep and got St Edmund's abbey re-organised. That occupies the whole middle third of Jocelin's book. Here I want to concentrate on Jocelin as cellarer and as critic — more in tears than anger at Samson's increasingly intemperate rule. This is mostly the matter of the last third of the book, but I begin with an example from fol. 128v, one-fifth of the way through. It seems to confirm my point about the purposes of Jocelin's *Chronicle*. Soon after becoming abbot in 1182, Samson usurped the cellarer's role; and Jocelin's tone, as he wrote of it, seems to be one of cautious approval.

'He took our manors of Bradfield and Rougham — the convent's manors as distinct from the abbot's — into his own hands for the time being, making good our rent deficit by paying out £40. These manors he afterwards returned to us, having heard that there were murmurs in the convent because he kept our manors in his hands. To run these manors, and all the others, he appointed new managers, wiser than the previous ones, and either monks or laymen, who both for ourselves and our estates would make more sensible provision.'

Fifteen years later, the abbey's administration was again getting out of hand:[18] I paraphrase again:

'*In the year of grace 1197*, certain innovations and changes were made in our church, which ought not to be passed over in silence. The cellarer's expenses exceeded his revenues, and Samson ordered the prior to find him a yearly increment of £50, to be paid in monthly instalments, so that all might not be squandered at one go: and *ita factum est uno anno*: this was done for one year.

'This was done for one year' is slightly misleading. Starting the paragraph

17   *Ibid.*, p. 23.
18   *Ibid.*, pp. 87–90.

in 1197, we are already thinking of the next financial year: Michaelmas '97—'98. But the year referred to concluded at Michaelmas 1196 and the innovations of 1197 have yet to be described. This chronology, difficult to follow in Jocelin's text, is important if we are to understand Jocelin's hazardous career at the cellary. (He should have used the pluperfect tense: 'this had been done for a year' would have avoided the confusion.) We are not surprised to read: 'The cellarer and his accomplices complained, and said that if only he could have the whole sum he could make much better provision', &c. The abbot reluctantly agreed, and, of course, the cellarer had spent everything by August.'

It is demonstrable that this was August 1197. Obviously, Jocelin was not describing himself as the cellarer who performed so miserably. One date in his career is fixed. On 18 May 1198, a cyrograph (written and signed) charter witnessed a grant of lands by the abbot and convent in full chapter and in the presence of, among others, *Joscelino cellerario*.[19] This is how his promotion came about. His chronicle continued:[20]

> The cellarer had spent everything by August, and £26 more, and he was like to owe £50 before Michaelmas. Hearing this, the abbot took it badly. [One can imagine!] He said in chapter he had often threatened to take the cellary into his own hands. He had put his clerk in to keep an eye on the cellarer, 'but neither clerk nor monk dares tell me the cause of over-spending. You see our burden of debt. Tell me how I should put matters right.
>
> Many cloister-monks almost smiled at this, and were pleased, seeing the truth in the abbot's words. The prior turned the blame on to the cellarer, the cellarer on to the guest-master. We did indeed know the truth, but were silent and afraid. On the morrow the abbot again asked our advice. No idea. On the third day, someone asked the abbot to advise. He said: 'Since you do not know how to govern your house, I take into my hand your cellary and all expenses of your guests.' He thereupon deposed the cellarer and guest-master, and set in their place two other monks, entitled sub-cellarer and guest-master, in association with Master G, a clerk from his own table, without whose assent nothing was to be done.

This new appointment, 'entitled sub-cellarer', was Jocelin of Brakelond's. It *was* an innovation, implying cellarer acting *sub* the abbot. It was made soon after August 1197, and he presumably made a good impression on Master G. In his chronicle, he reports with admirable fairness the reactions in the cloister. 'One monk, holding up his hands to heaven, said "Blessed be God who has inspired the abbot with such desire to set things right." Many spoke thus. But the knights wondered, and the people wondered, at the things that were done.' One of the common folk said (and how you can still hear the intonation): ' "Tha's a wonder, them monks, being so many, and with all that book-learning, to have to put up with having their property and their income all muddled and mixed up with the abbot's property . . ."

19   Davis, *op. cit.*, pp. 109—110.
20   Butler, *loc. cit.*, pp. 87—89.

'And so we are become a reproach to our neighbours, a scorn and derision to them that are round about us.'[21]

In September, the brethren more ostentatiously than usual celebrated the anniversary of abbot Robert (1102−07) who had separated the convent's property from that of the abbots.[22] The abbot had ignored the gesture. But at Michaelmas (still 1197), partly to curb the murmurings, 'he who had been acting sub-cellarer was made cellarer'. Jocelin's attempt at concealment caused himself to express himself quite awkwardly! Furthermore, Samson appointed a new sub-cellarer to replace Jocelin. Perhaps he was impressed by the need to strengthen the 'department'. There was now trouble with Master G., the clerk-overseer, who became drunk and overbearing. Someone spoke to Samson about him, who quietened him down.

Jocelin's troubles as cellarer were by no means over. We reach an ostensibly cheerful passage[23] about Samson saying he will spend more time at home and would improve the buildings in the abbot's court, replacing thatch by tile to remove danger of fire, and then:

> Behold, at the abbot's command, the court resounds with the noise of picks and mason's tools for the demolition of the guest-house, and it is now almost all down: this is the long-awaited day, of which I write not without joy. I who have charge of the guest-house.

What is this? No longer cellarer?

More detective-work — all unerringly done before me by Ralph Davis in preparing *The Kalendar*, but double-checking anything so complex is always rewarding — and it appears that Jocelin was reduced to sub-cellarer and guest-master for the year Michaelmas 1199−1200, and then restored as cellarer, in the following circumstances. (The present tense in the passage about rebuilding the guest-house shows that fol. 148, two-thirds of the way through the chronicle, was being written in 1199−1200.)

> Geoffrey Ruff, a monk of ours, though he conducted himself in too worldly a fashion, was useful to us in his management of four manors — Barton, Pakenham, Rougham and Bradfield — where in the past the rents had often fallen into deficit.[24] The abbot, hearing disquieting reports of his conduct, for a long time pretended not to have heard, probably because Geoffrey seemed so generally useful. Then, learning the truth, Samson suddenly had Geoffrey's chests impounded in the vestry, ordered a close guard on all stock in those manors, and locked Geoffrey up. A huge amount of gold and silver was found — 200 marks' worth — all of which Samson put to the work on the front of the shrine. At Michaelmas (1199), it was decided in chapter that *two* of our brothers should succeed to the management of those manors. Yet *one* of them, Roger of Hingham, who publicly engaged his readiness and fitness to take on

21 *Psalm 79*, verse 4.
22 Butler, *op. cit.*, p. 90.
23 *Ibid.*, p. 96.
24 *Ibid.*, pp. 122−3.

both the cellary and the manors, was thereupon confirmed in those *two* positions by the abbot, against the will of the convent. The other one of our brethren, Jocellus, was deposed, although he had carried out his duties providently and well and — unlike other cellarers — for two years without debt. He was made sub-cellarer [and, as we saw, guest-master]. But at the end of the year, Roger (Hingham) the cellarer, when he presented the account of his receipts and expenditure, admitted that he had taken sixty marks of stock from the manors to make good his deficit. After consultation, therefore, the said Jocellus replaced the cellarer, and furthermore Mildenhall, Chippenhall (in Fressingfield) and Southwold were made over to him, while the other manors were entrusted to Roger and Albinus and were separated from the cellary, lest the manors should be impoverished by the cellary or the cellary by the manors.

So Jocelin is vindicated. At Michaelmas 1200 he should have been feeling pleased. Far from it. The demotion had naturally upset him. If it had been justified by his ineffectiveness in, presumably, turning a blind eye to Geoffrey Ruff, there had also been a stand-up row between himself, as cellarer, and the abbot over the affair of Ralph the porter, who was responsible for seeing who went into and out of the abbey through the great Norman gate-tower.[25]

Ralph had upset some senior obedientiaries (monastic officials): although a servant of theirs, he had given evidence against them at the law-courts. They reduced his wages. He complained to Samson that he had been unfairly treated, and Samson took up his case. Opposed by the entire chapter, Samson resorted to a display of his power, publicly ordering the cellarer (Jocelin) to restore Ralph to his full salary and to drink nothing but water for one day. Next day the abbot forbade him both meat and drink until he had obeyed. The abbot then wisely went away for eight days. Jocelin says, 'there was a great uproar in the monastery, such as I never saw before, and they said that the abbot's order ought not to be obeyed'. But they were Benedictine monks, and it was, 'and we humbled ourselves before him. Seeing that we were overcome, he was himself overcome.' Ralph kept his full wages.

Then, during Jocelin's year of demotion, in 1200, Robert the prior died and there was renewed tension over the appointment of young Herbert, very amiable, but unlettered. He had been Samson's chaplain till promoted, a month or so ago, to be subsacrist. Samson clearly saw him as untroublesome. Jocelin, as Ralph Davis remarked, was so bitterly disappointed and upset at not being elected himself, that 'he slipped into the first person singular'.[26] The appointment over,

I, the guest-master, sat in the porch of my guest-house going over what I had seen and heard. A handsome fellow, dignified, elegant, young, strong, quick

25 *Ibid.*, pp. 117–120.
26 Davis, *op. cit.*, lvi.

to work for the needs of the church: a solemn man, voluble in French, for he was a Norman: a man of middling intelligence . . . I wept for joy.[27]

The grapes were sour. As Davis says: 'he had to console himself with a most unusual spate of quotations'. He proceeded to enlarge on

> another blemish of wrong-doing which, God willing, the abbot will wash out with tears of penitence, that one transgression should not besmirch such a multitude of good deeds.[28]

Samson raised the level of the fish-pond of Babwell, just outside Bury's north gate,

> by the new mill, to such a height that owing to the damming up of the waters, there is no one — rich or poor — with lands by the waterside from the north gate round to the east gate but has lost his garden and orchard. The cellarer's pasture is destroyed . . . the cellarer's meadow is ruined, the infirmarer's orchard is submerged, and all the neighbours are moaning.

It begins to look as if Samson was growing tyrannical in his old age. There follows a splenetic reflection on the general wisdom of appointing an abbot from among the brethren of another house! It was not a principle Jocelin supported when Samson's successor was considered (see *Electio Hugonis*, below).

We reach the last episode in Jocelin's *Chronicle*, in 1201 or 1202, when Samson was sixty-six or sixty-seven. His health was failing. King John sent for him to discuss some orders sent by the pope. Samson knew that, whatever he said, he would offend either king or pope.

> He actually asked our advice,[29] a thing he had hardly ever done before. Coming into the chapter-house on the day before his departure, he had all his books brought with him, and made a present of them to the church and convent.

At that moment, three brethren, not men of tact, suggested that Samson had been zealous in upholding the liberties of his barony but had never said a word in support of the liberties of the sacrist regarding the appointment of the town reeves with the consent of the convent.

> When the abbot heard that, he said things that should not be said, swearing that he would be master as long as he lived. But, as evening came, he spoke more gently with prior Herbert. Next morning, in chapter, just before he set out, he said — hoping presumably, for sympathy and peace — that his servants were all paid and his will made; as though he were not going to live long. And he excused himself for modifying ancient customs, on the grounds that he had thereby prevented a weakening of the king's justice.

He was not allowed to get away with that.

27 Butler, *op. cit.*, p. 129.
28 *Ibid.*, p. 131.
29 *Ibid.*, p. 135.

We asked what was to be done concerning the loss of the cellarer's court, and more especially of the halfpence he used to receive for the renewal of pledges. And when he countered by demanding our authority for exercising a royal right, we told him we had possessed that right ever since the foundation of our church, and even during the first three years of his own abbacy. ·

Samson could not find a satisfactory answer, and wishing to start on his journey without more fuss, he made the promise with which Jocelin, openly sceptical, ended his chronicle. It is to be doubted whether Samson underwent any change of heart in the remaining nine or ten years of his rule, which were beset in 1208 by the even greater troubles of the papal interdict. If Jocelin's chronicle had really been the 'biography' of Samson it is often said to be, then it would have been continued to the old lion's death. We know from the *Electio* that Jocelin, become Jocelin of the Altar, outlived him by at least a few years.

His chronicle closes with Samson at the moment of his departure for John's court, promising

that on his home-coming he would in all things work with our counsel, and would make just disposition, and restore to everyman his own. With this declaration, calm was established; but no great calm, for, as Ovid noted: 'in promises there's none but may be rich'.

'To everyman his own — *unicuique redditurus quod suum esse debet.*' There, fifteen years or so before *Magna Carta*, is Jocelin's last reference, in his own Chronicle, to the rights and liberties he wrote to defend. His political interests were local, narrowly confined to the affairs of St Edmund's abbey. His passionate involvement in that small world brought it — incomparably — to life. When Samson died, the election of a new abbot plunged them all into much broader questions of liberty — as between the monastery and the lord king, the lord pope and the lord king, the archbishop of Canterbury and the lord king, many of the barons and the lord king. Jocelin's part — a decade after he had written his Chronicle — was still transparently honest and undissimulating, engagingly so. The lord king's rearguard action is protracted all through the next Bury chronicle, the sequel to Jocelin's — less exclusively domestic, yet staged to a surprising extent in the chapter-house, and even in the cloister and the blood-letting room, at Bury: the *Chronicle of the Election of Hugh*.

* * * * * * *

The Chronicle of the Election of Hugh

Within the hour of Samson's death, late one evening after Christmas in 1211, in the fourth year of the papal interdict, all the monks, seniors and juniors, were called by the wooden clapper to a meeting in the blood-letting parlour. The *Cronica de Electione Hugonis Abbatis,*[30] was accurately titled. It moved straight into the occasion of the protracted and bitterly disputed election of Samson's successor. The perfunctory references to his 'venerable' memory, and to their being 'not without' heavy sorrow at losing so great a pastor, suggest concern with the problems created by the old man's death (he was about 76), and do not dispel feelings that there may have been profound relief. An alarming cantankerousness was already visible in 1201 or 1202 at the end of Jocelin's book, and may easily have grown worse. In any case, his 'greatness' would have been fresh in all their minds when they met that winter's night in the blood-letting room: they would think twice before electing another obviously strong man.

That night, there had of course been no time to inform King John of the abbot's death or to get his consent to elect: in any case, such elections were in abeyance during the interdict. It is slightly disquieting that the first thing St Edmund's monks all found it sensible to do was to pass, with a formal 'Amen', the proposal that no one should try to procure his own or another person's promotion to the abbacy by improper disposal of the church's goods. That reveals their awareness that misappropriation and bribery were possible, as, sure enough, the 'villain of the piece' later demonstrated. With allegations of this kind, we need to know the credentials of the author, and whether there is a reliable edition of the text.

Dr Rodney Thomson of the University of Tasmania has edited the *Electio Hugonis* for the 'Oxford Medieval Texts' series with exemplary thoroughness.[31] He begins his introduction to the *Electio* by referring to the great fame of the abbey of St Albans in the realm of medieval historiography, inaugurated there by Roger Wendover in the 1220s; and he observed that, at that date, in the writing of history the abbey of St Edmund at Bury was 'already without peer'. He remarked, and was the first to do so, that the *Electio Hugonis* was the third of three works distinguished by the vividness and the volume of contemporary eye-witness, the first being the *Relatio de Pace Veneta*, a description, apparently by a Bury monk, of the 1177 negotiations between Frederick Barbarossa and the pope, Alexander III: the second, as we know, was Jocelin of Brakelond's *Chronicle*. Rodney Thomson's judgement is that, in this

---

30   R. M. Thomson, ed., *The Chronicle of the Election of Hugh, Abbot of Bury St Edmunds and later Bishop of Ely,* Oxford, 1974. B.L. Harl., 1005, folios 171–192v.

31   More recently, he has compiled and edited an admirable volume on *The Archives of the Abbey of Bury St Edmunds,* Suffolk Records Society, Vol. XXI, 1980.

special business of concentrating in great detail on a particular subject, 'Bury achieved a lasting notoriety, unapproached by any other house.'

In correspondence, Dr Thomson says he is inclined to think of the *Relatio* as a more casual piece of work, 'springing from the deep impression made upon the writer by the events at Venice of which he was presumably an accidental eyewitness'. My own conviction was that Jocelin's *Chronicle* got written almost by accident — the accident being the strength of Jocelin's personal feeling, about the works of Samson and about his own identification with the cellary. However, I see that a description by a Bury monk of that papal negotiation of 1177 soon after Jocelin himself had joined the abbey might well have given him historiographical ideas. Dr Thomson makes it clear that the *Electio* was written — probably not till about 1220 — with Jocelin's book in mind, if not as an exact model. Professor Ralph Davis thought Jocelin *could* have written the *Electio*[32] (his italics). Rodney Thomson argues persuasively against this, basing himself first on the differences of vocabulary and construction. One reflects that Jocelin would have been twenty years older, in 1222, than when he wrote the *Chronicle* — a man of about 60 did not necessarily write the kind of Latin he wrote when he was 40. He had become 'Jocelin of the Altar': with age, unlike Samson, he had fewer responsibilities, and presumably was able to spend more time in the library. Thomson noted that Jocelin indulged in twenty-six classical quotations in the *Chronicle* — all but a couple taken from a *florilegium*, a book of quotations, whereas the *Electio* runs to a mere half-dozen tags. (That *could* be a sign of maturity!) The *Electio* has over a hundred Biblical quotations, but then Jocelin's *Chronicle* has seventy-three, not significantly different, given changes in reading habits of twenty years. I am no Latin scholar, but I confess that the *Electio* does not read like the work of the author of Jocelin's *Chronicle*. The thinking is *denser*, less direct and clear. The interests of the author of the *Electio* seem more legalistic, more concerned with pedantry (as revealed for example in criticizing the 'enemy's' sermons), than Jocelin had been. That could indicate advancing years too. But I think it betokens a genuine difference of character. Jocelin of the Altar, as Jocelin of Brakelond had become, was on balance, and by inclination, on the same side in the election dispute as the author. As we shall see, there is one episode,[33] at a critical point in the struggle, in which Jocelin appears with a comic loss of dignity: the description is that of a friend rather than himself.

Dr Thomson has done some very elaborate computing; has identified five episodes away from Bury where the kind of detail argues the presence of the author, and in which one monk satisfies all the conditions. He turns out to be Master Nicholas of Dunstable, then a relative newcomer among the brethren at Bury. Not much is known of him outside the pages of the *Electio*, except that for a short time, round about 1220, he held the high office

32 *Kalendar*, p. lvii.
33 p. 117 below.

Jocelin had held, the cellary.[34] Thomson makes out a convincing case for Master Nicholas's having been trained in the civil law, and possibly in Bologna. Certainly a major distinction between this book and Jocelin's *Chronicle* is the introduction into this text of documents used in the dispute, and almost beginning with the actual letter Nicholas was himself deputed to take to the archbishop, Stephen Langton. I think it is reasonable for us to accept appreciatively that Master Nicholas of Dunstable is the author of the *Electio*.

Rodney Thomson's analysis of the way ecclesiastical elections, in Bury or elsewhere, came to be documented in response to the decree of the Lateran Council of 1215 is very impressive.[35] He naturally recognises the precedent contained in Jocelin's full account of Samson's election.[36] At this point in his Introduction to the *Electio*, he says Jocelin's choice of 'material relating to the rights and customs of the abbey, especially the cellary, is largely determined by its relevance to the theme'[37] of the biographical portrayal of a remarkable abbot. The Carlyle view of Jocelin as Samson's Boswell was surprisingly influential and dies hard, but biographically inclined monks entitled their biographies *Vita*, not *Cronica*, and, with the exception of such a national hero as Alfred the Great, tended to choose more saintly subjects than Samson. Rod Thomson tells me he no longer agrees with the first half of his dictum: 'Jocelin's *Cronica* is a biography, the *Electio Hugonis* is apologia.' ('Apologia' he uses in the legal sense of 'vindication', not the modern sense of 'an expression of regret'.) His perception of the protagonists in the *Electio* as the embodiment of abstract principles is of the utmost value as we read the work: the abbot-elect, Hugh of Northwold, and his opponent, the sacrist, Robert of Graveley, 'never come alive', as Thomson says, because Hugh represents the conventional virtues of a defender of the church's liberties, while Robert symbolises 'the unrighteousness of the oath-breaker, and assailant of monastic privilege'.

There are, nevertheless, some delightfully lively pictures, And because the bias of the book is towards the church — the pope and the archbishop — and because the 'villainous' Robert ostensibly represents the customary rights of the crown, one might expect King John to come badly out of it all. In fact, as has often been remarked, you find yourself, as you put the book down, astonished to feel so much sympathy with King John — as well as with the abbot elect, Hugh. Indeed the author has written a story with a happy ending — the king and the abbot sitting down together for a private talk on the royal couch after dinner at Windsor, a day or two before the concord of Magna Carta. What makes this book so readable is the clear identification of local particular causes with great national, and inter-

34   *Electio*, p. 187.
35   *Ibid.*, xxi—xxii.
36   See pp. 103—104 above.
37   *Loc. cit.*, xxii.

national, causes. And if the figures of Hugh and Robert are not altogether life-like, that is also partly because we may have the freshness of Jocelin's work in our minds, and partly because Nicholas of Dunstable was a professional lawyer.

We remember, from Jocelin,[38] how Samson was elected, with the party from Bury taking three names in a box, so that the king might choose one from those three names. That might have been expected to be repeated in the electing of Samson's successor. The king certainly expected it, and this is how one immediately moves to his side. The convent chose a different way. And to understand their action it is necessary to glance at the famous election, back in 1205–1207, of the archbishop of Canterbury, Stephen Langton.

Stephen was already 'the most illustrious living churchman of English birth',[39] the friend of the king of France, Philip Augustus, and of the pope, Innocent III. Innocent had made him a cardinal-priest in Rome, where he taught theology. In 1205, Archbishop Hubert Walter died and John was determined to replace him at Canterbury by John de Grey. Sixteen Canterbury monks presented themselves in Rome with a promise of the king's assent to their decision (they had secretly agreed with John to elect de Grey). The pope bade them choose 'a fit man, and an Englishman'. With Langton sitting among the cardinals, his name was naturally suggested. The Canterbury monks confessed their deal with John, were absolved, and fifteen of them voted for Stephen Langton.

John, furious, saw himself saddled with an 'unreliable' archbishop, a friend of his enemies. All the Canterbury monks rallied to Stephen, and were driven into exile by John. The pope replied by placing England under the dreadful interdict. The people of England were denied the services of the church — the sacraments, burial in consecrated ground, practically everything — for over six mortal years. In January 1213 the pope sentenced the king to be deposed, entrusting the execution to Philip of France. John capitulated, welcomed Stephen home as archbishop, and the life of the church was resumed, including, nineteen months after Samson's death, the election of his successor.

These were the circumstances in which the Bury monks, on 1 August 1213, received John's letter (text copied in full into the *Electio*)[40] ordering them to send, without delay, as many of the wiser men of the convent as seemed to them necessary, with letters of authorisation, well-prepared and instructed 'to choose [i.e. elect] for you an abbot according to English custom'. The *Electio* immediately went on to reveal that they had taken advice from Archbishop Stephen and his 'papalist' friends, bishops Eustace of Ely and William of London. They naturally recommended a unanimous

38 See pp. 103 above.
39 Kate Norgate, *Dictionary of National Biography*.
40 *Electio*, p. 7.

choice of one person by the convent (such as Stephen had had, virtually, for Canterbury), which would give John no chance to impose his own candidate. What was more awkward, and the cause of the long dispute, was that it gave him no element of choice at all — such as his father had unquestionably exercised in the election of Samson.

Without more ado, host and relics were brought to the chapter-house. At once the dispute was brought into the open, the fangs were bared. Master Nicholas — author, as we believe, of the book — stood up and denounced Robert of Graveley, the sacrist, with ample evidence, as someone soured and ruthless, derisive and contemptuous of the brothers, ambitious, neglectful of his duty to maintain the fabric of the monastery, and much else; and proceeded to move that Robert the sacrist be ineligible either as elector or for election. The motion was seconded with similar charges. The sacrist was, on any showing, a controversial figure (as Master Nicholas already shows himself to be).[41]

The brethren pressed on, electing three uncontroversial brothers unanimously, whose duty was to go outside and quietly choose the seven electors. They returned with seven names, including 'Jocelin of the Altar, the former cellarer', his friend John of Lavenham, the victualler, and five others, not including Master Nicholas but including the tiresome sacrist and Hugh the sub-cellarer, who ended up as abbot elect. But not until Robert the sacrist had been appealed against and replaced by the chamberlain. The seven then vowed, on the host, that, according to the rule of Benedict, they would consider each of their own number and of the whole convent, and choose as their abbot one of the more compassionate, good-natured and prudent (*misericordior, benignior, discrecior*):[42] not qualities readily applicable to Samson in his old age. Out they went, and set up an interview-room in St Saba's chapel, one of the apsidal chapels behind the high altar: each monk was interviewed, two of the electors taking notes. Returning to the chapter-house, they joyfully announced the name of Hugh of Northwold, 'a man good-humoured and upright, learned enough in the Old and New Testaments, full of grace and compassion, utterly without bitterness, sober, chaste, modest, devout, calm, reliable and prudent in action'. Rodney Thomson says these are 'catalogue virtues, offering little real appreciation of Hugh's individual characteristics'.[43] It may be so, but these are the virtues the convent was probably looking for. Later, as the dispute developed, a meeting took place between the abbot-elect and 'the good bishop of Ely', at his manor at Biggin, near Cambridge: the bishop advised the abbot-elect and his two friends to present themselves to the papal legate and the archbishop would mediate with the king. The author of the *Electio* continued: 'Now the abbot-elect was of a wonderful simplicity and

41   *Ibid.*, pp. 7−8.
42   *Ibid.*, p. 11.
43   *Ibid.*, p. 11n.

gentleness.' I have seen no reason to doubt it. And I understand why, apart from the political wrangle over his election, and his good works at Ely, there is so little to read about Hugh.[44]

When he had been elected and nominated and the rite performed canonically, the whole convent, one after another, rushed up to give him the kiss of peace, and blessings to God. And when he was seated on the left side of the monks' choir, on the raised part where the abbot and prior are placed, side by side, they appealed against anyone who by trickery or malice might undermine this election. This was all done on 7 August, the day after the feast-day of the Lord's Transfiguration.

Early next morning, Hugh with a party of senior brethren, including Master Nicholas, but also the sacrist, set off to the court, probably at Corfe, to ask the king's favour on the election. Irate, he declined to give assent. The monks, aggrieved, sent Master Nicholas with a letter from the prior to the archbishop, explaining that they had chosen an abbot according to God and the canons, by unanimous consent. When this was read out to archbishop Stephen, he raised his hands heavenward, saying 'Glory be to the Most High: winning in this affair, the Church has now triumphed.'[45] The details here bear out the theory that the writer of the *Electio* had actually witnessed Stephen's reception of the prior's letter. (Admittedly, Master Nicholas could have reported the details to a different author, but there are too many similar instances for it to be likely.)

Back home, the sacrist made out that they were all in grave disfavour with the king. There was much fluttering, alarm and recrimination. Richard the precentor sounded everyone out, and found forty standing by Hugh, as well as the seven electors. The convent was divided down the middle. The 'faithful' rallied round Hugh in the prior's house, the sacrist's party shut themselves into the infirmary chapel, placing guards at the doors!

20 November was the Feast of St Edmund's 'Passion', his martyrdom. On the 19th the archbishop came to the abbey 'on account of his devotion to the saint, whom he venerated'.[46] On the 21st he came into the chapter-house, revived with the word of God the flock of the blessed martyr, exhorting them to persist in their original unanimity in the house of God, saying: 'Divided, we shall be ruled; united, we shall find ourselves insuperable.' He concluded: Whatever the character of the ruler of a city, such will be the character of the inhabitants.' Prior Herbert, and after him the chamberlain, pleaded with Stephen on behalf of the abbot-elect. The archbishop rejoiced in their unity, and promised to give their affairs as much time as his own. All this passed in the chapter-house, in the presence of earl Roger Bigot and

---

44 *Ibid.*, p. 25. In 1251, three years before he died, Hugh had a wonderfully detailed survey made of the Ely bishop's estates: the 'Old Coucher Book of Ely'. The idea goes back to Samson and Baldwin at Bury. Three copies exist (in B.L., C.U.L., and Gonville and Caius), but no edition. The degree of detail is new and extraordinary.

45 *Ibid.*, pp. 12–13.

46 *Ibid.*, pp. 20–21.

many clerks, laymen and monks from elsewhere. The archbishop moved on.

Impeccable advice, but there was no unity. It had already been destroyed by John's inevitable fury and by their fear of John, worked on by that 'controversial' sacrist.

This visit by archbishop Stephen on St Edmund's Day, 1213, 'out of devotion to the saint', has some bearing on the tradition that he and the rebellious barons met at Bury on 20 November the following year, on the pretext of pilgrimage to Edmund's shrine, to further their plans for the Great Charter of their liberties the following year. The furtiveness of the 1214 occasion naturally left it inadequately documented: the *Electio* makes no reference to it, though it has this full account of Stephen's 1213 pilgrimage.

The next grand visitor to the abbey was the cardinal legate, on 21 December.[47] Next day he preached in chapter-house before a great crowd, which he then asked to leave so that he could talk privately with the convent. The legate, naturally in favour of the election, went into it all very thoroughly. A day later Master Nicholas recapitulated the whole business 'ydiomate modum'.[48] He was followed by the precentor, who made an ass of himself and occasioned the suggestion that Nicholas had trained in Bologna. At the conclusion of this visit by the legate, the sacrist behaved like the most venomous snake-in-the-grass. According to the *Electio*, he now set about bribing courtiers with the kind of gifts they had all set their faces against on the very night Samson died. Alarmed by the news of the sacrist's work on John's entourage, Hugh, with archbishop Stephen's advice, sent Master Thomas of Walsingham and two other trusty members of the Walsingham family, to the papal curia in Rome, presenting the pope with all the facts of the case. It was late in January 1214. Because of 'imminent danger', the archbishop advised Hugh to leave Bury; and he sought safety overseas.[49] Sure enough, the king was enraged by the news of Master Thomas's visit to the pope, and (happily) vented it on the sacrist who had found some pretext to be at court: 'If the sacrist and his convent want me to restore them to my former favour, they had better begin by conducting their election according to the ancient, well-tried custom.'[50]

In the convent, the sacrist stirred up every kind of trouble. He also sent two villains, named the Mole and Hugh the Dog, after Thomas of Walsingham to the Roman curia, to see if they could discredit the Walsinghams.[51] His next scheme was to try to persuade the legate to side with the king against the election.[52] One begins to wonder if the sacrist was sane. These

---

47 *Ibid.*, p. 27.
48 Was he admitting that the people of Dunstable spoke differently from East Anglians? When Jocelin said Samson preached to the people in English, but in the Norfolk dialect, he used the expression '*linguam Norfolchie*', which one might perhaps translate as 'the lingo of Norfolk'. If Nicholas really had been trained in Bologna, it may be that he had acquired a Bolognese inflection, and that this is what he meant.
49 *Electio*, p. 53.
50 *Ibid.*, p. 39.
51 *Ibid.*, p. 48.
52 *Ibid.*, p. 61.

pages show the most appalling division, and seething unpleasantness, in the abbey.

On 18 May, one of the Walsinghams returned safely with letters from the pope setting up a commission of enquiry into the election — presided over by an abbot, a prior and a dean. On 4 June these 'justices' held their first sitting in the chapter-house. The king was represented by old William the Marshal, who appealed to the convent's sense of the benefits derived from the king and his predecessors. He ordered the supporters of the king's liberties to divide off from those consenting to the election as performed. Thirty brethren moved over to the left side of the chapter-house to signify their anxiety to support the king's liberties. This was the moment when Jocelin of Brakelond appeared in a rather undignified scene, from which he managed to emerge with courage and much credit.

'Suddenly, and with unseemly shouts in front of the barons and many other laymen present they dragged over to their side the reluctant Jocelin (of Brakelond) and John of Lavenham. Members of the rival factions were then, by order of the nobles, carefully listed. Jocelin and John of Lavenham rose in the middle of those present, and declared they stood and would always stand with the king and his liberties. But if it was a question whether the election had been properly canonical, there should be no doubt that it was; and they neither wished, nor would be made afraid, to cover up that fact.'[54]

This was the point at which the earl Roger Bigot spoke of his duty as St Edmund's hereditary standard-bearer.[55] The cellarer spoke rather dimly, failing to see that there is a difference between 'right of election' and right to a certain customary form of election, as practised at Samson's election in 1182. The court of enquiry was adjourned to St Albans, where it got more and more bogged down. On 5 August, 1214, the abbot-elect Hugh and Richard of Hingham set out to meet King John in Poitou.[56]

They found him unapproachable,[57] but later, the French legate calmed him down. He received Hugh, went so far as to describe him, in a letter to the prior and convent, as 'abbot-elect'. 'On our return to England, we will discuss it with you amicably.'

On 25 October, Hugh was back at Bury. On the 27th he met the king near London and got nowhere. He was back in Bury on 1 November and John followed on the 4th. In the chapter-house, the king began with a heavy, clipped sort of joke — the kind the late Field-Marshal Montgomery might have attempted. 'Although I have not formed the habit of visiting the chapter-houses of monks . . . I have made my pilgrimage here to St Edmund . . . and I felt I should visit you in your chapter-house. In the

53   *Ibid.*, pp. 84–85.
54   *Ibid.*, pp. 84–87.
55   See pp. 64 above.
56   *Electio*, p. 101.
57   *Ibid.*, p. 107.

matter of your election, which was not managed tactfully, I must ask you to proceed in accordance with my customary rights. If you do this, and abide by my advice, then — without dangerous delay — I will receive, as your pastor, whoever you choose, and admit him to my favour. But be warned of three dangers. 1.) These quarrels over the election threaten the poverty of your house. 2.) Your reputation will be destroyed. 3.) You will incur the hatred of your prince.'[58]

Hugh replied briefly, and very bravely, with overtones of Becket. 'I will cheerfully obey the Lord King's will in all things — *saving the law of the Church.*' The Lord King remembered that.

Then the king, assured that his presence would terrify the opposition into acquiescence, ordered the two parties to divide. 'But a marvellous and quite wonderful thing happened. The faithful party on the right outnumbered astonishingly the sacrist's party on the left. The sacrist's party was stunned. So was the king.' Long speeches followed. The king, still stunned and able to put up with this no more, left the chapter-house muttering threats.[59]

Next morning, Hugh offered to conduct the king out of town. The amazing sacrist appeared again, denouncing Hugh, accusing him of working 'to relieve you of your crown'. To this Hugh, 'of angelic disposition, pious, modest', quickly answered: 'All deceit and all lies devour horribly all lovers of such things.'

On 9 December, yet another meeting was held at Bury. The *Electio* breathed no word of baronial convention-pilgrimage on 20 November, but that is no guarantee that it was not held. The election enquiry went on, and on, with no less rancour. Richard Marsh, the revenue expert, represented the king. Master Nicholas stood up, as Samson once did against the Exchequer Barons, and placed the convent seal under the pope's protection. Ralph of London added: 'What's more, we who are sustained by the endowments of our patron Edmund, claim for him, as his sons and executors, the priceless ruby ring our sacrist gave you, Marsh!'[60] The dispute, unresolved, was re-convened at Reading in January and returned, like something in Dickens' Chancery Division, to Bury on Valentine's Day.[61] The author comes into his own. It could not be Jocelin. It has to be a lawyer!

The breakthrough came from the pope. Addressing his three churchmen-judges, he wrote on 26 January 1215,[62] 'Our dear son, Hugh, elected to rule the monastery of St Edmund, has made known to us that, after we had committed to you the examination of his election, you protracted the business unduly, with impediments placed by our venerable brother, Winchester, and with the quibbles and wrangles of the sacrist and some fellow monks, contradicting their own action and oath. From this, danger threatens the

58   *Ibid.*, pp. 118–119.
59   *Ibid.*, p. 127.
60   *Ibid.*, pp. 136–137.
61   *Ibid.*, p. 149.
62   *Ibid.*, p. 155.

monastery. We order you to bring the business to an end, or be accused of negligence and contempt.'

At last they crossed themselves and got down to a decision. As they pronounced sentence in the chapter-house in favour of confirming the election of Hugh, the sacrist, precentor and other opponents of the abbot-elect all rushed forward to give him the kiss of peace, and promised him canonical obedience from that day on.

Poor Hugh, thinking that might be that, had another shot at getting the king to receive him into his favour. With the prior, the cellarer, the precentor, Adam the infirmarer, Richard of Hingham and Master Nicholas — a considerable cavalcade — Hugh tracked down the king in Sherwood Forest. As the king drew near, they all dismounted and got down on their knees beseeching his favour. 'Wonderfully appeased', he helped Hugh up and said 'Welcome, lord abbot elect, saving the rights of my realm.' John had not forgotten Hugh's speech in Bury chapter-house: Hugh was having it thrown back at him. One can only marvel that they all continued to care about these rights!

No nearer a settlement, Hugh had to try again at the council at Oxford on 6 April, where again he was fobbed off. Returning home again on Good Friday with Master Thomas of Walsingham and Master Nicholas, he received a visit from the bishop of Evreux and then transacted some of the business we read so much about in Jocelin's *Chronicle*.[63]

> With the advice of the prior, sub-prior, sacrist, Jocelin the almoner, and Richard the precentor, the abbot-elect appointed John of Diss and Adam the (then) infirmarer managers of all the cellary manors, as well as Bradfield, Pakenham, Barton, Rougham, Herringswell, Horningsheath and (in Northamptonshire) Warkton. They were to take care of the external business on the cellarer's behalf, while Peter of Tivetshall and Robert of the hospital had care of the internal business, namely the provision of adequate funds for the monks' sustenance and hospitality. Peter the cellarer was set over the hospital,[64] Walter Gale over the infirmary and Roger fitzDrew over the buying of food for the guest-house. After these dispositions, he ordered Master Thomas of Walsingham and Philip to travel round with John of Diss and Adam, and record the number of ploughs and the amount of stock in each manor, and also which of our lands were sown or unsown.

This was an extraordinary act of trust and reconciliation. From the valuable lists Rodney Thomson has supplied of the members of the two factions of the previous two years, one sees that only three of Hugh's own supporters were included in these new appointments: Peter the cellarer, Roger fitzDrew (a former well-to-do layman) and Master Thomas of Walsingham.

Later that April, archbishop Stephen, who naturally used all his influence

63 *Ibid.*, p. 164—165.
64 This was St Saviour's hospital, founded by abbot Samson, just outside the former north gate and beside Bury's present railway-station.

to bring Hugh's business to its conclusion, sent for him to come at once as he still was neither blessed nor admitted to the king's favour. Because of the commotion between the barons and king, Stephen said Hugh should be blessed without delay. The bishop of Rochester blessed him at his palace near Rochester, where he celebrated solemn mass in sandals, mitre and ring. London was captured by the barons on 16 May, and Hugh went home to Bury, celebrating with a great feast for whoever wished to come.

The position between king and barons was so unsettled that Hugh sent his supporter, Richard of Saxham, to the barons to keep him informed. Archbishop Stephen said he should come at once and entreat the king's favour unceasingly. Meeting the king at Staines, Richard was told, pleasantly, 'Order your abbot-elect in my name to come to me without delay. For by God's grace I will do such a thing when he is here as will redound to the praise and honour of your house and the entire English church.' The abbot came to Windsor on 9 June. On the 10th in the famous meadow between Staines and Windsor, after much sending of messengers, the king at last admitted Hugh to favour.[65]

The king 'followed Hugh', and said he had one more demand to make on Hugh's good nature: 'Do not deprive us of your company at table, since the divine mercy has today restored you to my favour.' Hugh accepted, and they dined together at Windsor.

As they sat together afterwards, talking privately on the royal couch, there was an unbelievable interruption. The sacrist was suddenly there in front of them, throwing himself before the king on his knees and, with loathsome sycophancy and obtuseness, he said: 'Blessed is God, the Father of our Lord Jesus Christ, who has so visited the heart of our lord the king that not only does he admit the abbot to his grace, but he also wipes our former disagreement from the record.'

'As in a rage, the king replied: "By the Lord's feet, but for you I'd have received him into my favour and love six months ago!" Turning to the abbot, the king said: "O abbot, this sacrist has won you many enemies at my court." Then he went on to explain how, the previous August in Poitou, the French legate had almost persuaded him to take Hugh into favour, "but those round me, working against you on the sacrist's behalf, actually intensified my anger with you" '. He told Hugh quietly what the sacrist had found out and used against the abbot. The sacrist, watching them, reddened; unable to face the royal look any longer, he slunk away, without the king's leave.

The abbot did homage to the king the next day and hurried home, leaving the king to the barons. The process of the *Electio* was completed, though not before its author, the redoubtable Master Nicholas as we think, made reference to the abbot's kind bearing towards those of 'the household of faith' who had stood by the original election; and a wistful (I think)

65 *Electio*, p. 171.

reference to Hugh's studious promotion, 'to high office and dignity in our church, of others — not to say enemies, but if only one could say friends.' Curiously, as with Jocelin before him, one senses a touch of jealousy, or at least a feeling of being not quite adequately appreciated, in the very last lines of this remarkable chronicle.

How silent the abbey seems when the story of Hugh's election stops. Yet no silence fell for three more centuries. If we feel a sense of blankness and sudden deprivation it is because, after these two rather political clashes of rights, and of their respective human upholders, the life of Bury abbey went on, through testing times and slack, without ever again eliciting such spirited personal expression in its own chronicles.

EAST SUFFOLK: CLIFFTOPS, ESTUARIES AND CLAYLANDS

9

Southwold: St Edmund's Offshore Island

Southwold mans a cliff, a natural look-out twenty-five feet above the beach, bracing to the holiday-saunterer and invaluable to men on watch through the centuries for sprat and herring shoals, for sea-borne friends and enemies. Catching the first gleams as the sun lifts clear of the waves, the town holds the light of the great sky with the skill of some elaborate solar device. This is largely an effect of the ancient, very open lay-out, with the urban High Street running south-east towards the cliff and widening into, and forking off towards, a series of varied and very delightful village greens.

On the map, Southwold looks like one of those moated towns created for Louis XIV by Vauban. Although it had a grandstand view of one of the most shocking sea battles of the age — Sole Bay, in 1672 — its moat is partly creek, partly river. In fact, Southwold is an island. Only one road crosses to it, and that from the north. Approaching from the south, we first drive north over the Blyth at its lowest crossing, Blythburgh. There we soon see both the strategic importance of that early royal manor and — in the grandeur of its church — the late-medieval prosperity it shared with Southwold.

The early history helps to explain. Blythburgh's priory (now private ruins) was an Anglo-Saxon minster, the shrine of a good king and his son, St Jurmin, until, c. 1044–1065, Jurmin's bones went to Bury, qualified to lie alongside Edmund's and Botolph's. About the same time, the bishop of East Anglia gave Southwold to Bury; and Domesday Book, soon after, gave details. Southwold supplied Bury with herring from five-eighths of a sea weir; 20,000 fish in 1066, 25,000 in 1086. Whether the fishermen lived on the cliff or down by the river, the essentials of Southwold are there, the sketch for the picture today.

The hazards of tampering with their saint's endowment were effectively illustrated by one of the Bury writers, c. 1097. 'In the troubled year 1088,' he wrote, 'Robert de Curzun persuaded the sheriff to let him take possession of St Edmund's manor of Southwold. He was foiled by a truly frightening storm. Two followers, Turolf the Steward and a knight called de Mouneyn, pressed their attack on the manor despite the tempest; became frenzied, then permanently demented.' Miracles may still be asked of Southwold's weather, though seldom in connexion with such barefaced breaches of the peace.

Another entire century Southwold survived without chapel or chaplain. The unneighbourly Cluniac monks of Wangford possessed Reydon church and they profited greatly by seeing to it that Southwold's fishermen and farmers went to Reydon for marriage, baptism and burial, right down to 1430, when their present great church of St Edmund was begun. In 1206, the redoubtable abbot Samson of Bury established a chapel and chaplain for everyday worship. Then another Bury abbot secured for Southwold at least one of her two markets and fairs. Soon, Bury sensibly swapped Southwold for Mildenhall (more in Bury's orbit) with the earl of Clare, from whom it descended to the Duke of York and Edward IV. In York's day, the great church was built. After the battle of Bosworth (1485), Southwold was Henry VII's, who in 1505 made it a chartered corporation so as to be able to hold its own in disputes with Dunwich.

Dunwich lies three miles south, and mostly under the sea. Looking south now from Gun Hill across the present harbour mouth, and past a low cliff to the square hulk of Sizewell power-station, it is hard to believe that the low cliff once bore a town of eight parishes. In John's reign and all through the thirteenth century, Dunwich was the leading Suffolk port. In those days, the Blyth river came to Southwold from Blythburgh as the Alde comes to Aldeburgh from Snape, then turned south, exactly as the Alde does, met the little Dunwich river, and entered the sea on the north side of Dunwich — providing a superb natural harbour.

Superb it stayed for little more than a century. In January 1328, a storm more terrible than that of 1088 undermined much of Dunwich cliff, engulfed 400 houses. Even more grimly crippling, the sea choked that fair harbour with shingle, through which the river made a new mouth 'a large mile' towards Southwold. Four further shifts occurred, and the Blyth now meets the sea conveniently at 'Southwold Harbour', created in 1590. Steadily through those years, Southwold and Walberswick were attracting Dunwich's fisheries and her trade.

The spectacular declaration of Southwold's new fortunes is her church, dedicated loyally to Edmund. I wish we knew as much of its builders and its decorators as we do of Walberswick's. Here at Southwold the whole work seems to have been conceived and completed in one sustained effort, in one generation, that of 1430—1460, with the furnishings going on after 1460 and the south porch added twenty years later.

As in the town, so in its church: the abiding impression is of light. It is like the most elaborate architectural lantern, some huge Gothic lighthouse, which was exactly the intention. This impression is gained from outside as you stand to the north, looking *through* the building; but most over-whelmingly as you enter.

Apart from the glass, the outside decoration is done, with great restraint, by limiting the flushwork patterning to the buttresses (and to the porch and tower). This is masterly. Inside, the spell is composed of light and patches of colour, and length, and height. The uninterrupted roof-line, from tower-arch to east window, re-affirms that the building was conceived in one piece (as at Blythburgh, St Margaret's Lowestoft, and St Peter Mancroft above Norwich market). The roof would never have been attempted at that height without reliance upon the buttressing effect of the long aisles. Its height preserved the roof from the vexations of the Puritans who, unable to reach it, affected to ignore it and went for the stained glass: 'We brake down 130 superstitious pictures' &c. The height of the altar above the congregation must also have infuriated the Puritans: the sedilia, the stone clergy-seats, beside it, show that it occupies its original position — elevated six full steps above the level of the nave.

By some means, hard to guess at, much of the rood-screen and its decoration survives, and is the church's chief treasure. Before the vaulted lofts and the roods themselves (two, side by side) were pulled down, they must have been a dazzling sight indeed. Wise visitors make time to look closely at the entrance into the chancel, with rich original paint, green, white, red and gold; and with delicate glittering gesso-work. The south aisle panels, the least gifted workmanship, display Prophets. The central group, the richest, shows the apostles marvellously, though their faces (Bartholomew, for instance) still express a faint Tennysonian melancholy from the time when George Richmond tried his hand at restoring them. The point about their quality is that they are effectively three-dimensional, so as to be identified and admired by the throng in the nave. The north aisle panels, the most enchanting, display the shimmering Orders of Angels, some depicted in the feathered costumes of the guild actors, others in the silks and furs of rich merchants: they are perhaps the work of Norwich painters. There are certain Flemish undertones. The community of the North Sea is epitomised in this skylit, heaven-lit, church, as in its town.

Not satisfied with Dunwich, the elements almost obliterated Southwold too. 'It was pitifully defaced with fire in 1596, upon a Friday.' Then in April 1659, within four hours, a terrible fire consumed 238 houses, ruined 300 families, wiped out town-hall and market-place and broke the old civic order. A century later there were only 140 houses: the town had been effectively halved. In those years of recovery, Dutch influences were strong — in the gables of the museum, the entire row of cottages along Church Street, in Old Bank House in High Street with its steep hipped roof and dark blue pantiles. Those influences permeate John Evelyn's comment on the loss of Lord Sandwich and the two young friends who chose to perish with him in his blazing ship in the thick of the Sole Bay battle: 'the folly of hazarding so brave a fleet, and losing so many good men for no provocation but that the Hollanders exceeded us in commerce and industry, and in all things but envy'.

Southwold built a new life for itself in the Victorian years. Its increase from a thousand in 1801 to two in 1851 and almost three in 1901 — its heyday — is reflected in good traditional building and houses with an emphasis on holiday enjoyment: 'the pick-nick adventures on the pebble beach' described by Dr Wake in his *Southwold* in 1839. His Tamarisk Villa, and South Green House, Acton Place, Centre Villa and The Lodge still give a delightful dignity to the green cliffs: so indeed does Centre Cliff, built for the accommodation of nine lodgers. Wilson Steer painted on the beach in the 1880s, Stanley Spencer in the 1930s.

The real Victorian life of the place, its tradespeople and its seafarers, is powerfully contained in *The Southwold Diary of James Maggs, 1818—1876,* edited by Alan Bottomley, (Suffolk Records Society, 2 vols., 1983—4). For that busy Victorian townsman, the perennial interest of St Edmund's great church seemed to be whether the Georgian pews should give way to the more open wooden benches. They did, in 1878, two years after Maggs stopped chronicling and a year after P. B. Cautley came to the vicarage: his grandson, Munro Cautley, became diocesan architect and compiled the standard work on *Suffolk Churches and their Treasures.*

10

Dunwich, and its Defences[1]

Henry James, bicycling in Suffolk with Edward Warren, was bemused by Dunwich in August 1897.[2] 'A month of the place is a real education to the patient, the inner vision', he wrote. It moved him to much incohérence. But like many reflective visitors in Dunwich, he saw that 'there is a presence in what is missing — there is history in there being so little'. He was well content with the sensation, with the presence of absence, with the incentive to brood.

After a while such sensaticns wear off, the spirit of prosaic and disinterested enquiry returns, one is resentful of the repeated assertions that Dunwich's church bells may be heard ringing out beneath the waves, that there lies a submarine city of no less than seventy churches, and so on. It was 'the common fame and report of a greate number of credable persons' as early as 1573 'that there hath been in the town of Donewiche, before any decay came to it, LXX pryshe churches, howses of religion, hospitalls, and chapelles, and other such lyke'. In our own day guide-book succeeds guide-book, and with the appearance of each the number of Dunwich parishes fluctuates more wildly than the wildest seas could warrant. As we stand on the edge of the crumbling cliff, with the sea below gnawing the last fragment of the last of the medieval churches, grey truth is fabulous enough to stir the frailest imagination.

Dunwich was called Dommoc by Bede early in the eighth century. The name is a Celtic one, its survival an indication that the place was still inhabited by Romano-British people when the East English settled on this stretch of coast. Roman roads still fan out from, or converge on, Dunwich. On the evidence of these roads it is now fairly generally accepted as a significant Roman port. The name, ironically in the light of its future, means deep water. To imagine this harbour, think of a north and west facing situation more like Harwich's or Burgh Castle's, with the present cliffs rising higher as they stretched out perhaps a mile farther into the sea; and the Dunwich river running from inland, as it still does along Blythburgh's southern boundary, becoming a deep estuary as it joined (presumably the Blyth and) the sea along the north side of the town.

1 I have left the first part of this piece uncluttered save by these first two footnotes and almost exactly as it appeared in the 1961 Aldeburgh Festival Programme Book.
2 Henry James' *English Hours* (1905) contains his essay on 'Old Suffolk' mis-dated 1879. He had originally written it for *Harper's Weekly*. An extremely comic account of his stay in Dunwich, with four female cousins and MacAlpine, his 'horrible young meek Scotch typewriter', forms Chapter 38, 'A question of speech', in Volume 2 of the Penguin edition of Leon Edel's brilliant biography, *The Life of Henry James*.

That was the position down to the disaster of 14 January 1328. That day a terrible storm raged, of the kind that as lately as 31 January 1953 caused the death of forty people down at Felixstowe. It seems to have coincided with one of those shifts of the land in relation to the sea that were occurring in the fourteenth century. It destroyed 400 houses at Dunwich and completely choked up the harbour with a great shingle bar, so that the river retreated northwards along the shore and broke out into the sea 'a large mile' away, not far from the present mouth of the Blyth, which — after further northward shifts — reached its present position in the later Middle Ages, leaving Walberswick as a peninsula, like Shotley.

The storm of 1328 marked the beginning of the city's decline. What was it in its greatness? It must have been rather a cultivated place in the golden days of the Sutton Hoo dynasty, the first half of the seventh century. St Felix first based the East Anglian see here, and founded a school on the model of Canterbury. The succession of the bishops of Dunwich comes to an end about the time of Edmund's death at the hands of the Danes in the ninth century. Suckling, in his history of Suffolk (1847), reproduced the last bishop's seal — a notable antiquity, then in private hands, now, by extraordinary good luck, in the British Museum. It was dug up in a garden about 200 yards from the site of the monastery at Eye, and thrown into the fire by a child. It appears to be of bronze, mitre-shaped, of two rows of arches, surmounted by a rude fleur-de-lis, and supported by nine wolves' heads in the interstices of the arches; the eyes formed of small garnets, of which only one remains since its being recovered from the fire. (See Plate 7).

Domesday Book reveals Dunwich as a borough, not very flourishing twenty years earlier at the time of the Conquest, and with only one church, presumably St Felix's minster, restored, dedication unknown. But by 1086 two churches had been added and the population had increased to perhaps 3,000, though it is clear from the record that already the sea was devouring valuable plough-land. About this time Robert Malet, the real founder of Eye, founded Eye priory and bestowed on it 'all the churches that then existed or might subsequently be built in Dunwich, the tithes of that town, and a three-day fair on the feast of St Lawrence, and also the schools of Dunwich.' This is surely how the last bishop's seal came to be at Eye. Unluckily for our knowledge of Dunwich's wealth in its heyday as revealed through the revenues of Eye priory, the monastic officials of that house seem to have numbered tax-evasion among their accomplishments.

In Henry II's reign, Dunwich was clearly a rich, moated and perhaps inadequately palisaded town. In the course of the twelfth century, the three churches increased to eight, apart from the Templars' church of St Mary: these were the churches of St Leonard, St John the Baptist, St Martin, St Nicholas, St Peter, St Michael, St Bartholomew and All Saints. St Leonard's, the first to be eroded, c. 1300, was not necessarily the oldest. St Peter's or St Martin's or St Michael's are more likely to have been East

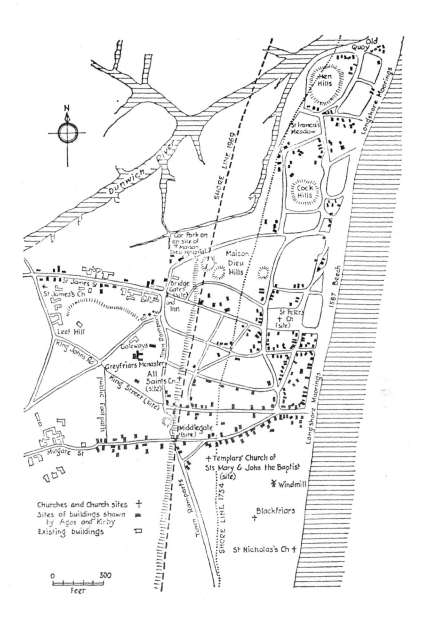

Old Quay

Hen Hills

Longshore Moorings

St Francis's Meadow

Cock Hills

DUNWICH River

SHORE LINE 1969

Car Park on site of Maison Dieu Hospital

Maison Dieu Hills

1587 Beach

St James St

St James's Ch

Lect Hill

King Johns Rd

Bridge Gates (site) and Inn

St Peter's Ch (site)

Gateways

Greyfriars Monastery

All Saints Ch (site)

King Street (site)

public Footpath

Middlegate (site)

Longshore Moorings

Midgate St

Templars' Church of Sts. Mary & John the Baptist (site)

Churches and Church sites +
Sites of buildings shown by Agas and Kirby
Existing buildings

Town Ramparts

Town Ramparts

SHORE LINE 1754

Windmill

Blackfriars +

St Nicholas's Ch +

0   500
Feet

Anglia's mother-church. As we stand today on that desolate cliff, we might imagine ahead of us, in the twelfth and thirteenth centuries, a town very nearly the size of medieval Ipswich.

In the time of king John, five galleys were stationed at Dunwich, five at London and two at Ipswich. Like Ipswich, Dunwich acquired a Charter from John in 1200. In 1216 he confirmed and supplemented it. In 1229 the Bailiffs were required to send forty ships, armed and manned, to Portsmouth for Henry III's passage across the sea. By 1232 the port was showing its fatal inclination to move northwards. In 1279 the Dunwich men 'took farm' of the town from Edward I, and owned eighty 'great ships'. That seems to have been the city's climax of prosperity.

St Leonard's went under c. 1300. St Bartholomew's and St Michael's c. 1331. The last institution to St Martin's was made in 1335, and to St Nicholas' in 1352. An Elizabethan writer revealed that at least the outlines of the fabric of St Nicholas' church were still remembered in his day.

In the first half of the fifteenth century there was a remarkable builder in Dunwich — Richard Russell, who seems also to have been one of the town's two M.P.s in 1427. How good he was! He collaborated with a Blythburgh man on the steeple at Walberswick, and probably on that of Kessingland as well. (Steeple was the word for church-tower in fifteenth-century Suffolk.) Whether any of his buildings helped to repair the ravages of the fourteenth century in his own town we cannot know. John Hopton, lord of Blythburgh 1430 – 78, lies beneath his Purbeck marble tomb in the magnificent church constructed at Blythburgh in his day: his widow lies at Yoxford (see p. 152). He was in constant feud with the Dunwich men over their claims to control the river that led to his quay. One day they broke up the quay and destroyed his mussel-beds.

Dunwich became one of the leading ports in the Iceland fishery in Henry VIII's reign, but that activity was a further subject of dispute. And the sea pushed forward relentlessly, demanding yet more parishes. At the time of the Dissolution of the monasteries, Leland wrote of the men of Dunwich desiring succour against the rages of the sea. John Daye, the great printer of the English Reformation, was born in St Peter's parish in 1552. Its turn came a century later. Meanwhile the Elizabethans fixed their eyes on the past of Dunwich and produced the first historical surveys. Not only were they looking back intelligently for the first time, but they provide us with our first substantial picture of the town as it stood in 1573, in 1589, and with other glimpses from that age of quickening discovery.

The first of these descriptions was written anonymously in 1573, and addressed to Master Deye. Suckling thought it might have been the work of Stow addressed to Daye the printer. But Stow describes the place only sketchily in his *Chronicle*: 'tottering fragments of noble structures, remains of the dead exposed, and naked wells, divested of the ground about them by the waves of the sea'. The writer in 1573 had known the place over a period, and was almost certainly from the district. And Master Deye is surely one of the Deyes of Eye, who lived there at Moor Hall and Stairhouse. In 1636 a collection of the records of Eye priory was in the hands of 'Thomas Deye of Eye'. The description of Dunwich in 1573 was presumably addressed to his forebear.

1570 had been a disastrous year. The Gilden Gate and the South Gate were swallowed. St John the Baptist's church had been dismantled in 1540, obviously to anticipate the sea: 'I thynke yowe doo remember', says the author of this manuscript to Deye, 'the maner, fourme and faysshen of tbe Byldinge and makynge of Seynt Johns cherche and Seynt Nicholles cherche, how they ware crose Eilled [i.e. had transepts] bothe northe and southe, and the steples in the myde lyke cathedrall churches.' St Nicholas' was the richest parish, but the mariners' saint was not to be propitiated: only six acres of that parish were left in 1573.

In 1643, St Peter's church, still unvisited by the sea, was visited by Dowsing the iconoclast: it was a church 'near as long as Blyburgh', and 'curiously glazed with painted glass quite through'. It was taken down in 1702, before Kirby described the mean cottages and mean weekly market there (*The Suffolk Traveller*, 1735). Thomas Gardner's *Historical Account of Dunwich, Blithburgh and Southwold* appeared in 1754, one of the most useful as well as delightful pieces of local history performed in Suffolk. He described at first hand the calamitous storm of 1740, as well as the evidences of the medieval religious houses: the cell of Eye priory that vanished in the time of Edward I, the fine vaulted church of the Knights Templars, the priories of Blackfriars and Greyfriars, the hospitals of Holy Trinity (or Maison Dieu) and St James.

What Henry James called 'the immense cincture' of the priory of Greyfriars is not the only survivor from Dunwich in its thirteenth-century greatness. The Leat Hill survives, and lines of old suburban streets running towards the town that isn't there: Midgate Street, King Street, St James's Street. Impressive remains of the apsidal chapel of St James's leper hospital, with its Norman arcade and south window and admixture of septaria, date at least from Richard I's reign. It stood, on account of its frightful function, on the outskirts of the town. Beside it now stands the last fragment of the tower of All Saints' parish church, taken down stone by stone from its perch on the brink of the cliff and removed here at the instance of the Suffolk Institute of Archaeology in 1923. The fifteenth-century memorial brass of Thomas Cooper, Bailiff of Dunwich, was also saved from All Saints': it rashly claims that he 'enclosed is in clay'. The brass is now in the plain little church of St James, erected 1827–32, beside the chapel of the leper hospital. Michael Barne, who contributed largely to the building of this church, has a memorial by William Behnes. It describes his military service in the French Revolutionary war and his political service 1812–30 — Member of Parliament for this decayed and submarine borough. Another

Barne is commemorated, who restored this church, added tower and chancel, improved the dwellings of the poor and was the last Member for the borough.

Dunwich returned two Members of Parliament from 1296 to 1832, when it was disfranchised. Its corporation was abolished in 1886, and its affairs are in the hands of a Trust. Its admirable new museum contains a copy of that bishop's seal, a list of MPs, a mace of Henry VIII's time, a sergeant-of-the-mace's badge, and minute-books of the corporation from the time of Queen Elizabeth. There are hospital accounts of the 1630s and an oath-book of Queen Anne's time. A full photographic record of 'the passing of All Saints' ' is curiously touching. It recalls the visits of Henry James, of Edward FitzGerald, of his friend Charles Keene the artist, and of Algernon Swinburne, who stayed here with Watts-Dunton.

A recent essayist-visitor to Dunwich, the late Geoffrey Grigson, in his *English Excursions*, noticed the last legible inscription among the gravestones surviving in All Saints' churchyard upon the cliff. It is sacred to the memory of John Brinkley Easey, who died on 2 September 1826, aged twenty-three years. In name he represents countless local families of Brinkleys and Easeys, and he must stand for all the lost thousands of Dunwich families whose bones over the centuries have been irresistibly drawn into that last, unfathomable and inviolable cemetery, the sea.

A small excavation in 1970 by the County Archaeologist found three small pieces of Roman pottery in the town ditch. The main Romano-British site must be presumed well out to sea, which has advanced a quarter of a mile in the past four centuries. The section of the western fragment of town rampart proved to be of the early 13th century. Was this perhaps a solid replacement of a more makeshift palisade, erected in response to Leicester's threat in 1173 which I examined in the following note?

*   *   *   *   *   *   *

A Note on the Historical Records of Dunwich's Defences

The most circumstantial early descriptions of the town are Elizabethan. One, very brief, is a report by a well-known land-surveyor, Ralph Agas, and is mainly concerned with a recommendation about stabilising the town's haven, or river-mouth, at that time opposite Walberswick. Gardner printed it, from a manuscript in his possession, in his *History of Dunwich*,[3] together with a detailed map of the town to which the report relates. The

3   T. Gardner, *An Historical Account of Dunwich*, 1754, pp. 20–22. For Agas' career, see Diarmaid MacCullough, 'Radulph Agas: Virtue Unrewarded', *Proceedings, Suffolk Institute of Archaeology*, XXXIII, 1976, pp. 275–284, and DNB.

map he dated 1587,[4] the report 1589. It says the town is on a 'Cliffe fortie Foot hie . . . and is girte on the Weaste and South, near to the Bodie of the Toune, with an Auntient Bancke, whereof Parte is now builte with the Wall of the Graieffriers . . .'

The other Elizabethan description, very long and interesting, is among the Harleian MSS in the British Museum[5] and was printed, with minor misreadings, in Suckling's *History of Suffolk*.[6] Its anonymous author addressed it in 1573 to 'Master Deye'. Suckling thought it was the work of John Stow, the London chronicler and antiquary, addressed to Daye the printer, who was a native of Dunwich. 'Master Deye' is surely one of the Deyes of Eye. In 1636 a collection of the records of Eye priory (with large holdings in Dunwich) was in the hands of 'Thomas Deye in Eye'.[7] The 1573 author had known the place over a period, was almost certainly from the district, and includes a great deal of technical surveying information.[8] He begins by estimating the extent of the suburbs 'without the Palles Deike'. The town dyke was certainly called the Pales Dyke in 1573, which is at least presumptive evidence of an earlier palisade. On Dunwich's length from north to south, he refers to 'one end of the said town by Hithe upon the aforesaid Palles Dike towards the south'. And on Dunwich's breadth, he refers to 'the place called the mydle gattes' and also to 'the bredge gates coming from Seynt James street'. After enumerating six churches (there were certainly at least eight) and the friaries, Temple, and so on, he returns to the question of fortifications:

> Also ye know veri well the greate deike that is called the Palles Deike, and the gate spaces going throughe and over the same deike, from and oute of the subbarbes in to the said town, viz. the Bridge Gates, or Seint James's Strete Gates — the mydle Gates, the Gyldynge Gates, and the south Gates, the which gate spaces are now so called, and yet doth still there remain, and all the rest of the gates are now drowned in the sea, all the which aforesaid gate spaces there is a number of old auntient dedes and dyvers evidence to prove the same, and that doth soo name and call them as aforesaid.

This passage assumes a mutual knowledge of the sites not only of the Bridge

4 The late Col. Michael Barne of Sotterly Hall kindly lent me the MS. History of Dunwich compiled and illustrated for his family by Hamlet Watling in 1893—4. A map on pp. 24—5 is a reconstruction by Watling, in an old-fashioned Regency Gothick manner, that includes most of the town buildings recorded from earliest times, all extended from Agas' record of the Elizabethan town. By implying that it was based on a 'plat mentioned by Agas' he has misled readers into thinking that there was an original map earlier than Agas'. Watling was not averse to that kind of ambiguity. His harmless object was to produce a pleasing book. Unfortunately his reconstruction was published by H. E. P. Spencer, *Proceedings, S.I.A.*, XXII, 1935, pp. 198—200, with the equally ambiguous caption, 'From a tracing of an old map of Dunwich by Hamlet Watling, date unknown, but probably about 1300'.

5 Harl. MS. 532, fols. 53v—60.

6 II (1847), pp. 244—252.

7 Harl. MS. 639, fol. 68.

8 D. MacCullough (see note 3) suggests that, whoever he was, he was an old man in 1573, from his early-Tudor hand: neither Agas nor Stow.

gates (safe, 1985) and Middle gates (eroded in the 1960s), but also the Gilden and South gates which apparently disappeared before that century was out.[9] From the gate-sites, and from the name 'pales dike', the author made reasonable conjectures about 'a myghtie strong and long pale' in the west, and an even stronger one in the east, where 'all the chefe danger of the enemies was to be feared . . . or with some other such strong defence of walles, towers and castelles'. These conjectures supply at least negative evidence. No actual remains of pales, gates, or castle were known in 1573. This is not surprising, for three-quarters of a mile of the town may already have been drowned.

There is some very early support for these conjectures. It is provided by Jordan Fantosme and William of Newburgh, two remarkable contemporaries who were chronicling the rebellion in 1173−4 against Henry II. While Henry was abroad and his justiciar, Richard de Lucy, fighting the Scots' king, the earl of Leicester landed at Walton (the Bigod castle within the Roman fort of Felixstowe). Fantosme, a former official of the diocese of Winchester, wrote his account of the whole episode in metre, in Norman French.[10] He was present when De Lucy captured the Scots' king at Alnwick, but there is no independent evidence that he was present when De Lucy smashed Leicester's force of Flemings at Fornham St Genevieve, near Bury St Edmunds.

Fantosme described De Lucy's dismay at hearing of Leicester's arrival and of his concentration of strength between Orwell and Dunwich (lines 820−2). Hugh Bigot tried to persuade the people of Dunwich that Leicester was their friend, and that their heads would roll if they would not take his side (lines 843−6). They defied him and prepared for a siege. That day you could see burgesses like valiant knights sallying out to their defences, each knowing his job, some bowmen, others lancers, the strong helping the weak to have spells of rest. Inside the town there wasn't a girl or a woman who didn't carry stones for hurling from the palisade: 'Ki ne portast la piere al paliz pur gete' (lines 871−6). The earl of Leicester retired humiliated.[11]

Fantosme added (lines 1,000 et seq.) that the Flemings came for wool. Most were weavers and didn't know how to carry arms. 'They came for loot, for there is no better-provisioned place on earth than Bury St Edmunds.' If this assessment of the rebels detracts a little from the formidable effectiveness of the defences of Dunwich, it also suggests that Fantosme had personal knowledge of the places in his narrative.

9   Gardner, op. cit., p. 94.
10 Richard Howlett, ed., Chronicles of the Reigns of Stephen, Henry II and Richard I, Rolls Series, III (1886), and R. C. Johnston's admirable edn. of Jordan Fantosme's Chronicle, 1981. Fantosme's name implies that he was uncommonly thin, not that he lacked reality: alternatively, as a joke, that he was very fat (Johnston, p. xiii).
11 Gardner, op. cit., p. 7, recorded the tradition that the earthworks then visible 'on Westleton Heath, not two miles from Dunwich, were remains of the Barons' Fortifications when they besieged the town'.

William of Newburgh refers very briefly, in his prosaic but reliable way, to Dunwich's successful defiance of the rebels.[12] Confirming the event, he indirectly supports Fantosme's more circumstantial account, with its reference to the 'paliz'.

In John's reign, there is plenty of reference to Dunwich's importance and prosperity, none that I can find to its defences. They had need of them in 1216, when the baronial rebels under Prince Louis extorted ransoms from Yarmouth, Dunwich and Ipswich.[13]

For 13 May 1222 the Patent Rolls contain a grant of Murage for Dunwich, as the sea had flooded the town and there was need to build a barrier against it more quickly, 'cicius'.[14] Miss Hilary L. Turner tells me that because of this clear reference to the *sea* walls, she has dismissed the 'walls' of Dunwich 'somewhat lightheartedly' in her book on the fortified towns of medieval England.[15] Yet in the same Calendar of the Patent Rolls, under 1217, one sees a reference to Eustace de Vescy's custody of 'the castle and town of Dunwich'. It does not sound like an *unfortified* town; it might, I suppose, be that a small Norman castle stood within the walls of a Roman fort, as at Burgh Castle and Walton (Felixstowe).

The Close Rolls for 1253 refer to a building up against the South gate at Dunwich,[16] confirming the Elizabethan memory on that point. Finally, there is the licence in Mortmain, 25 August 1290,[17] quoted by Gardner, in which the Greyfriars of Dunwich were granted the King's Dike of Dunwich adjoining a plot (*'placee'*) given to them by the commonalty of the said town to build upon and inhabit; also licence for them to inclose the same. In 1290 then, the town's west rampart had occupied its present site long enough to be thought dispensable. Less than forty years later, in January 1328, the sea made its most devastating advance.

By destroying the town, the sea destroyed its corporation's need to preserve intact its official documents. Even in Ipswich, where the sea exerted no such dominion, it is hard to provide documents for a history of the town ramparts. At Dunwich, we must manage with these scraps, and look the more carefully at the evidence of the spade.

12 Howlett, *op. cit.*, I (1884), p. 178.
13 See above, p. 60.
14 *Cal. Pat. Rolls, 1216−25*, p. 333.
15 Hilary L. Turner, *Town Defences in England and Wales*, 1970.
16 *Cal. Close Rolls, 1251−3*, pp. 311−2.
17 *Cal. Pat. Rolls, 1281−92*, p. 383.

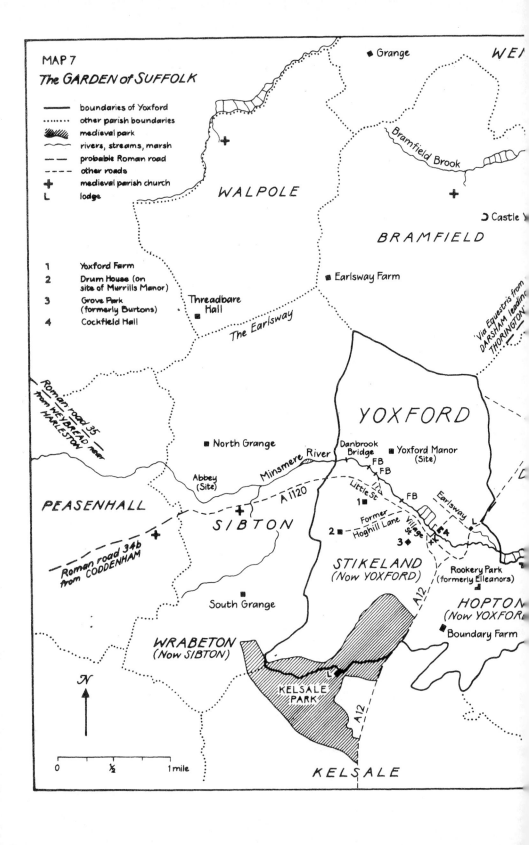

MAP 7

The GARDEN of SUFFOLK

— boundaries of Yoxford
⋯⋯ other parish boundaries
▨ medieval park
∿ rivers, streams, marsh
— — probable Roman road
– – – other roads
✛ medieval parish church
L lodge

1   Yoxford Farm
2   Drum House (on site of Murrills Manor)
3   Grove Park (formerly Burtons)
4   Cockfield Hall

• Grange

WE[...]

Bramfield Brook

WALPOLE

BRAMFIELD

⊃ Castle [...]

■ Earlsway Farm

Via Equestris from DARSHAM leading to THORINGTON

■ Threadbare Hall

The Earlsway

Roman road 35 from WEYBREAD near MARLESTON

■ North Grange

Minsmere River

Danbrook Bridge

■ Yoxford Manor (Site)

YOXFORD

FB
FB

Abbey (Site)

A1120

Little St.

FB

1■

Earlsway

L

PEASENHALL

SIBTON

Roman road 34b from CODDENHAM

2■

Former Hoghill Lane

Village St.

3◆

4■

L

STIKELAND (Now YOXFORD)

Rookery Park (formerly Elleanors)

■ South Grange

A12

HOPTON (Now YOXFOR[...])

■ Boundary Farm

WRABETON (Now SIBTON)

KELSALE PARK

L

N ↑

A12

KELSALE

0   ½   1 mile

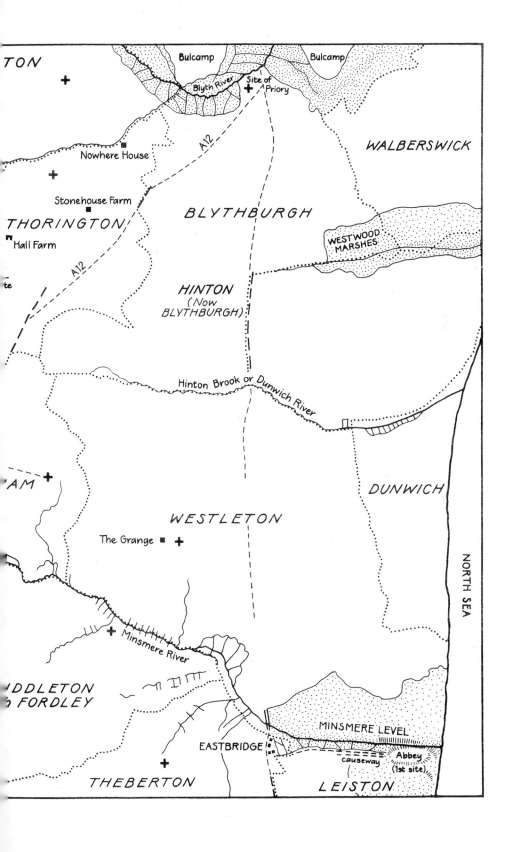

11

The Planting of 'The Garden of Suffolk': Yoxford's Origins

William White's first *Directory of Suffolk*, in 1844, declared Yoxford was 'a large and remarkably neat and pleasant village, seated in a fertile vale, sometimes called "The Garden of Suffolk" '. The appellation has become attached more to the village than the vale, and still seems appropriate. If there are rivals for the title — Earl Soham, perhaps, or Chelsworth, Denston or Stoke-by-Clare — they have never laid claim to it. The quality contributed by the vale itself may be judged by the fact that in Sibton, the next parish upstream from Yoxford, an abbey was established in 1150 by the Cistercians, as a grand-daughter of their great abbey of Rievaulx and a sister to the irresistible Tilty in Essex.

The very noticeable connexion between Cistercian monasteries and beautiful landscape sprang from St Bernard's austere renunciation of the kinds of disturbing beauty the Benedictines were up against from so often being established in or near towns and cities: the monks of Bernard's Order settled in remote valleys, practised vegetarianism (with a little occasional fish) and became very skilful farmers. Though their abbey at Sibton has been in ruins since the time of Henry VIII, their rural idyll still pervades the neighbourhood, where several of their farms survive both in name and as going concerns. In Sibton itself, Northgrange Farm and South Grange lie on opposite side of the valley. Northgrange is approached up its medieval drift-way. Its records (a selection has been published by the Suffolk Records Society)[1] include those of the dairy under Katerine Dowe in 1508−9. A few years earlier, in the late 15th century, Suffolk cows, 'Countryware', were being crossed here with a 'Northernsteer', perhaps from one of the Rievaulx farms in the Yorkshire Dales: the object was to improve the yield of a less creamy milk in the interest of Suffolk's serviceable, winter-keeping (and notoriously disagreeable) cheese.[2] Their other local granges, all with us still, included Cookley Grange, Wenhaston Grange, Abbey Farm at Linstead Parva, Rendham Grange and probably Rendham Barnes, and Westleton Grange. It seems reasonable to imagine that during much of the Middle Ages these served as model farms — in a district celebrated for model farms in Arthur Young's day, and more recently.

1   A. H. Denney, (ed.), *The Sibton Abbey Estates, 1325−1509*, Suffolk Records Society, Vol. II, 1960. The Society's Charter Series has now (1985) published Part I of Philippa Brown's edition of the Sibton Abbey Cartularies and Charters. Rendham Barnes represents the Barneys manor purchased by the abbey before 1325 (Denney, p. 61).
2   *Op. cit.,* pp. 37−38.

So this was a fertile vale all right, in the Middle Ages as when White described it in 1844. Its stream is generally called the Minsmere river after the place — now a famous Nature Reserve and Bird Sanctuary — where it flowed into the sea. Suffolk rivers often take their names from their places of origin, so that each tributary is easily and immediately identifiable. This stream, flowing from the site of the medieval Badingham Hall, through Sibton and Yoxford, has no very significant tributaries, so took its name from the large mere at its mouth. Here, on an island in the mere, connected by a causeway to the 'mainland' of Leiston at East Bridge, Leiston abbey was founded in the early 1180s by the Justiciar, Rannulf Glanville, for Premonstratensian canons. (Plate 24 and map 7.) The founding canons came from Welbeck Abbey in Nottinghamshire and their abbey at Durfold in Rogate on the Hampshire edge of Sussex. Laying the site out took over two months.[3] By the 1340s, the aggressive sea-surges that had in 1328 wrecked Dunwich, immediately north of Minsmere, were making life intolerable for the Premonstratensian canons. They moved inland, to the site of the present noble ruins, which date from the 1360s and 1380s. They left a small chapel at Minsmere. Its walls retain masonry that looks about a century earlier than 1182. Here, as, for instance, at Blythburgh, and Butley, Rumburgh and Mendham, there are reasons for thinking the Norman grandees, whose 'Foundation Charters' survived, may have been building on existing smaller institutions, beneath their notice in these impressive documents, registering their lavish contributions to the glory of God, and the King, and to the advantage in heaven of their own souls and those of their wives.[4]

In 1810, an Act of Parliament was obtained for draining Minsmere. The job was accomplished in the years 1846—1850, by Messrs Garrett and Son of Leiston Iron Works, and the resulting fine marshlands are known as the Minsmere Level. The straight line of the New Cut may be seen in the air photograph, Pl. 24, running close to the corner of the sea-defence earthwork bastions dug by the desperate medieval canons. The importance of river-drainage and meadow-making over the years since the Middle Ages is apparent as soon as we start to look at the making of Yoxford.

Yoxford takes its name from a ford across the river — probably a ford wide enough to be passable by 'a yoke of oxen abreast' (Ekwall). Where was this eponymous ford? Its location may tell us something of the structure of the place. Was it where the A12, the old main road from London to Yarmouth, crosses the river at the east end of the village street and just north of

3 *Leiston Abbey Cartulary and Butley Priory Charters*, Richard Mortimer (ed). Suffolk Records Society, 1979, 2.
4 Editing *Leiston Abbey Cartulary* for the Suffolk Records Society in 1979, Richard Mortimer thought the chapel could 'hardly be the remains of the first monastery' (p. 4). He had not seen the aerial photograph BYZ 29 taken by Dr J. K. St Joseph on 3 July 1976, when the monastery's layout around the chapel was revealed in Richard Rope's cereal crop, ripe after a period of drought.

the church, near the rustic Darsham Road gate-lodge entrance to Cockfield Hall, the entrance to that Hall from the A12 and the east? Or was it somewhere near the west end of the village street?

A village street is by no means a common feature of Suffolk's 500 parishes: so many scattered parishes seem to have managed through the centuries without one. Yoxford's is the central feature of the whole parish: broad, lined with a delightful variety of houses, cottages, and small business-premises, and terminated gracefully at the east end by the medieval church of St Peter, with its tall leaded spire. The variety is partly a reflection of the different ages of the buildings. There is perhaps a general feel of the first half of the 19th century, but some of the shapes and plaster-coats look 17th-century, and one or two earlier still. The most casual visitor sees that this is an ancient street, perhaps ready-made for the village. Indeed, it may occupy the line of a Roman road.

Yoxford's street-framework is unusually simple. The village street is part of a 'main' road, the A1120, running across from Stowmarket in the south-west to join the A12 'trunk' road, running north from Ipswich to Lowestoft. These are virtually the only roads of any importance in the village. Yoxford through the first half of the present century congratulated itself that its village street was on the quiet A1120 and not on the trunk road. The recent large increase in cross-country lorry traffic has diminished the village's quiet and its safety, but it remains less pulverised than any part of A12. If Sizewell 'B' Power Station is authorised in 1986, the contractors will greatly increase the volume of heavy traffic along the A1120 and all through 'the Garden of Suffolk'.

Much of the A1120 occupies straight stretches of Roman road: Margary's 34b,[5] which he shows running from the junction of five Roman trunk roads at Coddenham, through to Peasenhall. In Peasenhall, 'it runs in rather a deep hollow: here it meets another road coming from the north-west, and it is evident that both were intended to serve some settlement near, or a little to the east of, this point, perhaps near Yoxford'. (Cf. map 7.) Margary thought that the 3rd-century Antonine Itinerary *Iter IX*, starting out from *Venta Icenorum*, Caistor-by-Norwich, went through this Peasenhall junction, along his road 35, on its way to *Sitomagus* before cutting back westward to Coddenham.[6] If *Sitomagus* was, as professional archaeologists begin to think, in the heathland of Knodishall, between Kelsale and Aldeburgh, the *Iter IX* at Peasenhall would have gone straight for it, heading directly south-west for *Sitomagus*, then changing direction for Coddenham via Stratford St Andrew and Wickham Market. The question concerning Yoxford is, did Margary's 34b, from the south-west, run straight across the *Iter IX* route at Peasenhall, fording the Minsmere river at, say, the Sibton abbey site, and going on towards Blythburgh with a fork to

5   I. D. Margary, *Roman Roads in Britain, I, South*, 1955, 234—235.
6   *Op. cit.*, 242—244.

Dunwich; or did it follow the line of the A1120 round inside the curve of the river-valley from Peasenhall, through Yoxford village street to meet the ancient 'A12', and ford the river with it? There is, at present, no evidence for its continuing north-eastward, straight through the Sibton abbey site. There is no doubt at all that the A12 river-crossing was a major ford: here, presumably, was the eponymous *Yox-ford*.

Since I began to think of the origins of Yoxford, I have noticed that much of the A12 in this northern part of Suffolk has all the signs of being Roman, though Margary did not venture to include it in his standard survey. I had been content to assume that the A12 was the immemorial, prehistoric route skirting the dense clay forest edge where, in the lighter lands, a general north-south track — a sort of eastern version of the Icknield Way — would be easier to make. Looking at it now, immediately north and south of Yoxford, I see it has much straighter continuous lengths than appear to the south of Wickham Market, and that these look like Roman improvements. At two points, Yoxford's own boundary makes a significant turn in order to run, briefly, along a straight stretch of this road: in the south, bordering Kelsale, and just north of the river on the bounds of Darsham. So the road was already there when the boundary was made, in the Middle Ages. More significant still, about 1100 yards further north, the road from Halesworth tees into the A12 at right-angles, with parish boundaries on both sides of the right-angle. (These 1100 yards of straight road flank what looks, at first glance, like a Romano-British farm landscape in Darsham, immediately west of the A12: it would be worth closer examination.) At this stage in my scrutiny of the indispensable (but discontinued!) 1:25,000 Ordnance Survey sheets, I consulted the County Archaeological Unit at Bury. There the whole matter was clinched by a recent air photograph. 800 yards north of the turn-off from the A12 to Halesworth, the straight stretch of A12 suddenly veers from its NNE direction, and heads NE for Blythburgh. The air-photograph clearly shows a line of straight road *continuing due NNE* from that 22½° change in direction (see map 7 and OS map reference TM47-419721). At this point we are at a former fork in the Roman road, the vanished line of which continued straight across Thorington Park, as if making for Stonehouse Farm, Thorington, and Nowhere House on the Blythburgh-Wenhaston boundary (433746). There it met a road plunging through steep banks and labelled, in 1594, 'from Dunwich to Halesworth', i.e. to Stone Street (Map 4).[7] We are in danger of being enticed into the large subject of Romano-British Thorington and Wenhaston, and must return from the Blyth to the Minsmere river, and its ford at Yoxford.

The A12 swerves nowadays into a rather alarming double-bend just south of the little bridge over the Minsmere stream: car-drivers and passengers are usually so diverted by the bend that they have no impression of the bridge. It is certain that the Roman road would have indulged in no

7 'A plat of the Manner of Hynton in the parishe of Bliburgh, 1594': S.R.O.: HA30: 378/1.

such double-bend, but probably followed the line from the north straight across the river and along, roughly, the west edge of Rookery Park. The other great difference was the condition of the river. In Roman and medieval times, it was more formidable: in bad weather a broad and difficult crossing. The width of the flood-plain before such improvements as the drainage of the Minsmere Level in the 1840s can be seen easily by walking in the valley at the west end of the village; below the modern cemetery, for instance, where the edges of the flood-plain are still marked by (very miniature) cliffs moulded as the river swirled round and past. It is even more marked at the east end of the parish, as in the meadows below Beveriche Manor Farm. Perhaps the most telling modern demonstration, however, comes from Cockfield Hall.

Cockfield Hall is now Yoxford's great house: the principal manor-house and in many ways one of the most interesting houses in Suffolk. For the moment we are concerned with its situation, which is almost inconveniently low-lying. It stands immediately north of the river, and scarcely above its flood-level. Two arms of its medieval moats remain, the rest being filled in during 17th-century, and later, improvements to the house. The moat-filling may not have been such an improvement: dug deep, they keep the level of the damp down from the house-walls, as farmers all over clay-land in Suffolk still know. At any rate, the lawns near the house are sometimes too spongy, and the water stands too level with the top of the banks of the moat for the taste of Mr Roderick and Lady Caroline Blois, whose hospitable home this is. There is no question of maintaining an underground cellar. R. T. L. Parr, who devoted much of the time between 1907 and 1947 to writing the history of Yoxford in eight large typescript volumes,[8] recorded that the original Cockfield Hall, of the 16th and 17th centuries, was supported on wooden piles, like the city of Amsterdam. 'Entire trees' were found to have been used when the middle came to be rebuilt by Sir Ralph Blois at the end of the 19th century. 'Cylinders set in cement' were substituted for those great waterlogged oaks.[9]

This brings us to the manorial history of Yoxford, which contains many surprises. We have so far established that Yoxford's name refers to the once quite adventurous ox-waggon crossing of the Minsmere river on what had been a Romanised section of the A12; and that another Roman road came in from the west at right-angles to the A12, probably curving round inside the arc of the river-valley and supplying the line of the present village street. Cockfield Hall lies to the north-west of this ancient road-junction, Grove Park to the south-west, and Rookery Park to the east. One might be forgiven for assuming that this arrangement represents the manorial division of Yoxford, but it does not.

In Suffolk, it is easy to think of parishes or 'vills' (to use the Domesday

8   Entitled *Yoxford Yesterday*. A copy reposes in the Suffolk Record Office in Ipswich.
9   Parr, *op. cit.*, IV, 221.

Book term for the secular unit that often coincided with the parish) that contain more than one manor: sometimes there are three or four manors, or more: eight in Helmingham, for instance. It is also easy to think of ancient named settlements, or vills, that have been subdivided — like the three Bradfields whose splitting and labelling we considered in Chapter 6, or the three Stonhams, the four Creetings, the two Sohams, two Blakenhams, and so on. (Great Blakenham, lying as low in the Gipping valley as Cockfield Hall in the Minsmere vale, was known picturesquely as 'Blakenham super aquam' in the 14th century, to distinguish it from Little Blakenham in the chalky 'hills' above.) It is much more difficult to think of examples in Suffolk where the reverse of this has happened; where three considerable Domesday places, or vills — though one of them declined to the status of hamlet before fusion — have been amalgamated so successfully that they have for centuries seemed like one place. This is what has happened here at Yoxford. It is certainly an unusual story. It has come about through three main circumstances. The first, and perhaps most important, is that they shared one convenient church — Yoxford's present church, St Peter's. The second is, I think, that they had to hand a convenient, 'ready-made', village street. The third, though this could perfectly well have happened *without* unifying the three vills if, for example, they had had separate churches, was that in the 15th century the principal manors were acquired by John Hopton, and have remained in one family, or rather a sequence of three: Hoptons followed in 1597 by Brookes, followed in 1693 by Bloises, who continue.

Though traces of early Romano-British (and perhaps Iron Age) farms have been noticed at three points fairly high up the valley slopes towards the west side of Yoxford parish (all three, apparently, discontinued),[10] we would be wrong to imagine a discontinuance of settlement during the later Roman and early Anglo-Saxon periods simply because we have so far failed to spot the evidence. So fertile a valley would not have been neglected. Nor would the lines of Roman road have survived a whole generation of disuse: they would quickly have reverted to nature, as we noted in Chapter 1. The convenience of these roads, and an established river-crossing, would certainly not have been wasted on the 7th-century kings and missionaries whose activities we glimpsed in Chapters 2 and 3. But, as to the extent of any settlement in Yoxford between the 2nd and 3rd centuries and 1066, we must acknowledge complete ignorance for the present.

What we find in the Domesday record, describing landholdings in 1066 and 1086 in such gratifying detail, is this. In *Gokesford* was a manor of 600 'acres' and in *Iokesfort* a more modest manor of 100 'acres', with two small-holdings farmed by groups of freemen. What 'acre' and 'carucate' mean in

10 By Peter Warner in his extremely interesting unpublished Leicester University Ph.D. thesis: 'Blything Hundred: A study in the Development of Settlement', October 1982, p. 185. A microfilm copy, J440/1, is available in the Suffolk Record Office in Ipswich.

Domesday Book I will try to explain a little further on. We owe it to the late R. T. L. Parr that we are confident that these two manors represent Yoxford north of the river, and that Yoxford south of the river was represented in Domesday Book by two vills, now forgotten, but lived in as *Hopton* and *Stikeland* (occasionally spelt *Stikingland*, but generally later spelt the first way, and presumably pronounced as three syllables, *Stik-e-land*: see map 7).[11] Yoxford had these two manors, one of them a major affair, identified by Parr as Yoxford Manor in the early Middle Ages, the other he identified as Cockfield Hall, which became, from the early 15th century, the major manor it remains. Hopton also had two manors, and Stikeland three. The church was in Stikeland.

Domesday Book enables us to see something of the arrangements *before* 1066, particularly in the main Yoxford manor, the earthworks of which can still be located in the woods on the higher slopes north of the river (see map). Domesday Book[12] reveals this Yoxford manor in the hands, in 1086, of Robert de Todeni, or de Tosny, whose French headquarters were at Conches, near Evreux, and whose English castles were at Kirtling, near Newmarket, and at Belvoir. He displaced an Anglo-Saxon Dane called Manning Swartingson, whose father, Suen Swart, Suen the Black, he displaced in Essex at Upminster:[13] Manning had a son called Ulf the Thegn, a young grandee who features ignominiously in the chronicles of Bury abbey.[14] Manning gave Chepenhall (still remembered in Chippenhall Green in the southern part of Fressingfield parish: see chapter 8, p. 107), to St Edmund's abbey, but his son Ulf appropriated it, was frightened by a snake-bite, and guiltily offered St Edmund the choice of Syleham or Chepenhall. The monks chose Chepenhall 'because it abounded in woods'. Domesday Book confirms that Ulf, or Olf, had been displaced in Syleham by Robert de Tosny, and that Syleham had woodland enough to feed 150 swine.[15] Chepenhall woods could feed 160 swine.[16] Not much in it, but the Bury monks under Abbot Baldwin were not born yesterday.

I like this picture of the clayland woods of Fressingfield and Syleham, with swine-pannage high among their valuable products, but my excuse for this diversion is that it helps us to imagine the very people who owned the Yoxford manor in 1066 and 1086, grand absentee landlords both before and after the Conquest, possibly visiting the place once or twice, but dependent on a resident steward: Domesday Book specially recorded that 'Robert holds in demesne', did not have a sub-tenant.

11 For *Hopton*. see R. T. L. Parr, 'Two Townships in Blything Hundred', *Proceedings, Suffolk Institute of Archaeology*, XXV, 1952, 297–301, and for *Stikeland* and Yoxford, see *Yoxford Yesterday*, I, 1–20.
12 Fol. 419b.
13 Manning himself was sometimes called 'the Black' — see Domesday Book, fol. 292b.
14 V.C.H., *Suffolk*, I, 1911, 504n, quoting B.L. Add. MSS, 14847, fol. 24.
15 Domesday Book, fol. 429b.
16 Domesday Book, fol. 368.

Their manor-house is almost as clean departed from the landscape as its forgotten occupants. A beautifully full survey, or terrier, known as a 'Drag', was made for the amalgamated Yoxford manors in 1471.[17] Already only a few old tenants could remember anything of what the place was like. By a nice coincidence they included Piers Candler, whose direct descendant, the Rev Matthias Candler, vicar of Coddenham, himself made a remarkable survey of Suffolk church monuments and of the principal inhabitants of 400 Suffolk parishes in his day, the mid-1650s.[18] Piers Candler and his cronies recalled that, 'in very ancient days', Yoxford manor was 'walled about with walls and a moat, which said site was formerly built upon, and was then called the inner court of the manor. Men now living have seen jambs and posts'. The site was approximately square, the main entrance from due south along a ditched causeway, known as the Old Entry.

With his knowledge of the documents, Parr located this key site in the development of Yoxford. It stands high on those south-facing wooded slopes rising north of the river. Presumably the fork north off the A1120 at Little Street represents the Anglo-Saxon and Norman approach to a former main river-crossing — to the main manor from A12, village and church. On account of the importance of the manor, I began by wondering whether this was not the site of the 'yox-ford', but concluded that the name is likely to have been associated with the more general, immemorial crossing by the A12. (I also wondered if the neighbouring Danbrook Bridge might represent the original ford, as its name sounded vaguely ancient. In fact, as Parr explained, it takes its name from a Yoxford shopkeeper who, on 22 June 1801, shot himself at his breakfast table in the presence of his wife and the local surgeon, and was buried at the corner just across the bridge: unfit, 'of course', for a place in the hallowed churchyard.)

The OS map-reference to the site of the Yoxford manor is 389702. On the 1:25,000 sheet, TM37, 1956 edition, the site was marked as a small isosceles triangle of woodland immediately west of Yoxford Wood. This triangular wood still appears on the 1981 Sheet of the OS 1:50,000 map, though its sharp outlines have for some years been swallowed (happily) in more extensive woods. From the area of Little Street it is in some seasons possible to look across the valley at those wooded slopes and make out the more mature trees marking the ancient site. From the 'Drag' and from the earthwork remains, Peter Warner has reconstructed a convincing ground-plan,[19] a very valuable record of a vanished manor-house — with its 'walls and a moat', an early fortified manor. Nothing very like it survives in Suffolk: perhaps the nearest thing is Little Wenham Hall. There seems to be no trace of a Norman motte such as de Tosny raised at Kirtling.

Now we look at the second of the two Domesday manors in Yoxford —

---

17   S.R.O. (Ipswich), HA 30, 50/22/13. 15.
18   B.L. Add. MSS. 15520 (Microfilm in S.R.O., Ipswich, JC1/1/5).
19   P. Warner, *op. cit.*, figures 55a, 55b.

that is, north of the river. Here (in what became Cockfield manor), the Conqueror's tenant was Roger Bigot (later Bigod), the King's sheriff in Norfolk and Suffolk,[20] who acted as steward to many of the king's own manors in Suffolk,[21] and was building up for himself the most powerful position of any local Norman magnate. His second wife was de Tosny's daughter, and their son Hugh became earl of Norfolk. Here at Cockfield there is still a reminder of him. In that 'Drag' of 1471, the manor was described as '7 acres in all, lying between the river on the south and a certain way called Earlsway on the north'. This Way seems to correspond to the present approach to Cockfield from the A12. This neighbourhood has rather a profusion of 'Earlsways', as may be seen from the map (7). The one running along, and perhaps providing, the northern boundary of Sibton and aiming at Earlsway Farm, appears to refer to a different earl — the Count Alan of Richmondshire and Brittany. The *'caput'* of *his* large local estates in Kettleburgh and 'Earl' Soham seem to be directly connected by the Sibton 'Earlsway' with his adulterine castle at Bramfield.[22] In several of his estates in this area, Bigot succeeded someone called Norman. Sometimes he was 'Norman the thegn', as he is here;[23] and there is a reference in neighbouring Darsham to 'Norman the sheriff',[25] who is very unlikely to be a different person. Most of the references are simply to 'Norman', and since the Conqueror's sheriff Roger succeeded the Confessor's sheriff Norman in so many estates, particularly in this neighbourhood and in Colneis (the Walton-by-Felixstowe peninsula), it looks as if Roger may have been succeeding to land held by Norman *as* sheriff — transferred to him from the Confessor's sheriff as reward for the job. Many of these estates are characterised as being small holdings by large numbers of freemen, which might explain the need for involvement by the sheriff.

In relation to Norman (whose name proclaims him some kind of Northman who settled hereabouts ahead of the gang from Normandy), Domesday Book records an almost unparalleled act of clemency by the Conqueror. Describing the smaller of the two good Saxmundham manors, the scribe commented: 'This is one of the three manors the King gave back to Norman: now Norman holds it of Roger.'[25] Another is clearly Walton,[26] which adjoined the site at *Burch* (Old Felixstowe), where the massive walls of the Saxon Shore fort stood, in which the Bigots soon erected their own castle. The third is probably Peasenhall,[27] where Norman held two fair-sized manors in 1066, and held them in 1086 as one. Other small estates,

20 G.E.C., *The Complete Peerage, IX,* 1936, 576.
21 Domesday Book, fols. 281b — 284b, 290 — 290b.
22 *Proceedings Suffolk Institute of Archaeology,* XXXV, 1981, 85 — 86. A. H. Denney (ed.), *Sibton Abbey Estates,* 1960, 53 — 54.
23 Domesday Book, fol. 333.
24 Domesday Book, fol. 334b.
25 Domesday Book, fol. 338b.
26 Domesday Book, fol. 339b.
27 Domesday Book, fol. 331b.

including small manors, Domesday book shows he was able to hang on to. One wonders if Norman's fellow English and Anglo-Danes around here regarded him with envy, or with hatred as a Quisling. His keepings were not enormous, but his friends and neighbours were ruthlessly dispossessed: Ulveva, the freewoman at Kelsale, we remember, where the king granted Roger a new market.[28] Nor were members of Roger's household neglected. His chaplain, Ansketil, acquired in Darsham, adjoining Yoxford, a 'carucate' that had belonged to seven freemen (six of whom were named here in the record); and 16 'acres' and 1 'rood', which the same wretched Ulveva had owned and had to hand over; and 24 'acres' less 1 'rood' that belonged to Blakeman,[29] a freeman who was also relieved of small manors in Darsham and Sibton.[30]

The question of 'carucates' and 'acres' in Domesday Book and other early tax registers, like abbot Samson's *Kalendar*, causes much perplexity. We need not get heavily involved, but the two words appear in the majority of entries in such indispensable records of those times. The clearest and most dependable explanation, and one of the briefest, is given by R. H. C. Davis in his exemplary edition of *Abbot Samson's Kalendar*.[31] The simple point is that 'carucates' and 'acres' were units of assessment, not measurements of actual area. Davis is describing land taxable by the 'Hundred', the area of Anglo-Saxon local administration responsible for assessing and gathering taxes for defence and other government purposes. For these purposes, 1 'carucate' equalled, as a rule, 120 'acres'. (When referring to such measurements in Domesday Book or the *Kalendar*, I use inverted commas to show readers that these are not actual land measurements.) In fact, for ordinary reading purposes, as distinct from the writing of theses, it is not too misleading to think of an 'acre' as an acre, and a 'carucate' as 120 acres. Few of us anyway carry about with us a *precise* idea of an acre. If we wish to remember that a taxable carucate of poor land is likely to represent considerably more than 120 measured acres, and of good land perhaps rather fewer, let us do that.

I have, of course, oversimplified. Measurements anyway varied from one part of the country to another. Two small sums I once did. They consoled

28 Scarfe, *The Suffolk Landscape*, 1972, 167−171.
29 Domesday Book, fol. 334b. Ulveva is here recorded as 'Alveva, a freewoman'. I am only guessing that she is the Ulveva displaced by Roger from nearby Kelsale in fol. 330b. I am fairly certain neither of these refers to 'Alveva the mother of earl Morcar', since she has a tenants-in-chief section all to herself (fol. 286b). Appearing outside it, briefly, as at Brandeston, she is duly dubbed 'Alveva, mother of earl Morcar'. (fol. 373b − 374). Morcar's *father* was Aelfgar, son of Leofric of Mercia. Aelfgar became earl of East Anglia when Harold succeeded his father Godwin as earl of Wessex in 1053. In 1057, he succeeded Leofric as earl of Mercia, and Gyrth, Godwin's 4th son, became earl of East Anglia, 1057−1066. Morcar spent some time on the Isle of Ely with Hereward, but surrendered and was in prison in Normandy at the time of Domesday Book. He probably died in prison in Rufus's reign.
30 Domesday Book, fol. 313.
31 1954, xxxii − xxxiii.

me, though I do not suppose they are of universal significance. One was to check for myself the figures for the 4th and 5th *letes* (divisions) of Thedwestrey Hundred, near Bury, as set out in Samson's accounts and reproduced in Davis's edition on pp. 16−18: they deal with the Bradfields (see chapter 6), and some of their neighbours. It is reassuring (and fairly surprising) that in Bradfield St George, for example, the various tenants — Adam the huntsman, &c. — are assessed at 60, 15, 10, 15, 10 and 10 'acres' respectively, so that they do add up to 120 'acres', a 'carucate', and would know the proportion of tax each must find.

Then, in the world of real acreages, I made another check: this time in East Suffolk, at Thorington Hall, Wherstead, just above Belstead Brook to the south of the Ipswich borough boundary. This was among the many pleasant holdings in Norfolk and Suffolk of Robert, son of Corbutio. Domesday Book assesses *Torintun* at 2 'carucates' (240 'acres') of land held as a manor, with 20 acres of meadow and a church endowed with 50 acres (twice the average).[32] The church has vanished, except as the name of a field close to the Hall. But the point to be made is that this assessment (240 + 20 + 50) at 310 'acres' comes remarkably near to the real measurements of the Tithe survey in the 1840s. The Thorington estate then amounted to 298 acres, only 12 adrift from the 1086 tax assessment. The 'acre' is, at least here, not very different from the acre.

This is a fairly simple estate to choose; small, and, from the making of its physical boundaries, unlikely to have experienced any major change over the seven and a half centuries. The trouble with attempts at this kind of comparison is that the larger the sample, the more uncertain the calculation: what acreages are missing from the Domesday descriptions — in woodland, for instance, and swamp, and other uncultivated area?[33]

We can now form an idea of the five Domesday manors in 'Yoxford south of the river'. These are relatively small. North of the river, de Tosny's manor was assessed at 5 'carucates', 600 'acres', with woodland enough to find pannage for 30 swine. The smaller, Bigot's was a mere 100 'acres'. The map shows *Hopton* flanking the river and Middleton 'Moor' — which in these parts means 'fen': this is right, for Hopton means 'farm (*tun*) in the valley or marsh' (as at Stanford le *Hope* in Essex). Here, one manor was held by a freemen with a mere 42 'acres' and 2 'acres' of meadow. The other was held by a freeman with 60 'acres' and wood to feed 2 swine and half a church; and he held it, not very surprisingly, of Roger Bigot. Parr reckoned,[34]

32 Domesday Book, fol. 426.
33 His calculation of Domesday measurements is one aspect of Peter Warner's very interesting thesis that I find I cannot agree with: *op. cit.*, 151−154.
34 *Yoxford Yesterday*, I, 42. He noticed in the Sibton Abbey Cartulary (B.L. Add. MSS. 34560) that a Sayer Beuerach de Jokeford, who was living in 1266, held a tenement in Hopton (*Proceedings Suffolk Institute of Archaeology*, XXV, 1952, 298). In the same article he noticed an Adam Beveriche granting 'a piece of land and the marsh called Meadowland' in an early Tudor hand.

persuasively, that this manor may be represented by Beveriche Manor Farm, and the ½-church may be the complement of the ½-church in Darsham listed among the lands of the king in the royal demesne which (quite by chance) Roger Bigot was keeping for him. This Darsham church was part of Bigot's great endowment of St Mary's Priory at Thetford. In that Borough he had considerable possessions which were looking particularly promising at the time of Domesday Book,[35] before the East Anglian bishop moved his cathedral from Thetford to Norwich (whither the Bigots were careful to follow).

The rest of Yoxford south of the river started as *Stikeland*, and by 1086 was in three manors. Only the third is fairly easy to locate in modern Yoxford. The first and largest is another of those 'Lands of the King in the royal demesne' which Roger Bigot so willingly 'kept' for him.[36] It was not large compared with Yoxford manor across the river: one 'carucate' and 40 'acres' — 160 'acres'. The only real clue as to whereabouts is that there were 3 'acres' of meadow — they certainly were beside the river. The stock included 1 swine and 16 sheep. Was it perhaps based where Yoxford Farm now stands? Parr can give no lead.

The next two manors are small. One, of 80 'acres', was part of the Honour of Eye, the huge cluster of estates run by the Malet family from Eye castle.[37] Here, all they had in addition to 80 'acres' was 1 'acre' of meadow and two freemen's smallholdings: at least the meadow was down by the river. The Malets also had here a 40-acre farm, not a manor and with no meadow.[38] No clue to whereabouts.

Domesday Book's record of the last of the seven Yoxford manors is perhaps the most interesting.[39] It certainly comes in one of the most detailed sections, the one headed: *Freemen under Roger Bigot*. We saw just now that he had planted his own chaplain Ansketil over a bunch of freemen in Darsham. In Stikeland he has planted over this 80-acre manor two trusty freemen with the remarkable names of Cus and Akile Sufreint, the second one sounding like an 18th-century French admiral. There were 2 acres of meadows down by the river, and 4 beasts, 8 swine and 24 goats. Then the measurements of this manor are given, and they are surprising: 1 league (1½ miles) x 5 furlongs. As with the 'acres', these are useful only as giving some idea, at least, of proportions.

Now this same entry goes on, and we realise that the commissioner is describing the village street. Five freemen are named, who hold 60 acres, and they include Bunde the smith. They, too, had 2 'acres' of meadow. Then there was a freewoman with 20 'acres', and 1 'acre' of meadow. She is not named, but she seems not to have been displaced. So with a half

35   Domesday Book, fol. 173.
36   Domesday Book, fol. 282b.
37   Domesday Book, fol. 313b.
38   Domesday Book, fol. 312.
39   Domesday Book, fol. 334b−335.

freeman, whose condition would be clearer written 'half-free man': he had 8 'acres'. Finally, and this is no uncommon discovery in these parts: here in this little *Stikeland* manor, owned and run by freemen and a freewoman under the Confessor, is a church with 24 'acres', an average endowment, and an 'acre' of meadow. We reach the last sentence: 'Hugh de Corbun holds it of Roger Bigot.' Roger has put a Frenchman in to keep an eye on things. I doubt if it was a happy relationship, and hope Bunde applied his hammer only in the forge.

The Bigots established a park in the woods on the Kelsale-Stikeland boundary (see map 7). What remains of it I have already described, including some formidable bank-boundaries.[40] It is easy to imagine those jubilant French Normans in full cry after boar and stag. But the Bigots went too far. They antagonised the Lord Edward who succeeded as Edward I in 1272. By the time Edward died in 1307, the Bigot (or Bigod) earldom was over, their vast estates reverted to the Crown. The market that William I granted the Bigots at Kelsale was transferred to Saxmundham. In Edward I's time, the name Cockfeud supplants that of Bigot at 'Cockfield Hall', and the name of Adam de Merihil appears at Stikeland, to be followed by Richard de Muriel who died in that most terrible year, 1349. And now, somehow, the parson of Stikeland beomes the parson of Yoxford.[41]

The later history of these manors is not to be attempted here. Robert Parr did what he could in eight fat typescript volumes. He showed the Cockfeuds being replaced by John de Norwich in 1349. When John and Maud Norwich sold, in c. 1430, the proceeds went into a major rebuilding of Yoxford church. Cockfield was bought by John Hopton, a bastard of the Yorkshire house of Swillington, which had owned Yoxford manor since the 13th century, and which came to John Hopton under a complicated settlement. His purchase of Cockfield from the Norwiches' executors brought the main Yoxford estates together, and simplified the story. His laudable quiet life has been meticulously pieced together by Dr Colin Richmond.[42] His third wife Thomesine, something of a character, is shown in her shroud, c. 1497, on a brass memorial in the church. Dr John Blatchly has suggested that she was responsible for the remarkable armorial of 22 small wooden shields-of-arms, of which 15 survive, in the south aisle and chapel. By her second husband, her great-grandson Sir Henry Sidney was much the ablest of Queen Elizabeth's governors of Ireland, *and* was father of Sir Philip Sidney. At Cockfield, her Hopton descendant Arthur was custodian to Lady Jane Grey's sister, Lady Catherine Grey, whose foolish marriage to the earl of Hertford, and offspring by him, threatened and naturally incensed the Queen. Catherine died here, in January 1568, and was embalmed. After a month, on 22 February, she was buried in the church. In 1621, when her

40   *Suffolk Landscape*, 171–172.
41   Parr, *op. cit., VII*, 183; I, 20.
42   Colin Richmond, *John Hopton*, Cambridge, 1981.

husband died, and was buried in Salisbury cathedral, her mummified corpse was removed to lie near his.[43] The beautiful gatehouse and brick-fronted, step-gabled north wing are parts of the house that would have been only too familiar to this great-grand-daughter of Henry VII, the next in succession to the crown had Elizabeth died before her. The rest of the house was rebuilt in the late 17th century, modified in the 18th, and largely reconstructed, with a new and splendid 'Caroline' great hall of the 1890s (designed by the diocesan architect, E. F. Bisshop).

The only other manor-house R. T. L. Parr succeeded in identifying, apart from the earthworks of the original Yoxford manor, was Murrills, or Meriels.[44] When Parr photographed it (Pl. 25) before World War II, it was a charming reed-thatched and plaster-coated timber-framed house with an Elizabethan or Jacobean chimney-stack rising between the former hall and parlour, converted into two cottages. It was called Fife-and-Drum cottages, after the inn that was established in it during the Napoleonic Wars. As the manor went back into the earlier Middle Ages, so some features of the house may have done. But it has been completely pulled down in recent years and replaced by an imposing new building called Drum House.

Characteristically of our day, the old approach to it has also changed. A new housing estate was built half-way up the steep climb to Fife-and-Drum cottages, up what had been called, longer than anyone could remember, Hog Hill Lane. On 7 February 1950, a note in *The Times* newspaper was headlined *Hog Hill Disgruntled*, and informed its readers that Blyth Rural District Council had decided the previous day to change the name of the new housing estate to *Strickland Manor Hill*. Strickland is a nice touch: people in the district had vaguely heard of Agnes Strickland, who lived over at Southwold and was author of the *Lives of the Queens of England*, a very nice class of subject. It hardly mattered that this part of Yoxford was called Stickland, that the actual Manor at the top of Hog Hill Lane was called Murrills, or, if preferred, Meriels. Perhaps hogs are too countrified an idea for our suburban villagers to accept? Even if, as Robert Parr thought, the name was really a form of Hoo Hill — as in Sutton Hoo — a 'hoo' being a spur or ridge? The history of our times may prove more difficult to disentangle than that of the times of the first Roger Bigot.

But as we walk back along the village street from the bottom of Strickland Manor Hill towards old Stikeland church, it is encouraging to see, immediately on the left, the sturdy old brick 'shaped' gable-end of the house, end-on to the road and known as Payn's from its 16th-century owners, which serves the present 'Approved Coal Merchant': its authentic panelled plaster-work along the east front is still unspoilt by the modern fatal substitution of cement for the old lime-and-sand mix. George Cade,

43 Parr, *op. cit.*, III, 227.
44 Parr, *op. cit.*, I, 214.

knacker, lived here at the end of the last century, a successful preacher at the very attractive Primitive Methodist Chapel, 1856, next on the left. It was recorded by an observant neighbour that he preached one of his best sermons: 'Owe no man anything', from *Romans*, 13, 8 the week before he was declared bankrupt.[45]

Similar good old pargetted plaster-work enriches, quietly the walls of the next two cottages on the south side (right). *Caxtons*, is called after (a misreading of) Roger de Croxton's name, who bought a messuage here in 1401, but which was the 'Mayd's Head' in 1616, probably when the present building was fairly new (it was made into two cottages before 1800, and reunited between the World Wars).[46] It presents a properly rustic front. Then *Wisbech's*, too, is found to have a very well pargetted old lime-plaster coat, and bears the name of its Tudor owners. Between the two, Hope House has curved brick gable-ends of c. 1700, and a brick front that has suffered the indignity of being painted: this served as vicarage in the second half of the 18th century. The vicar, though resident, was a liability, to put it no lower. Much neighbouring brickwork has been painted, some unfortunately. The superb demonstration in Yoxford street of the benefit of cleaning brick instead of painting it comes on the right, at Milestone House, which also displays good stone-masonry in its front. William Calver, stonemason and bricklayer, had it during the years 1857−63, and presumably remodelled his frontage as a piece of excellent advertising. Yoxford's heyday was the 1840s and '50s, and in White's *Directories* for 1844 and 1855 one glimpses a village life that seems ideal. Here were five academies, including the National School, four bakers, three blacksmiths in place of old Bunde in 1086, six boot- and shoe-makers, three butchers, three milliners, two watchmakers, and so on. The Yoxford Mechanics Institution was established in 1850, with a library of more than 500 volumes, and about 70 members: in the 1870s it moved into the east end of Milestone House. The population of Yoxford had risen steadily from 851 in 1801 to 1272 in 1851, and then just as steadily declined; as it did almost throughout arable central Suffolk. Today, at just under 700, it is well below the level of 1801. Only Smyth's seed-drilling manufactory in Peasenhall and Garrett's steam-engine works in Leiston kept employment and population in those nearby places. Their machinery contributed to the reduction of farm-work in all the other villages.

The milestone itself, carved in the lettering that was nowhere less than handsome in the days of the Georgian turnpikes, now bears this message:

'From London 93 miles
To   Hall 5 miles.'

The word Heveningham was obliterated in the excitement of the invasion dangers of the summer of 1940. Next on the right, the name of 'Magnolia

45   Parr, *op. cit.*, VII, 125.
46   Parr, *op. cit.*, VII, 131.

House' hints at its character. The private walled garden behind is one of the best small gardens not only in the Garden of Suffolk but in England. It was a dower house of Grove Park, a building of the 1770s standing away to the south, in the park, on its own. It was built by Eleazar Davy, a late successor, in 1770, to Roger Bigot as sheriff. James Wyatt was consulted over the design, but as Davy was not good at paying the tradesmen, Wyatt cannot properly be thought of as his Architect. When he died in 1803, his nephew and heir, the invaluable Suffolk antiquary, David Elisha Davy, lived on here until 1822, and then moved away, to live less grandly in Ufford.[47] Now we approach a nicely conceived old ironwork signpost, and come to the church. It deserves a whole essay of its own, but at least we have got it into a long perspective.

47   John Blatchly (ed.), *David Elisha Davy's Journal of Excursions through the County of Suffolk, 1823–1844*, Suffolk Records Society, 1982, 6–8.

12

Wingfield, Fressingfield, the Hundred Years War and the Funding of Medieval Church-building

In 1971, the Aldeburgh Festival reached out into the rich clay landscape beyond Framlingham. In the church at Wingfield, choristers of Ely cathedral sang anthems and a *nunc dimittis* by Christopher Tye, their predecessors' Master from 1542 to 1562, who did so much to see English church music through the Reformation. At Fressingfield, the organist of Norwich cathedral played the organ built by Henry Willis, who in Victoria's reign supplied or renewed at least a dozen of the great cathedral organs of Britain. Another muse was casting her spell during those performances. The designers and craftsmen of those churches are now remembered only by their surviving works: their names have evaporated. But something is recoverable of the grandees for whom they created two of Suffolk's most splendid places of worship and of commemoration.

Sir John Wingfield, of Wingfield, served as senior staff officer to the Black Prince, Chief of his Council. His despatches from the Prince's headquarters in Bordeaux and the lower reaches of the Dordogne reveal the co-ordinated strategy of attrition, from October to Christmas 1355 that prepared the way to Poitiers the next year and the sensational capture of the French king. It was economic warfare, aimed at cutting off some of the king's main supplies of money, the wages for his men-at-arms. Without the evidence of Wingfield's despatches, the Prince's raids right across Gascony and Guyenne, and as far as Narbonne on the Mediterranean, seem a mere catalogue of adventure, of pitiless (but profitable) destruction. Robert de Ufford, earl of Suffolk, was another commander of the chivalry in that campaign. Already a patron of the nunnery at Campsey Ash, he retired to Suffolk in 1362 and devoted himself to rebuilding Leiston abbey on its present site. Wingfield had died the previous year. His funeral was paid for by his Prince (£57 13s 4d). Then his executors founded, as he intended, a college of secular chaplains in the parish church at Wingfield.

So a charter of the bishop of Norwich named three chaplains, and allowed for an increase up to nine, and three choristers. The church was to be 'in great part built anew', on an ampler scale, with campanile, bells, houses and other necessary offices, *'sumptuoso'*. The chaplains were to say matins, etc., daily, and celebrate masses for the dead and for the health of King Edward III and the Black Prince, and that of Wingfield's widow Eleanor Glanville, and of their only daughter Katherine and her husband, Michael de la Pole.

The alliance of the Wingfield heiress to Michael de la Pole lies behind the main building-story of the churches of Wingfield and Fressingfield. The heraldic arms of this marriage, 'impaled' on a shield, were displayed by an angel over the apex of Fressingfield's south porch, though both shield and angel are now crumbling to nothing. Michael, like his father-in-law, fought beside the Black Prince and John of Gaunt. His own father, a Hull merchant, was made a baron of the exchequer after lending great sums to Edward III; and his grandfather had married the affluent Eleanor Rotenheryng of Hull. When Michael got on too well with the Black Prince's son, Richard II, his fishy origins were unchivalrously recalled by his political opponents. In 1382, after the Peasants' Revolt, Richard allowed him to build the castle at Wingfield. That year, Robert de Ufford's son and sole successor died, and by 1385 Michael de la Pole had acquired the earldom of Suffolk. But Richard II's friendship had its drawbacks. Accused of treason, Michael fled and died in Paris in 1389.

In 1415, restored to royal favour and the Suffolk earldom, his son Michael sailed with Henry V for Harfleur and the renewed war. Before Harfleur fell, there was fearful dysentery. Michael died of it, and was buried at Wingfield. His second son, William, was invalided home for a short time. The heir, the brief young third earl, went on to Agincourt. There, on Crispin's day, some five weeks after his father's death, he plied his battle-axe, and was killed. His body was parboiled that night, and the bones taken to England for burial, probably at Butley priory.

His brother William, nineteen, succeeded to the earldom and returned to the wars, apparently 'without coming home or seeing of this land' for fourteen years. He became lieutenant-general of Caen, the Cotentin and Lower Normandy, and count of Dreux. (I think we should look to these long periods lived in Normandy by Suffolk land-owners and their tenants to explain some marked similarities of detail in several of the timbered houses of the two districts.) By 1429 William was one of the most experienced soldiers of his day, and was just tightening his grip around the walls of Orleans when he was totally outmanoeuvred, in a few, simple, breathtaking moves, by a very unconventional soldier, a girl of seventeen. Joan of Arc not only released Orleans from his grasp, she trapped Suffolk in Jargeau, a little way up the Loire. At Jargeau he and his brother John were taken prisoner, their rashly-named brother Alexander (who had been 'scolatized' at Ipswich school) killed. As prisoner John may have died, for no more is heard of him. His own ransom cost William £20,000 (more than a million in our money), as well as his only brother Thomas, who died four years later, apparently still a hostage. After this débâcle, it is not really surprising to find that Suffolk returned to England, became the leading 'dove' at court, married the widow of his old commander, Salisbury (she was Alice Chaucer, the poet's grand-daughter), and set about commemorating his parents and their children at Wingfield.

About 1430 he extended the chancel and its chapels at Wingfield eastwards, providing the church with its most striking internal feature, the creamy stone arcade between chancel and (S) Lady Chapel. There, under the easternmost arch, his parents are now represented in wood on a magnificent stone tomb-chest (after Harfleur the father had lain at first under a plain slab). Eight empty canopied niches for the 'weeper' statues line the S side of the tomb. These were William's three unfortunate younger brothers and their five sisters. He and his elder brother, and perhaps their wives, were presumably represented in the niches at the end of the tomb. He spent £75 8s 4d on this extension of the building to house 'my Lord's fader's and his moder's tombe'. Thirty-eight tons of 'Lyncolnshire' stone were brought, presumably from Ancaster by water through Sleaford and Boston, round to Yarmouth and up the Waveney.

William, now duke of Suffolk, owed his flight and assassination in 1450 to the failure and high unpopularity of his peace policy. As he left England the people sang: 'Now is the Fox drevin to hole; hoo to hym, hoo! hoo!' His touching farewell to his young son John is preserved among the Paston letters. John and his mother abandoned the crumpled Red Rose of Henry VI, and he married Elizabeth of York. Soon after his brother-in-law, Edward IV took the crown, his mother Alice moved from Wingfield castle to Ewelme, near Oxford. The inventory of 'stuff' she took with her including her books, ended with 'a head sheet of miniver [white ermine] doubled with crimson cloth for a cradle' and 'a mattress of blue buckskin for a cradle'. These may well have cradled John, who was later laid, so very disillusioned, alongside Elizabeth of York, north of the main altar at Wingfield. Their side had lost finally at Bosworth, a decision their children were fatally unable to accept. But they themselves lie here under effigies majestically modelled in alabaster. We can now look in detail at the two churches.

Wingfield

St Andrew's is best approached from the S, its flintwork, clear glass and tall, unbroken roof-line seen above the trees and cream-plastered walls of the farmhouse that incorporate magnificent medieval remains of the college. From outside, notice the delicate flowing lines of the tracery of the 1362 windows, each with moulded hoods ending in a couple of small, finely carved human heads, contemporaries of John and Eleanor Wingfield. The best is at the W end of the S aisle. The 1362 E windows of the aisles were kept and re-installed when the church was extended eastwards c. 1430. The join of the later building is visible beside the chaplain's door on the S. Those later ('Perp') windows are more mechanical, more difficult to appreciate with their brilliant glass gone. (Some coloured fragments survive in the big E windows.)

Inside, the eye soon goes to the carved stone and woodwork of the chancel, which is almost as large as the nave. (A corner of the nave houses a sort of portable sentry-box conceived to shelter the priest at the graveside in rough weather.) The font, c. 1430, bears the arms of Wingfield (wings), De la Pole (leopard's heads) and Stafford (a knot). Duke William's mother was a Stafford, and the knot is among the emblems about her tomb. Impressive staircases lead eastwards from the nave to the vanished rood-loft. But the base of the screen survives, and happily the parclose screens, at right-angles to it, are almost intact; they reward careful examination.

We come in some awe to the chancel and its chapels and tombs. By himself, north of the chancel, lies Sir John Wingfield, by whose will the collegiate church was built. In 1812 Thomas Kerrich, a local antiquary, scraped off the whiting very carefully, found the Wingfield arms painted on the surcoat, and left notes (in the British Museum) of the detailed painting and gilding of the whole effigy. Beside this tomb the crocketed doorway leads into the Trinity Chapel, with sacristan's watching-chamber over, whose view of the altar involved breaking the line of cresting over duke John's tomb when that was installed. William's creation of the great arches of Lincolnshire stone for his parents' tomb has already been described. I think the chaplains' carved wooden stalls must have been new-made at this time, and certainly the handsome stone seats N of the tomb. The candle-holders on the stalls were designed by J. N. Comper in 1911. The stone knots and leopards' heads preserve part of the decorative scheme, but the shields have lost all their painted heraldry. Before 1863 the names of some of the eight children were legible on the S side of the tomb. There is old paint in Trinity Chapel, but the best remains of original colour are pre-served on duke John's tomb. The 'funeral armour' helmet suspended over the tomb tallies with the crested helmet on which the effigy's head rests. This is one of the very finest examples of the appearance of a robed Knight of the Garter and his lady in Henry VII's time. The faces are probably por-traits.

Fressingfield

SS Peter and Paul's stands, unlike Wingfield church, in a clustered village. A medieval market was held in the little valley below the NW side of the churchyard, opposite the Swan. And a medieval guildhall, with carved wooden figure of St Margaret, lines the S side of the churchyard (it is now the Fox and Goose). 'Merry Fressingfield' is the scene of much of Greene's play *Friar Bacon and Friar Bungay* (1594), in which fair Margaret of Fress-ingfield captivates most of the male characters, four of whom slay each other: '. . . the damsell is as fair, As simple Suffolk's homely towns can yield'. This parish contained several manors. One was owned by the family of William Sancroft, whose conscience forced him to renounce the arch-bishopric of Canterbury and retire here rather than accept the Revolution of 1688. His marble tomb lies just outside the S porch of the church.

This porch, and the sight and feel of much medieval carved woodwork inside the church, are its chief physical attractions. The porch is a beautiful combination of freestone and flint, with sacristan's upper chamber, sur-mounted by the eroded Wingfield/De la Pole shield. The chamber window, and canopied niches and blank panels on either side of it, are very fine. (Some curious floral patterns in the spandrels below may date from repairs of Sancroft's day.) The arched outer doorway, embossed with shields and a winged heart, remind one firmly of the 1430 arcade over earl Michael's tomb at Wingfield. One of the bench-ends inside is carved with a chalice and the initials 'A.P.'; another bears the initial 'H'. All this may well be work promoted by William de la Pole on his return from Orleans and Jargeau — 'A.P.' being the initials of his wife (Alice Pole), and 'H' that of Henry VI. No documents have yet been found to further this speculation.

Before entering, notice the clerestory with its good dark flintwork and red brick decoration over the windows. The elaborate stone sanctus bellcote was added to the nave roof in the 1490s. The inside of the porch raised the great question about restoration. The stone figures the Victorians restored are readable but ugly, while the original stone bosses are now so far eroded as to be almost meaningless.

In the nave, one first rejoices in the broad single-hammerbeam roof, with its rich cornice running along the junction with the wall (the fretted work pegged on). Beneath the oak roof is a nave full of oak benches, carved to an overall design and arranged in two main blocks framed in a curb on the floor. Many of the arm-rests are broken off, like the one where St Dorothy sits with her rose-basket, eaten by worms. The most impressive are at the W end, where the whole length of the backs is carved. Look especially at the one with all the emblems of Jesus's rejection — the crowing cock, the buffet-ing hand, the seamless coat, and the dice-board (with the dice lately and happily renewed). The N arm-rest of this bench bears a baffling piece of symbolic heraldry. In the chancel, the top of the NE window retains enough of its fourteenth-century glass, gold, deep-green and grisaille, to suggest the original scheme. Here the brass effigies of William and Elizabeth Brewes, 1489, survive to represent all the families in these parishes whose names were not Wingfield or De la Pole.

* * * * * * *

These most evocative of Suffolk's parish churches remind one that here, as all over Christendom, churches were built out of the spoils of war and military adventure, as well as the proceeds of more peaceful trades. The point is worth making, for the cliché has long gained a hold that Suffolk's famous churches are 'wool churches' — by which are meant, or should properly be meant, churches enriched by the successful manufacture and marketing of textiles. The weavers' skills never seem quite adequately conjured up by the phrase 'wool churches', a phrase more appropriate to the Cotswolds or the Yorkshire wolds, the source of such marvellous fleeces.

So we bear in mind these local successful warriors and members of the kings' households in the decades before and after 1400. Looking at Dennington, we notice Henry V's lord Bardolph, but it may be that the light-filled chancel there was built for another of the Wingfields — William, who seems to have been Sir John's nephew, buried in 1398 in the chancel, where the indent of his brass effigy and inscription remains. At Playford, near Woodbridge, one of the most distinguished tower-designs benefitted in 1409 from the will of the widow of Sir George Felbrigg, a military squire of Edward III's household. He was a descendant of the Norman Bigot earls: indeed his brass effigy at Playford, with sword and dagger, drooping moustaches and rampant red lion, may be the only surviving visual representation of a member of that potent East Anglian family. The truly vertical 'Perpendicular' of Stowlangtoft church seems to be the work of Robert Davey de Ashfield, 'a servant to the Black Prince': he died in 1401, leaving £20 to the finishing of the south porch, and his arms, a fesse between three fleurs-de-lis, are on a spandrel of the screen. Peter Northeast has shown that at Westhorpe, near Stowlangtoft, Dame Elizabeth Elmham gave instructions in 1419 that a chapel, two aisles and the steeple should be built at her expense. She provided £40 more for the bells. Her husband, Sir William Elmham, was another 'career soldier' in Edward III's wars. Incidentally, the leopards' heads on the shield of the de la Poles appear not only at Wingfield but also at Eye, Stradbroke and Wattisfield, and they probably represent more than mere badges of allegiance.

We need not overstress this theme. No doubt most people contributed what they could to these proud buildings that seemed to increase in splendour until a climax was reached with the great campanile at Lavenham in 1525. Southwold, erected completely in the decades c. 1430−1460, reflects the capricious behaviour of the Blyth river, withdrawing its favour from Dunwich in 1328 and bringing its harbour and trade to Walberswick and Southwold in the 15th century. Needham Market's famous roof rose under the aegis of the Ely bishop, but with the people contributing: 'Pray we all for grace', as the stone inscription says. Though the de la Pole arms appeared with the angel on the south battlement of Eye's magnificent tower, we know it was completed in 1470 'chiefly' with the help of the parishioners. If we remember John Clopton and his butler, Loveday, from the inscription over Long Melford's Lady Chapel, we also read, in the north clerestory, of 'the help of the well-disposed men of this town'.

The clothing trade, for all its crises, financed some marvellous churches in those ancient industrial villages beside the northern tributaries of the Stour — from Clare right along to East Bergholt. We always remember the 'wool' churches but somehow forget the grandeur created by the coastal trade and the fisheries: we seldom hear of the Suffolk 'fish-churches', though St Peter himself was a fisherman. Lowestoft and Beccles are not often thought of in the same way as Blythburgh: nor are Mildenhall and Lakenheath, but the fenland fisheries were as important as the coastal fisheries in the medieval food-economy.

One catches oneself thinking cynically of church-endowment as a form of rich man's insurance for the hereafter. At such moments, I like to think of John Baret's tomb in St Mary's church at Bury. As our endpapers show, its celure, or canopy, is handsomely made and painted, sparkling with ingenious little glass jewels and epitomising the feeling of endowment and devotion with the repeated motto: 'Grace me governe'. His long, meticulously detailed will was made in 1463. It was proved in 1467, amid the tremendous activity of the rebuilding and restoration of the abbey church after the fire that swept through the roofs at the beginning of the previous year. Baret was himself clearly an official of the abbey during the first two of the four decades when the great Simon Clerk was Master Mason at Bury, as he also was at King's College, Cambridge. No wonder the crafts-manship is fine. Baret listed each item for his own memorial: the rebuilding of the Risby Gate at the west entrance to the town, 'in flint if Symkyn Clerk' advises: the painting of an altarpiece, the 'prick song' and masses to be sung, a dinner to be given, on the day of his interment, to the chief townsmen, 'gentlemen and gentlewoman with other folks of worship, priests and good friends', and fourpence, 'to drink', to each of his tenants, 'for they have been right gentle and good to me at all times'.

TALES BEFORE THE REFORMATION

13

The Re-telling of Two Strange Tales from the Chronicler Ralph of Coggeshall, and of a Moral Tale from the Hundred Mery Talys

When Jocelin of Brakelond was writing in Bury, Ralph of Coggeshall, abbot of the idyllic Cistercian monastery at Little Coggeshall near Colchester, was writing his *Chronicle of England*.[1] He was an excellent narrator, and he reported, in engaging detail, the two best-remembered strange episodes in the life of medieval Suffolk.

The first occurred in Ralph's young days, when Bartholomew Glanville was custodian of Henry II's tremendous new castle at Orford, when Bartholomew's kinsman, Rannulf Glanville, was founding Butley priory in the marshes under the eye of Orford keep, and when Orford's majestic Romanesque church had just been dedicated to Bartholomew's own patron-saint. The Orford longshoremen were out fishing in the sea off Boyton and Hollesley when they found they'd trawled up in their nets what Ralph called 'a wild-man-of-the-woods'. They brought him up into the castle to show him to the lord Bartholomew. The man was entirely naked, and all parts of his body were apparently shaped like any human's. He grew hair, too, though on top of his head it looked as if it had been plucked out. His beard was thick and pointed, and he was excessively shaggy about the chest.

For a long time the lord Bartholomew had him guarded, day and night, in case he went back to the sea. Whatever food was set before him, he consumed it uncritically. He ate fishes, either raw or cooked; but when they were raw he pressed them hard between his hands till all the water was squeezed out, and ate them like that. He wouldn't — he quite obviously couldn't — form any words — even when he was hung upside down by his feet and horribly tormented. When he was taken into St Bartholomew's church, he made not the slightest motion of reverence at the sight of anything sacred; still less gave any indication of religious belief. He always got off to bed at sunset, and stayed there till sunrise.

Then one day, the fishermen took him out to the mouth of the estuary and released him into the sea, after carefully hedging him round inside a sort of pen, three nets thick. It didn't occur to them to put a bottom into the pen. He dived down deep under the nets, and bobbed up several times, away beyond them, disporting himself in the open sea. After they'd given up hope of getting him back, he returned to the Orford folk quite willingly,

---

1 J. J. Stevenson, ed., *Radulphi de Coggeshall Chronicon Anglicanum*, Rolls Series, 1875, pp. 117–119. The same tales are told in William of Newburgh, but seem likely to have been collected by Ralph.

swimming up into the estuary. He stayed with them two more months. Then he grew bored and disgusted with them. As they didn't trouble to watch him, he slipped off back to the sea, and never appeared again.

> Now my brothers call from the bay,
> Now the great winds shoreward blow,
> Now the salt tides seaward flow:
> Now the wild white horses play,
> Champ and chafe and toss in the spray.
>   Come away, away children;
> Come children, come down! . . .
> We will gaze, from the sand-hills,
> At the white sleeping town;
> At the church on the hill-side —
> And then come back down . . .
> Singing: 'There dwells a loved one,
> But cruel is she!
> She left lonely for ever
> The kings of the sea.'[2]

Ralph of Coggeshall's second record of the strange life of medieval Suffolk came from Bardwell and Woolpit, on the western edge of the old Suffolk woodlands. Right down into the 19th century, all the middle part of Suffolk was generally known as 'the woodland'. Even when the early farm enclosures had been made, the great hedges remained, studded with enough oaks to give an overall impression of close woodland, almost down to our own day. Here lies the explanation of all those 'woodwoses' (or 'wild-men-of-the-woods'), shaggy figures, often brandishing clubs, carved in church-doorways and on font-pedestals, and most densely distributed in this very woodland region. The wild man on Orford's font is thus a distant relative of the merman, whom Ralph specifically described as 'a-man-of-the-woods'. But such figures on fonts may presumably refer to John the Baptist's much publicised stay in the Wilderness.

Ralph's other story is brief. A boy and girl whose skins were green were found near the mouth of a deep hole in Woolpit. (The *Oxford Dictionary of English Place-names* says Woolpit means 'pit for trapping wolves', and this is a possible explanation of the 'deep hole'.) They were taken to Richard de Calne's house, Wicken Hall, 6 miles up the road from Woolpit.[3] Unlike the

2 No one would suppose that the most haunting of Matthew Arnold's poems, *The Forsaken Merman*, had any connexion with the Orford merman; superficially, the poet's experience of Suffolk seems to have been limited to an exhausting round of school-inspections in Ipswich and elsewhere in 1852. His immediate sea-links were with the Isle of Wight, where his grandfather, like the poet Crabbe's, was a customs officer, and where his uncle Matthew, a young army chaplain, was drowned in 1820. But his great-grandfather, Matthew Arnold, had moved to Cowes from the Lowestoft hinterland. In Lowestoft itself, generations of Matthew Arnolds stretched from the 18th century back to 1577, alternating with Thomas Arnolds who go back there, as herring-merchants and suchlike, to the 1520s.
3 Antonia Gransden, *Historical Writing in England*, 1974, p. 331, supposed this to be a reference to Wakes Colne in Essex, a good way from Woolpit. In the *Kalendar of Abbot*

merman, they could speak: but no one could understand what they were saying. Even more unlike the merman, they declined to eat. Finally some-one tried them with beans. These they ate, but the boy soon died. The girl, tougher, survived, adjusted to other food, ceased to be green, learnt English and was baptised. Ralph got this story direct from Richard de Calne, so it is presumably reliable; and it doesn't sound to us as supernatural as it did to them.

> The woods of Arcady are dead
> And over is their antique joy.
> Of old the world on dreaming fed:
> Grey truth is now her painted toy.

This theme of Yeats is the moral of one of the *Hundred Mery Talys* that Beatrice referred to in *Much Ado About Nothing*; the only one that is set here in Suffolk. It was published in 1526, the same year as Tyndale's marvellously colloquial English Bible, for which he was burnt. The simple Biblical form of the sentences you will notice at once, as well as the frank anti-clericalism that rings entirely true to Suffolk. So do the conies, which is the old name for rabbits — all too familiar still in our coastal heathlands. Tudor rabbits were prized for their fur as well as their flesh. The moral is spoken at the end, as in one of Thurber's fables for our time. It shows that, in Suffolk at least, medieval superstition was receding, a little, before the pressures of Renaissance and Reformation.

Of Him that played the Devil and came through the Warren and made them that stole the Conies to run away.

It fortuned that in a market town in the county of Suffolk there was a stage play, in the which play one called John Adroyns — which lived in another village 2 miles from this — played the devil. And when the play was done, this John Adroyns, in the evening, departed from the said market town to go home to his own house; and because he had with him no change of clothing, he went forth in his devil's apparel. In the way coming homeward, he came through a warren of conies belonging to a gentleman of the village where he himself dwelt.

At which time it fortuned that a priest, a vicar of a church thereby, with two or three other unthrifty fellows, had brought with them a horse, a net and a fetter to the intent there to get conies. And when the ferret was in the earth and the net set over the pathway wherein this John Adroyns should come, this priest and these other fellows saw him come — in the devil's rai-ment! Considering that they themselves were in the devil's service and steal-ing conies, and supposing that here came the devil indeed, they for fear ran

---

Samson, ed. Davis, 1954, p. 40, 'the heirs of Richard de Caune' held a quarter of the Bard-well lete. That was c. 1186 – 91. He was probably Ralph's informant about the children. A few years later Wicken Hall was sold by Walter, son of Sibila de Calna, according to W. A. Copinger, *Manors of Suffolk*, I, 1905, p. 266.

away. This John Adroyns, in the devil's raiment and because it was somewhat dark, saw not the net but went forth in haste and stumbled thereat and fell down and with the fall had almost broke his neck.

But when he was a little revived, he looked up and spied it was a net to catch conies, and looked further and saw that they ran away for fear of him, and saw tied to a bush a horse laden with conies which they had taken. And he took the horse and the net and leapt upon the horse, and rode to the gentleman's place that was lord of the warren, to the intent to have his thanks for taking such a prey. And when he came, knocked at the gates. To whom, anon, one of the gentleman's servants asked who was there, and suddenly opened the gate: and as soon as he perceived him in the devil's raiment was suddenly abashed, and sparred the door again and went in to his master and said — and sware to his master — that the devil was at the gate and would come in.

The gentleman, hearing him say so, called the steward of his house, the wisest servant that he had, and bade him go to the gate and bring him sure word who was there. This steward thought he would see surely who was there, came to the gate and looked through the chinks in divers places, and saw well that it was the devil, sat upon an horse, and saw hanging about the saddle on every side the coney-heads hanging down. Then he came to his master, afeared, in great haste, and said: 'By god's body, it is the devil indeed that's at the gate, sitting upon a horse laden with souls; and by likelihood, he is come for your soul purposely, and lacketh but your soul; and if he had your soul, I suppose he should be gone.'

This gentleman, then marvellously abashed, called upon his chaplain, and made the holy candle to be lit, and gat holy waters, and went to the gate with as many of his servants as durst go with him, where the chaplain, with holy words of conjuration, said: 'In the name of the fader, son and holy ghost, I conjure thee and charge thee in the holy name of god to tell me why and wherefore thou comest hither.'

This John Adroyns (in the devil's apparel), hearing them begin to conjure in such manner, said: 'Nay, nay, be not afeared of me, for I am a good devil. I am John Adroyns, your neighbour dwelling in this village, and he that *played* the devil today in the *play*. I have brought my master a dozen or two of his own conies that were stolen in his warren, and the thieves' horse and their net, and made them for to run away.

And when they heard him thus speak, by his voice they knew him well enough and opened the gate and let him come in. And so all the aforesaid fear and dread was turned to mirth and disport.

Moral: By this tale ye may see that men fear many times more than they need. Which hath caused men to believe that spirits and devils have been seen in divers places, when it hath been nothing so.

Index

120-21; trained in Bologna? 116
Norfolk, 16th duke of, 70
Norfolk, 17th duke of, 70
Norman the sheriff, 148-9
Norwich, 66, 92, 93, 127, 151

'open spaces', ancient, 18, 20-21, 76
Ording, abbot, 92, 94, 98
Orford, 66, 166
Orwell, 136
Orwell estuary, 6
Osbert of Clare, 42
Oslo Museum Christ, 86-7, 90, 91
Oswald, king of Northumbria, 42
Oswen, 58, 60n.
Oswiu, king of Northumbria, 40
Otley, 27
Oulton, 26

paganism, 10, 24, 30, 31
Pakefield, 21
Pakenham, 106, 119; Grimston End, 6
and n., 16
Paulinus, St, bishop of York, 32
Peada, under-king of the South Mercians,
40
Peasenhall, 7, 142, 148, 154
Penda, king of the Mercians, 40, 41, 42
Peter the cellarer, 119
Philip II Augustus, king of France, 113
place-names, Celtic, 7-8, 10; Danes and
Norsemen and, 5, 29; as evidence of
British presence, 5, 7, 8; eyes, 3; -feld
names, 13-26 passim, 76; lēah, 76; local
vegetation and, 1; patron saints and,
78; remaining suffixes, including -halh,
27-9; Roman, 9, 11; suffixes discussed,
13-14; survival of, 9; Sutton Hoo, 4;
from tumuli, 12-13; -tun and -stan, 5,
26-7
Playford, 161
Pleshy, 66
Pole family, Alexander de la, 157; John de
la, 157; John de la, 2nd duke of
Suffolk, 158, 159; Katherine de la,
156-7; Michael de la, 1st earl of Suffolk,
156-7; Michael de la, 2nd earl of
Suffolk, 157, 158; Michael de la, 3rd
earl of Suffolk, 157; Thomas de la,
157; William de la, 4th earl, later 1st
duke of Suffolk, 157, 158
Pole family shield, 161
Puritans, 127

Raedwald, king of the East Angles,
Aethelthrith and, 32, 33; Bretwalda,
40; conversion to Christianity, 30;
death, 40; Edwin and, 5, 31, 32, 33;

power, 35; and Sutton Hoo ship burial,
4, 31, 36
Raedwald's queen, 30, 31, 32, 34-5
Ralf Bainard, 73, 74, 75
Ralph of Coggeshall, abbot, 65, 66, 166,
167
Ralf Fitzbrien, 74
Ralph of London, 118
Ralph the porter, 107
Ranulf Flambard, 61
Relatio de Pace Veneta, 110, 111
Rendlesham, 4 and n., 30, 37, 46
Reydon (near Southwold), 24, 126
Rice, John Ap, 70
Richard de Calne, 167, 168
Richard of Hingham, 117, 119
Richard I, king of England, the Lionheart,
61, 89n., 95, 97
Richard II, king of England, 80n., 157
Richard of Saxham, 120
Richmond, George, 127
Ringmere (Norfolk), 77
Ringsfield, 21
Risby, 29
Robert, abbot of Bury, 106
Robert Blund, 17
Robert of Graveley the sacrist, and elec-
tion of Hugh of Northwold, 114, 115,
116, 119; and king John, 120; symbolic
figure, 112
Rockstone Manor, Cookley, 27
Roger of Poitou, 73, 74
Roman Britain, Dunwich, 129; farms, 8,
145; forts, 6, 7, 27, 41, 47, 136, 137;
house-site, 8; kiln, 16; roads, 5, 6, 7, 8,
18, 24, 28, 76, 129, 142-3, 144, 145;
settlements, 6, 20, 24; villas, 6, 7, 8, 9,
20, 76; wattle-and-daub, 16; woodland,
14
Roos, John, 5th Lord, 80
Rougham, 14, 57n., 104, 106, 119
Rumburgh, 141
Russell, Richard, 132

St Clare family, 79
St Edmund's abbey, after Samson's death,
110; Archbishop Langton at, 115, 116;
apsidal eastern chapels, 91; Bainard
exchanges land with, 73; Baldwin and
chapel furnishings, 91; cardinal legate
visits, 116; cellarer, 87 and n., 95, 110-
101, 104, 106-7; Chronicle of Jocelin,
87, 99-109; in debt, 92, 102; election of
Hugh of Northwold, 113-19; gifts and
bequests to, 28, 59, 77, 146; great fire,
69, 92, 102; holy relics, 50, 68; Hugo's
bronze church doors, 90; involvement
of king and barons in, 65; king John at,

Corrigenda and addenda

In the Preface, to the third paragraph from the end: *add* In 1997, Gracewing Books, of Leominster, published an interestingly illustrated little book by me, *Jocelin of Brakelond: the life of a monk and chronicler of the great abbey of St Edmund.*

p.7   para 2, line 4: *for* Roman villa *read* possible Roman villa

p.9   para 3, line 4: *for* Cleawanceeaster *read* Gleawanceeaster

p.10   para 2, line 5: *for* Eygptian *read* Egyptian

p.31   line 3 from bottom: *delete* ineffectual

p.41   footnote 9: *add* Burgh Castle's claim is strengthened by Blomefield and Parkin's *Norfolk*, VIII, 1801, p.4, which records a chapel dedicated to St Furseus in Aldeby church, where 'offerings were made to this saint, and certain titles belonged to it.' Aldeby was Aldeburg in Domesday Book, as Ekwall recognised, an OE pre-Danish name that later adopted the Old Scandinavian form. Aldeby lies about 7 miles up the Waveney valley from Burgh Castle. Across the Waveney from Burgh Castle, and 3 miles up the Yare, St Felix is recorded as founding a church at Reedham (*Liber Eliensis*, Bk 1, ch. 6).

p.46   line 2: Bede's silence may reflect his opinion that there were already too many monasteries in Northumbria, endowed by their kings to the neglect of their military defences.

p.47   footnote 33: *add* Or perhaps more probably something like the 'stepped stone late-4th-century font at Richborough in Thanet, where Augustine and his apostles first came to Kent: PDC Brown, 'The Church at Richborough', *Britannia*, II, 1971, 225–31.

p.55   footnote 2: *add* One may be the palimpsest of the brass re-used for a memorial to Anne Blenerhaysett in Frenze church, just north of the Suffolk border. See *MBS Bulletin*, 50, 1980.

p.66   footnote 46: *for* 1926 *read* 1826.

p.73   3rd para, line 2, after first sentence: *add* By the time of Domesday Book, Shimpling-with-Chadacre was already in three manors, with 2 churches. The largest, 6½ carucates (780 acres), with the best-endowed church, belonged to *another* lady – Ailith – till 1066. This was the manor that, after 1086, took Aelfled's name, Alpheton: fols 430b and 415b.

p.75   2nd para, line 8: *add parenthesis* (especially as the widow of ealdorman Brihthoth was Aelfflaed, probably the stepmother of Leofflaed, who was Thurston's grandmother).

Line 11: *for* beside *read* in

p.82   running heading: *for* SE EDMUND *read* ST EDMUND

p.90   line 2: *for* probably *read* probably not

p.91   top para: *delete last sentence and substitute parenthesis* (This point favoured acceptance of the Oslo Museum Christ.)

p.93   3rd para, line 3: *for* throne *read* throng

p.100   3rd para, line 4: *for* in his chronicle *read* in his official capacity as cellarer, when he was writing his chronicle.

p.106   2nd para, last line: 'someone spoke to Samson' is Jocelin being anonymous

p.113   footnote 38: *for* pp *read* p

p.115   bottom para, 5 lines up: *start inverted commas before* Whatever
3 lines up: *after* Stephen *add* to work

p.151   last line: *for* a half *read* half a

p.152   top line: *for* written 'half-free man' *read* if we knew which the other half of his holding was.

p.154   bottom two lines, sentence should *read*: The word Heveningham has got rather squeezed out by the carver, who was determined to get it all into one line.

p.169   *Index* Arnold, Matthew: *for* 167n *read* 3, 166n

p.170   *for* Bradfield-on-Sea *read* Bradwell-on-Sea

p.176   *insert* Warner, P, 24, 28, 145, 147

Also insert Watling, H, 135, fn 4

At Wingfield, *delete* Q